ATLANTA

Unforgettable Vintage Images of an All-American City

Note from the Publisher

Royalties from the sale of this book and the others in the Best of Series will be donated to the National Trust for Historic Preservation. These funds will be used to further their work and provide support to the preservation movement nationwide.

ATLANTA

Unforgettable Vintage Images of an All-American City

ARCADIA
PUBLISHING

ISBN 978-0-7385-9710-2

Published by Arcadia Publishing
Charleston, South Carolina

Printed in the United States of America

Library of Congress Catalog Card Number: 00-104650

For all general information contact Arcadia Publishing at:
Telephone 843-853-2070
Fax 843-853-0044
E-mail sales@arcadiapublishing.com
For customer service and orders:
Toll-Free 1-888-313-2665

Visit us on the Internet at www.arcadiapublishing.com

Contents

ACKNOWLEDGMENTS

Arcadia wishes to express its gratitude to these authors of Arcadia titles in the Atlanta area:

Atlanta History Center	*Central of Georgia Railway*
	Atlanta: A Portrait of the Civil War
	Atlanta Scenes: Photojournalism in the Atlanta History Center Collection
Kimberly S. Blass	*Central of Georgia Railway*
Tammy Galloway	*Central of Georgia Railway*
James B. Glover	*Marietta: 1833–2000*
Narvie Harris	*African-American Education in DeKalb County*
Scott McIntosh	*Central of Georgia Railway*
Jackson McQuigg	*Central of Georgia Railway*
Joe Mctyre	*Marietta: 1833–2000*
Herman "Skip" Mason	*Black Atlanta in the Roaring Twenties*
	African-American Entertainment in Atlanta
	African-American Life in DeKalb County: 1823–1970
Michael Rose	*Atlanta: A Portrait of the Civil War*
	Atlanta Scenes: Photojournalism in the Atlanta History Center Collection
Dee Taylor	*African-American Education in DeKalb County*
Elena Irish Zimmerman	*Atlanta in Vintage Postcards: Volume I*
	Atlanta in Vintage Postcards: Volume II

INTRODUCTION

The Best of Atlanta is a collection of images accumulated from ten books in Arcadia's *Images of America* series. Through some two hundred photographs, we have attempted to project a visual sampling of life in this Southern city, considered by many to be the jewel in the Southern crown. In order to honor the traditions, values, and essence of Atlanta, we have worked in cooperation with the many authors in the series who know Atlanta best, from the tip of Kennesaw Mountain to the sandy banks of the Chattahoochie.

Atlanta originated in the hustle and bustle of railroads. The geography of the city made it the perfect railway connection, channeling overland traffic from the seaboard through the city to travel on westward. Named Terminus, then Marthasville, and finally Atlanta, the city was officially born in 1837. During the Civil War, Atlanta became a supply depot for the Confederacy, and a prime target for northern military leaders. The name William Tecumseh Sherman to this day sends shivers of repugnance through some Atlanta residents, evoking as it does the acrid smell of fire baked into the red clay as the general made his infamous march to the sea, torching the city in his wake.

Atlanta eventually rose from the ashes to become the economic hub of the New South. The images presented here reflect that ever-present sense of pride and determination found in the faces and voices of Atlanta residents. From Oakland Cemetery to the house of Margaret Mitchell, Atlanta has thousands of stories to tell that can truly be seen through the eyes of the photographers represented here and to whose lenses we are beholden. The images portrayed in *The Best of Atlanta* try to focus on the smaller intricacies that make up a larger story, such as the tarnished brass of a young soldier's button, or the sweat on the brow of a Civil Rights leader.

We invite you to experience the rich and infinite variety of Atlanta's history for yourself. Take a walk down Peachtree Street to smell, taste, and breathe the history of this city. Imagine the warm air pulsing through the magnolia trees as it whispers the stories that make this city great. But in the end, as in any American city, it is the people who hold the fabric of their societies together, and Atlanta is no exception to this rule. Grab a glass of lemonade, come sit on the porch, and witness the history that is Atlanta.

Keith Ulrich
Editor, Arcadia Publishing

Facts about Atlanta

- Atlanta was named for the Western and Atlantic Railroad, which featured prominently in the city's origins.
- The population of Atlanta is 425,200.
- There are 182,754 families in the Atlanta metropolitan area.
- The city is positioned 33.76 degrees north of the equator and 84.42 degrees west of the Prime Meridian.
- The Georgia State Capitol was patterned after the United States Capitol.
- Atlanta is one of the largest and fastest growing metropolitan areas in the United States.
- Oakland Cemetery is the oldest active cemetery in the city.
- Only 400 of roughly 400,000 buildings were left standing after Sherman's burning of Atlanta.
- In 1973, Atlanta became the first major city in the South to elect an African-American mayor.

One

Business and Industry

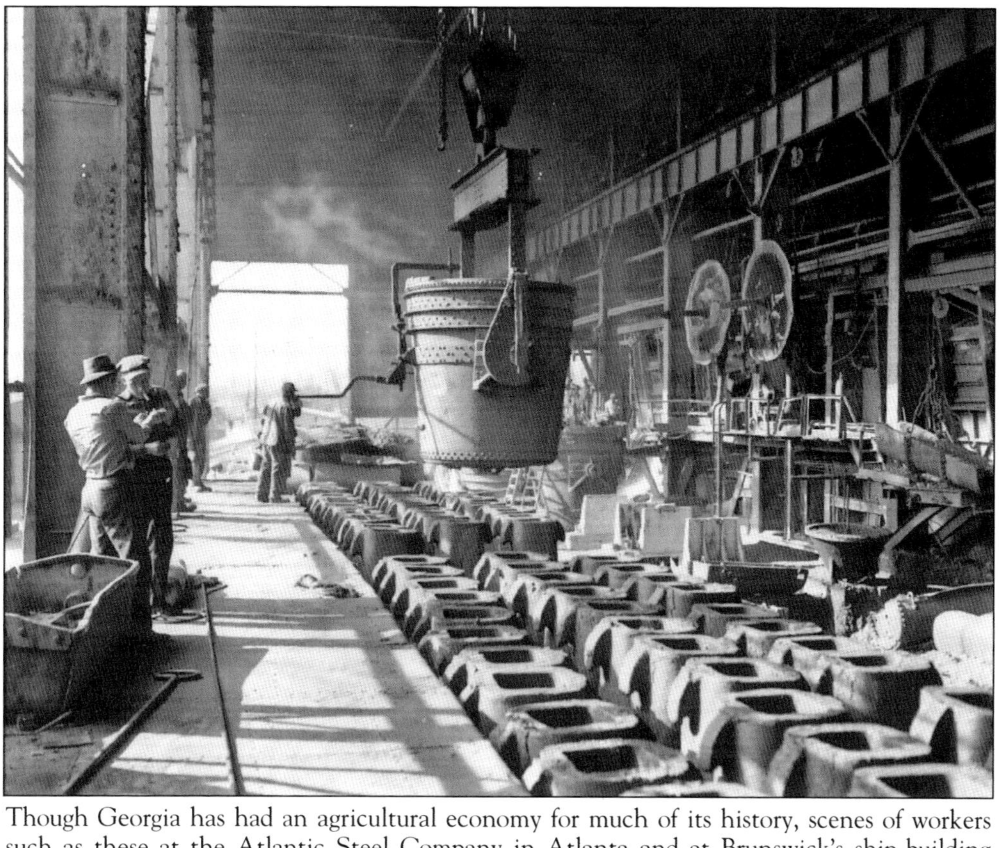

Though Georgia has had an agricultural economy for much of its history, scenes of workers such as these at the Atlantic Steel Company in Atlanta and at Brunswick's ship-building facilities display the state's industrial capacity. (Courtesy Atlanta History Center.)

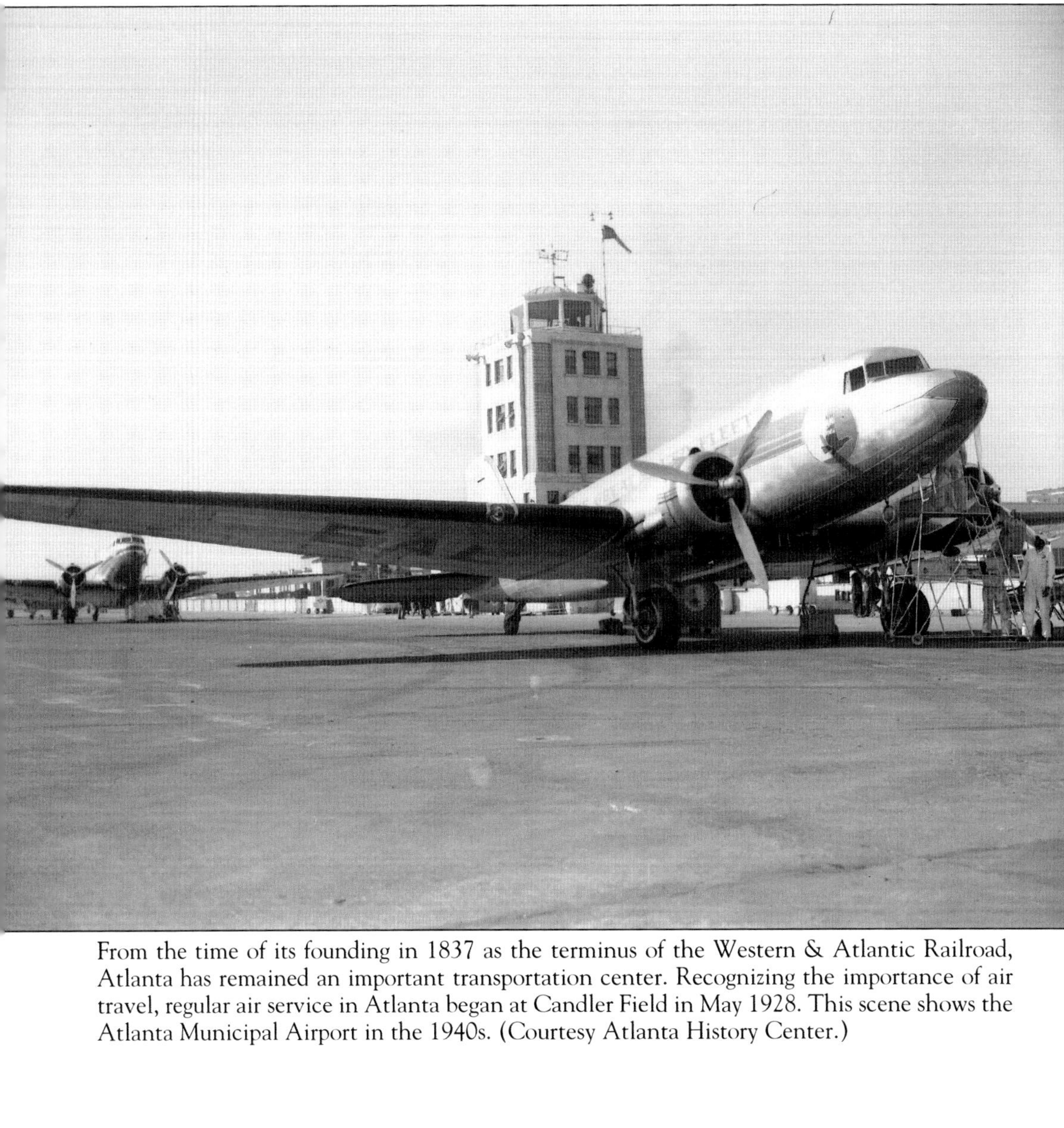

From the time of its founding in 1837 as the terminus of the Western & Atlantic Railroad, Atlanta has remained an important transportation center. Recognizing the importance of air travel, regular air service in Atlanta began at Candler Field in May 1928. This scene shows the Atlanta Municipal Airport in the 1940s. (Courtesy Atlanta History Center.)

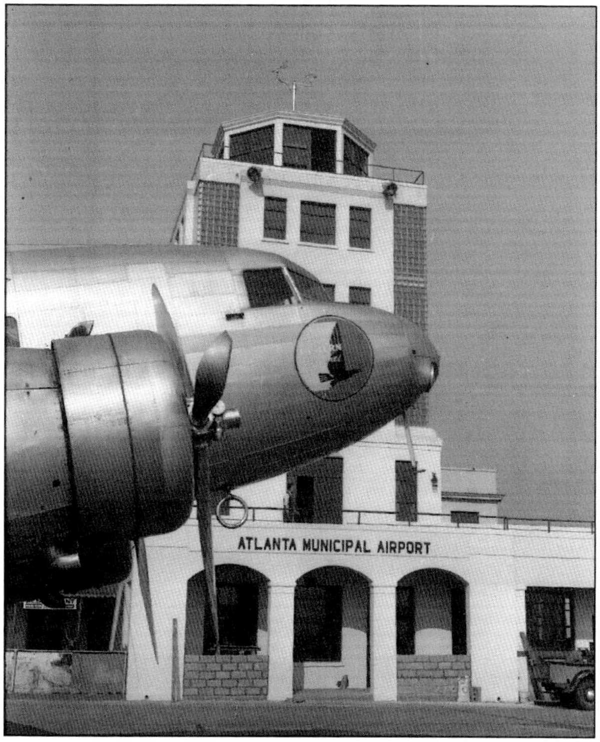

An Eastern Airlines plane appears here in front of Atlanta Municipal Airport at Candler Field. By the 1940s, Atlanta's airport was one of the country's busiest, and was the first with an air traffic control and instrument approach system. (Courtesy Atlanta History Center.)

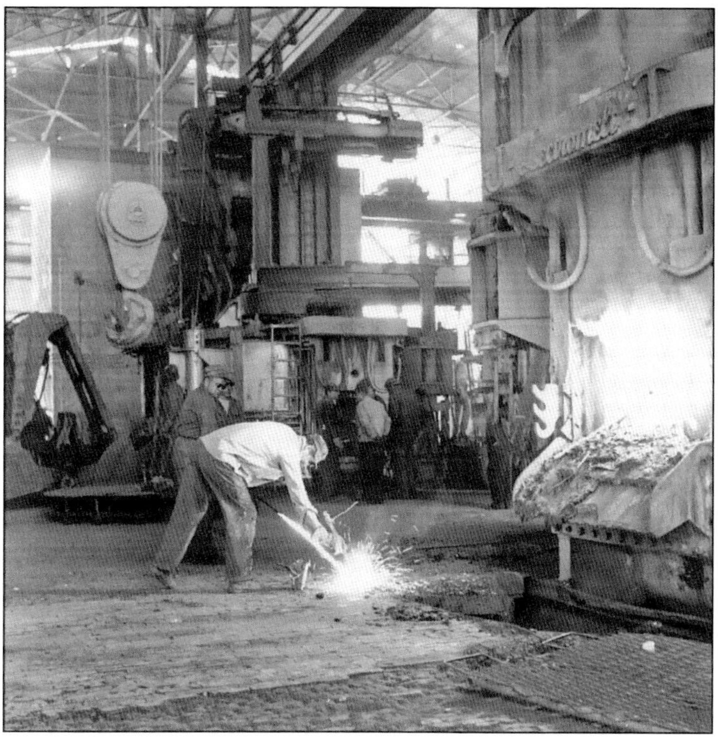

Red-hot steel, fiery furnaces, and giant machinery mark the interior of the Atlantic Steel plant, 1950. In the 1950s Atlanta's own steel mill processed thousands of tons each day. (Courtesy Atlanta History Center.)

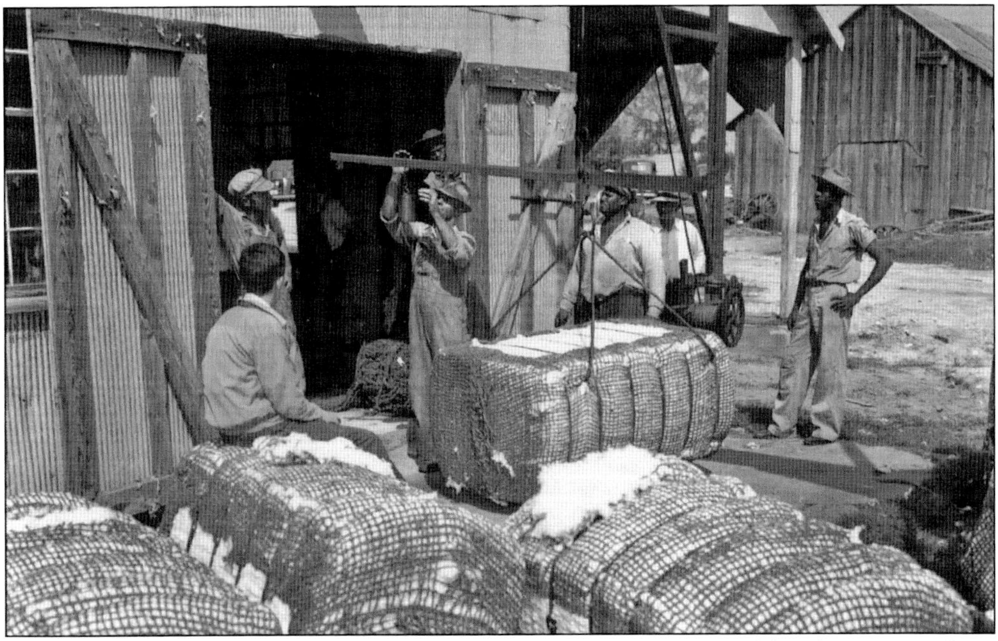

As New Deal programs reduced cotton acreage in Georgia, scenes like this one evoking the cotton culture of the old South—workers weighing and unloading cotton—became less prevalent. By the end of World War II, production had moved west, and Georgia's agriculture became more mechanized and diverse. (Courtesy Atlanta History Center.)

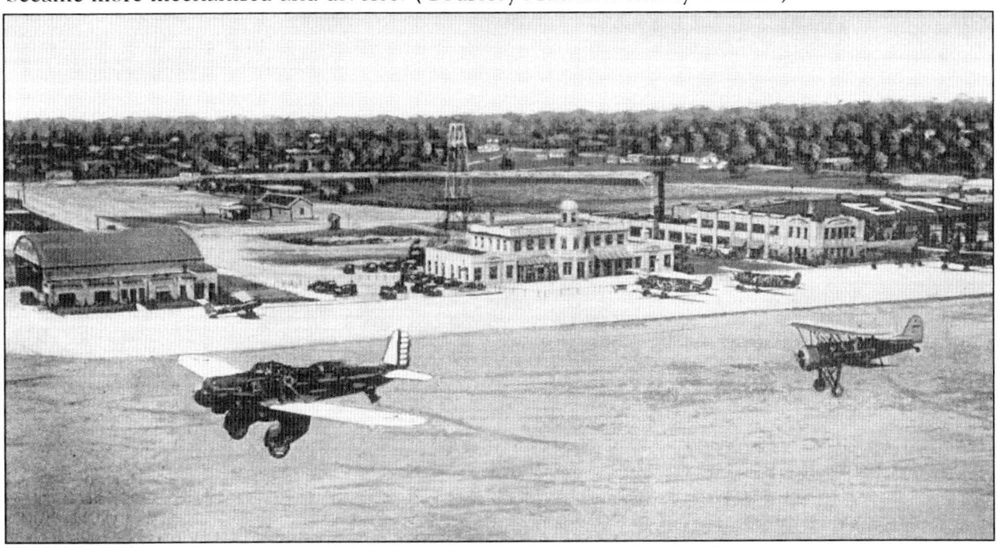

In November 1911, Georgia's first air meet was held on the Candler Speedway property in Hapeville, which became the nucleus of Atlanta's Hartsfield International Airport. The city purchased the property in 1929, and in 1930, Eastern Airlines began regular passenger service between New York and Atlanta. By the mid-1930s, when this postcard was printed, "twenty-six passenger and mail planes arrive and depart daily from Candler Field." (Published by R and R News Co., Atlanta.)

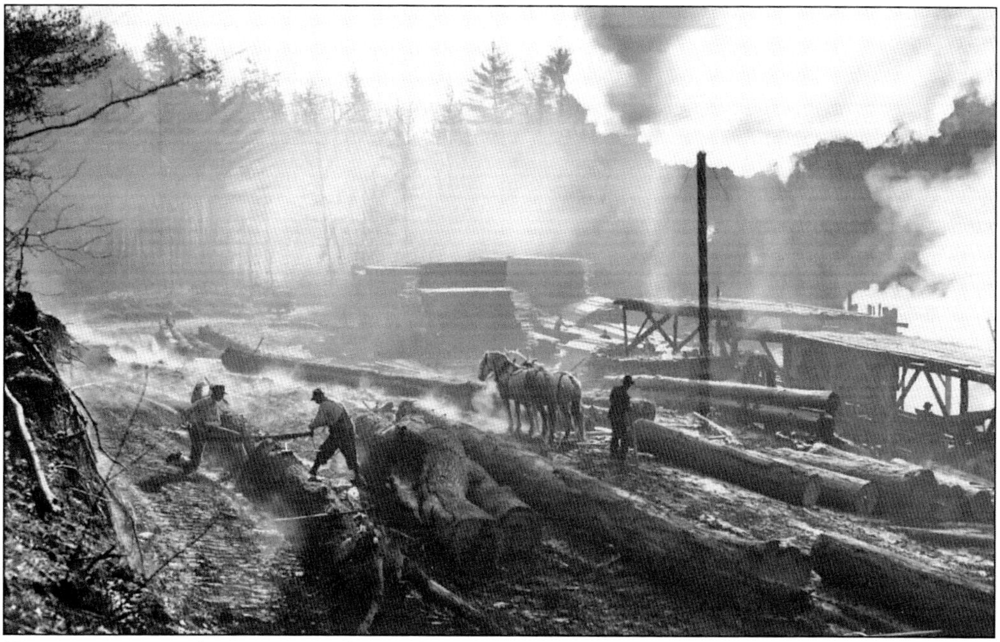

Two men are seen here sawing a log in the early morning mist. Lumbering had long been one of Georgia's main industries; in the 1940s and 1950s it enjoyed a boom period. (Courtesy Atlanta History Center.)

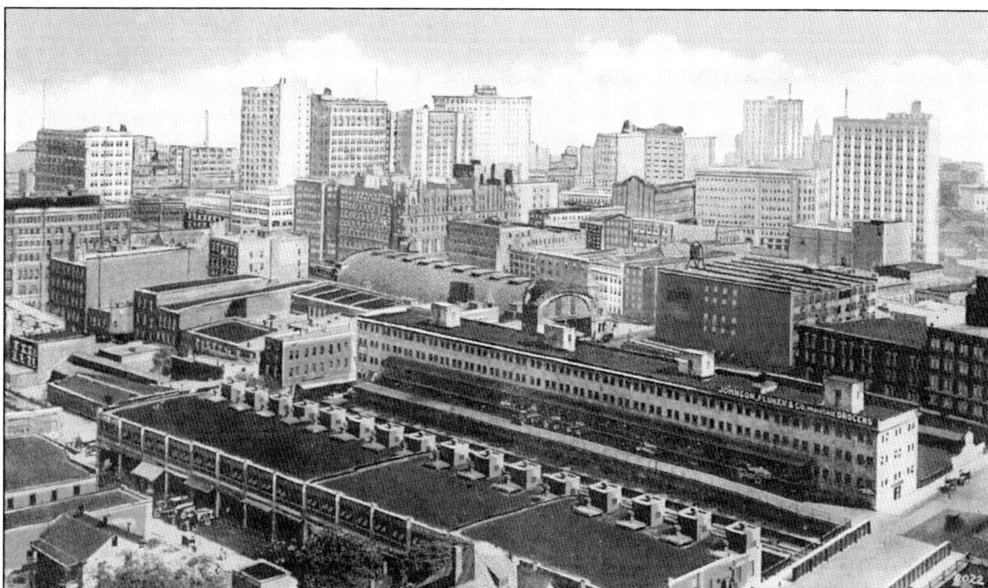

The size of these railroad buildings emphasizes the importance of Atlanta as a rail center. The building with the rounded roof is the Union Station. At the far end is the Kimball House. This shot was taken atop the state capital. (Published by the Chessler Co., Baltimore; card sent 1923.)

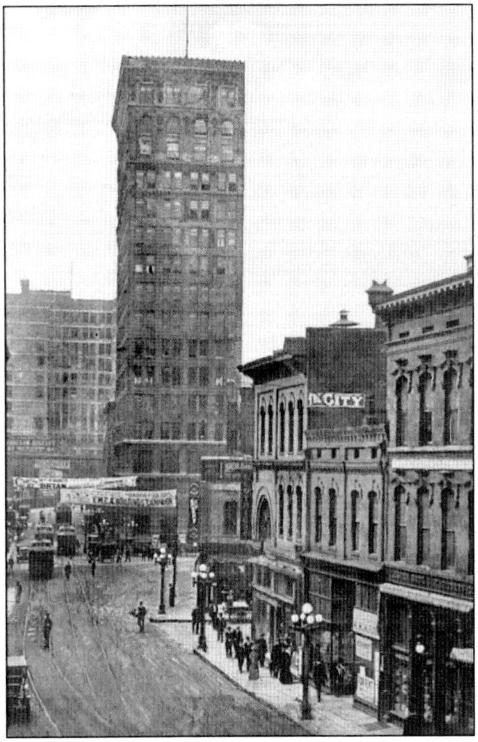

Standing like a lone sentinel at Five Points in 1908, the Fourth National Bank overlooks muddy streets, streetcars, and street banners relating to a YMCA Building Campaign and William Jennings Bryan, who ran a third time for president that year. (Published by Leighton and Valentine Co., New York.)

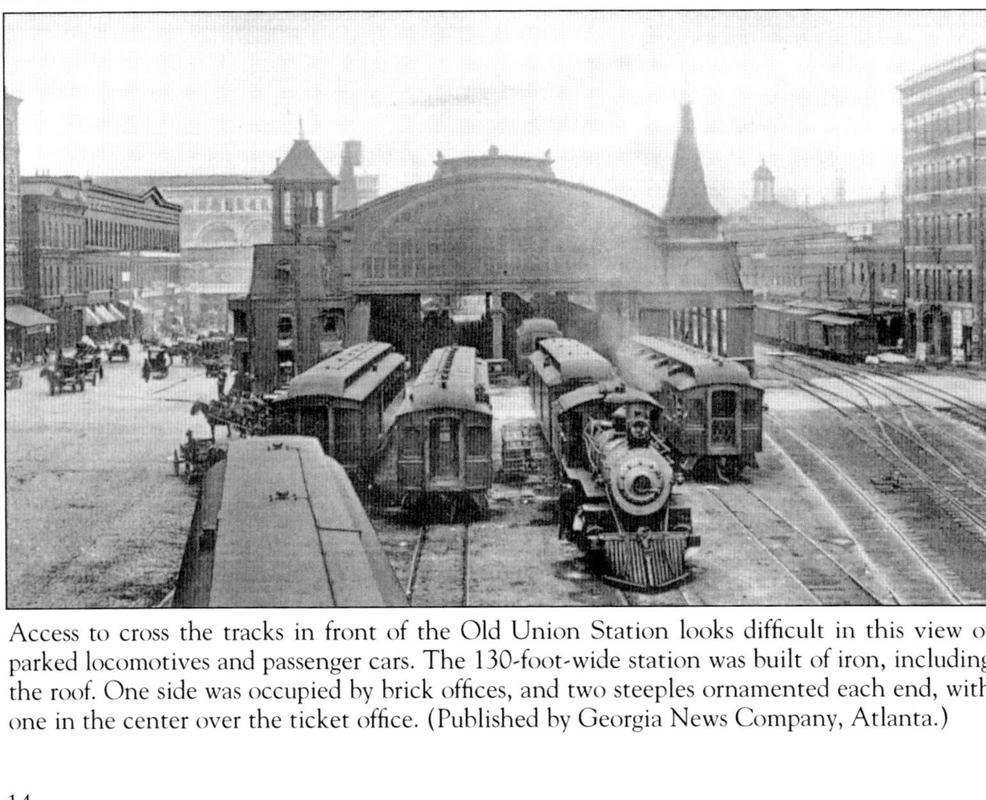

Access to cross the tracks in front of the Old Union Station looks difficult in this view of parked locomotives and passenger cars. The 130-foot-wide station was built of iron, including the roof. One side was occupied by brick offices, and two steeples ornamented each end, with one in the center over the ticket office. (Published by Georgia News Company, Atlanta.)

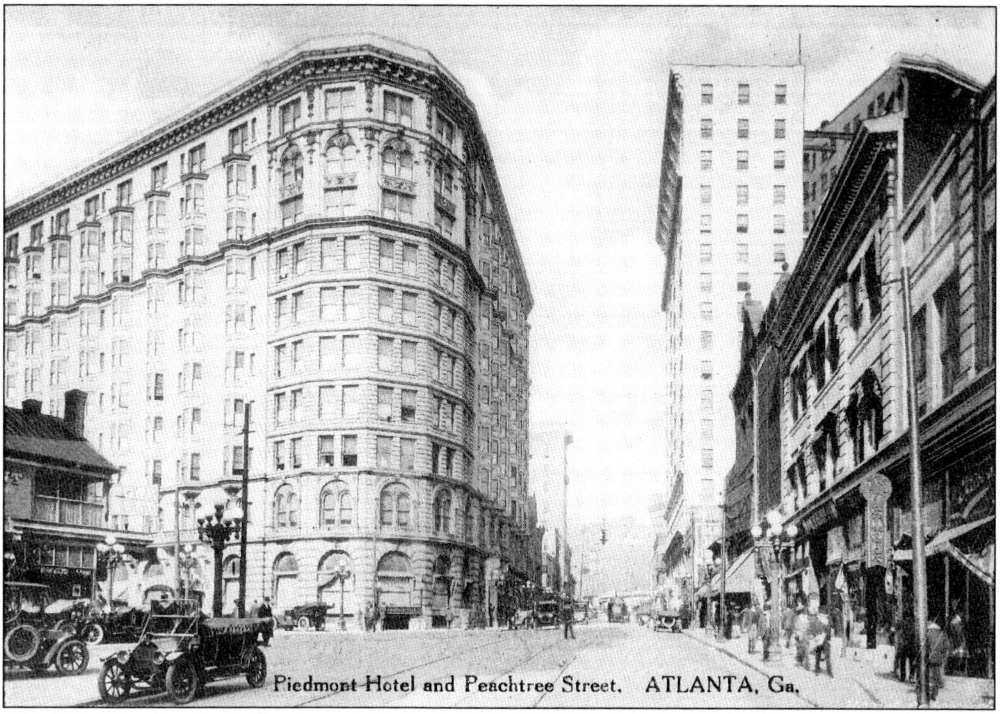

The handsome new Piedmont Hotel (above) at Luckie and Peachtree Streets opened January 15, 1903. On that day, there was an "open house" attended by hundreds of people who marveled at the beautifully decorated rooms and the elaborate menu in the dining room. It was called "our New York hotel." It was Atlanta's first hotel to emulate the modernity and sophistication of the east. (No publishing information available; card sent 1916.)

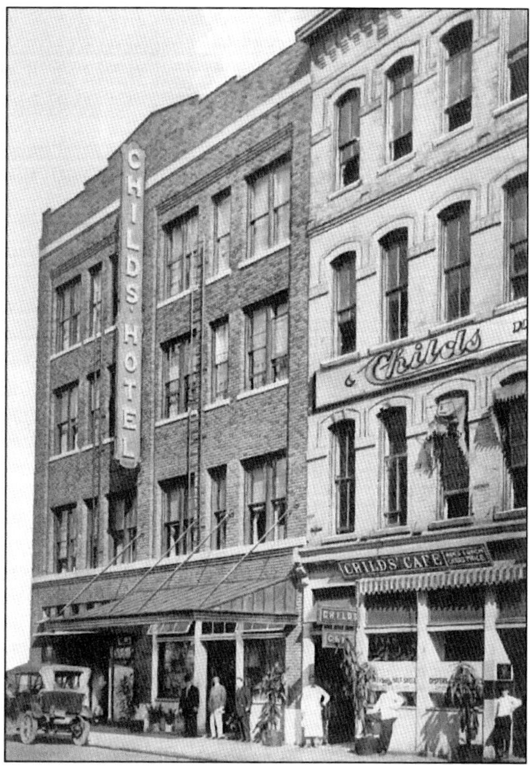

Child's Hotel (right) was located "in the heart of the city" and had "electric car service to and from all depots." Further amenities included single rooms with bath or "rooms en suite," hot and cold running water, electric lights, and a telephone. Rates were $1.50 "with privileges," and $2 with private bath. There was a private dining room for ladies. (Published by I.F. Co., Atlanta; card sent 1915.)

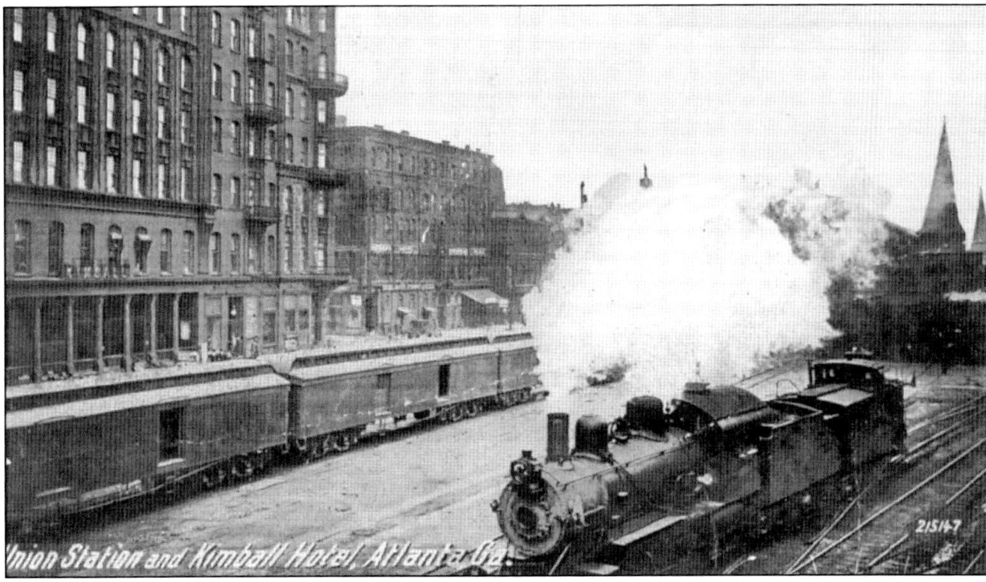

Next to the tracks and at right angles to the Union Terminal, the Kimball Hotel was subject to the noise and smoke of passing trains, as this picture demonstrates. Both Pryor and Whitehall Streets crossed the tracks here at grade. The new Plaza Park, achieved in 1949, now covers the area occupied by the trains. The Kimball was torn down in 1959. (Published by Leighton & Valentine, New York; card sent 1913.)

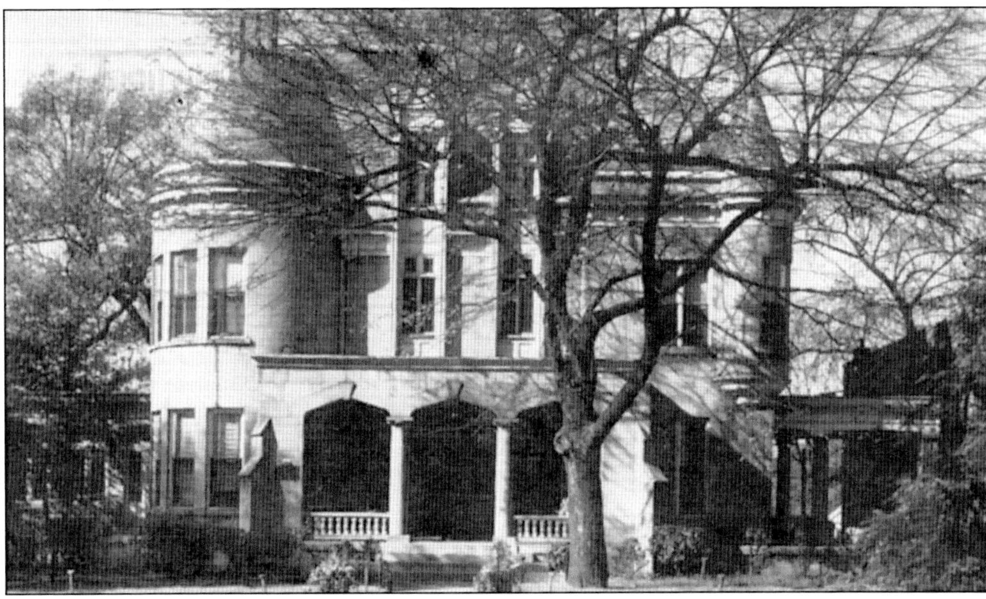

Morris Rich (1847–1928) came to Atlanta at age 19 and opened a modest dry goods store at 36 Whitehall Street. After years of successful merchandising and expansion, a new six-story building was occupied in 1924 at Broad and Alabama Streets. Expansion continued through the years. In 1990 the store closed, and in 1994 the Store for Homes was destroyed. (Published by I.F. Co., Atlanta; card sent 1918.)

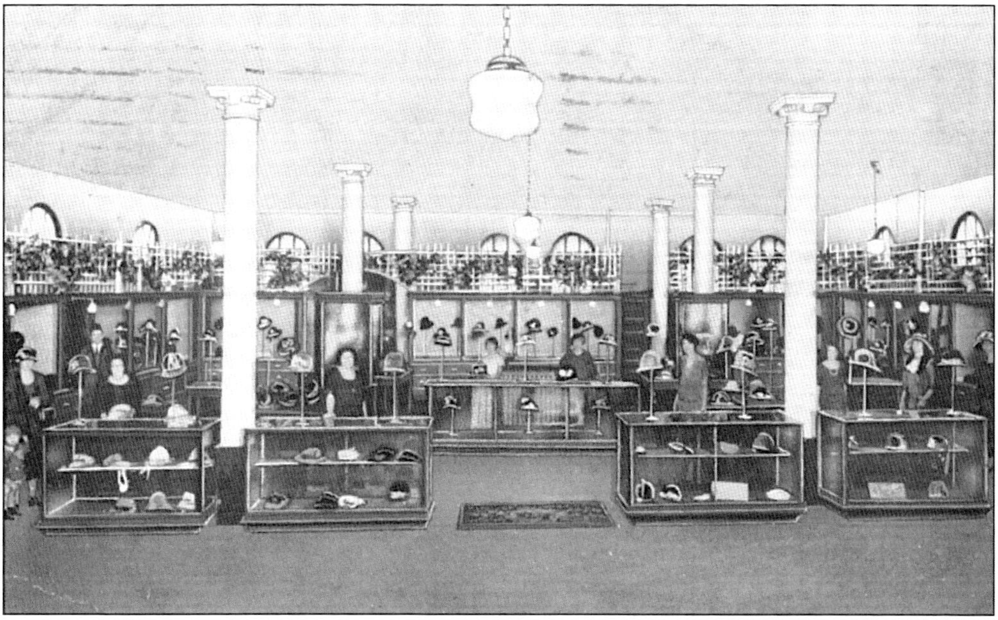

Obviously proud of its millinery department, Smith and Higgins, of 254 Peters Street, advises on the reverse side of this card, "Our fall hats are the best value in the city. Smartest styles are featured at popular prices. Our values throughout the store are always the best to be had." (Published by Imperial Post Card Co., Atlanta; card sent 1925.)

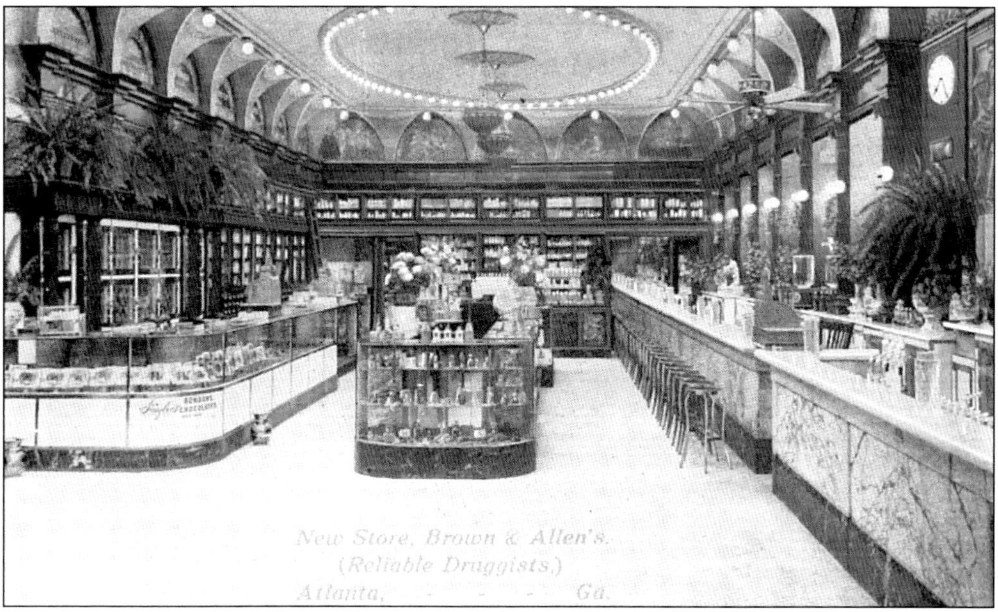

The picture shows a beautiful drugstore: bonbons and chocolates at left; boxes of cigars on display; a cosmetic island in the center; and a lengthy soda fountain at right. The Brown and Allen's pharmacy is evidently in the rear, and necessary brass spittoons are seen at left. The ceiling seems rather elaborately special. (Published by S.D. Zacharias, Atlanta.)

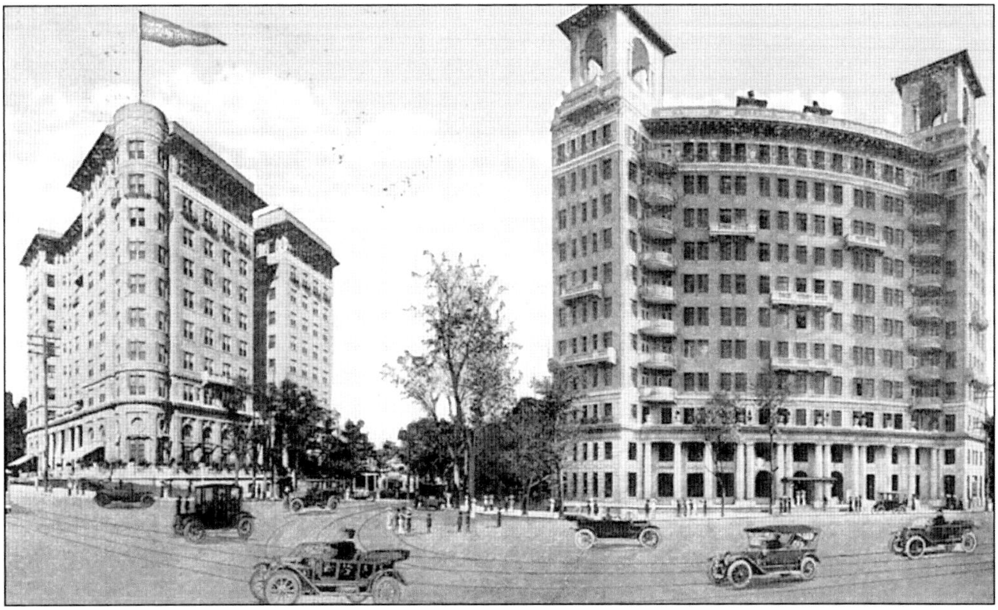

Located at Peachtree Street and Ponce de Leon Avenue, the fine establishments of the Georgian Terrace Hotel and the Ponce de Leon Apartments display impressive architecture by W.L. Stoddard. The Ponce de Leon, 11 stories tall, sports twin turrets on the roof. Atlanta's first penthouse was here; the year was 1913. The automobiles were superimposed on the picture but nevertheless delineate the era accurately. (Published by I.F. Co., Atlanta; card sent 1917.)

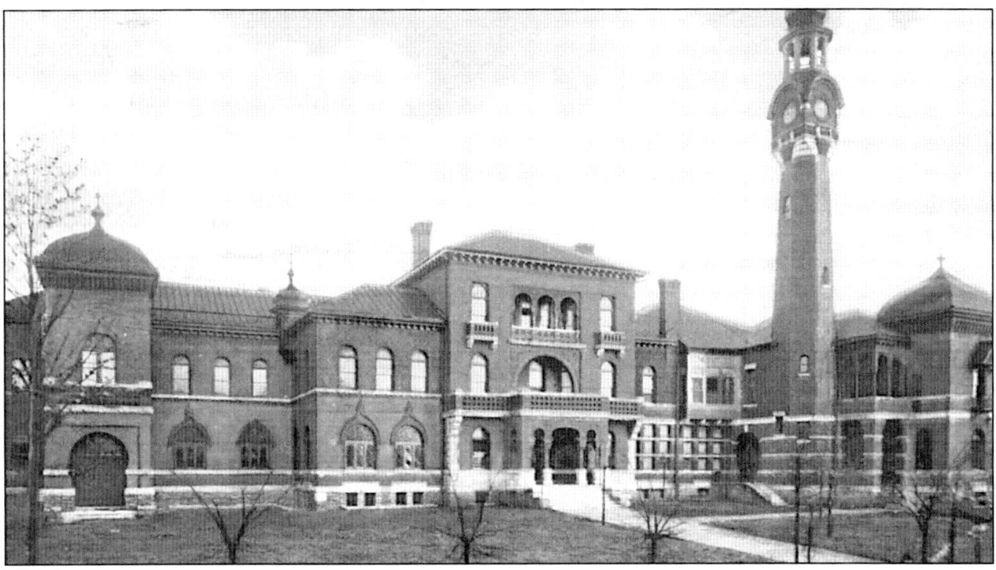

Opened in 1888, the Jewish Orphans Home was a large rambling structure on Washington Street. By 1911 the home accommodated 150 children. In 1930 the program was extended to provide a foster home for every child, and the name was changed to Children's Service Bureau. This building was demolished in 1974. (Published by Georgia News Co., Atlanta; card sent 1909.)

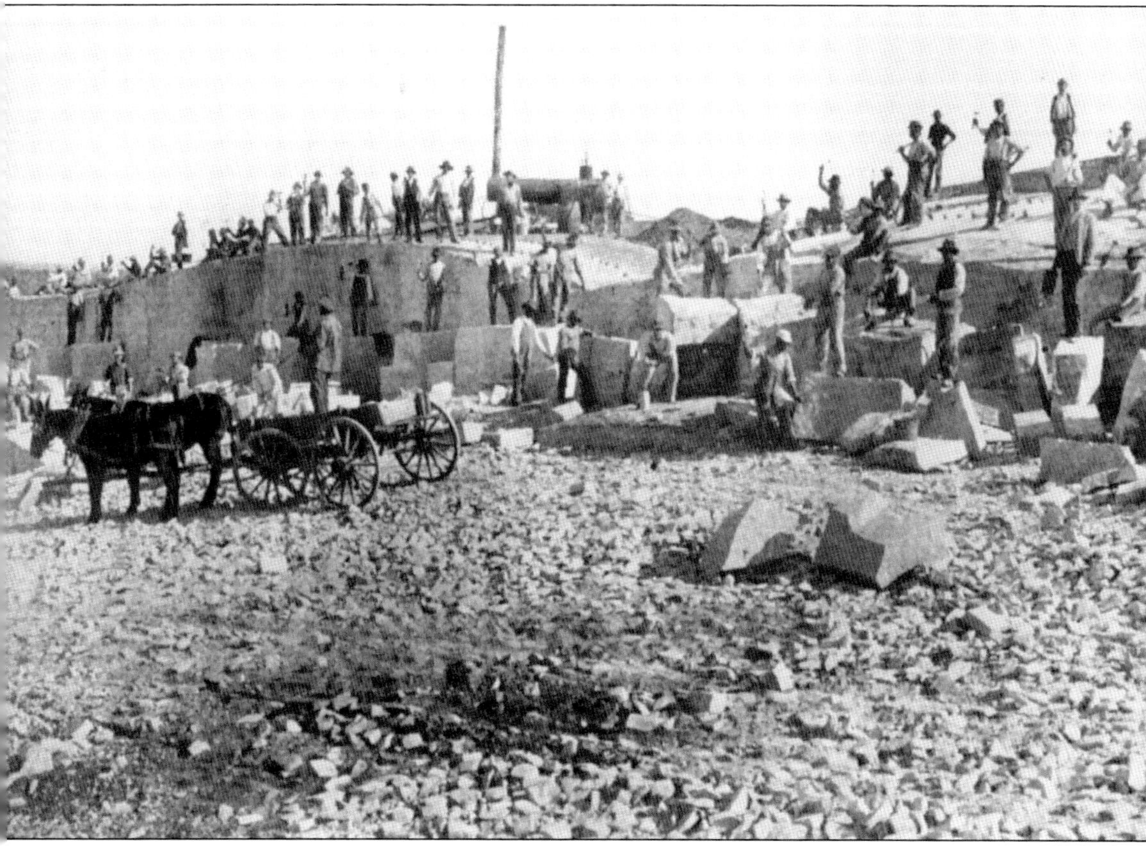

Located in the southeastern section of DeKalb County was an area known as Crossroads. It was later renamed Lithonia, taken from the Greek word "lithos," meaning "rock." The ground was extremely hard to till. A post office was established as early as 1832 and a tavern was operated for stagecoach stops on the Augusta-Nashville route. From Lithonia comes the only woman to have served from Georgia as a U.S. senator, Rebecca Latimer Felton, a white woman and daughter of Major Charles Latimer, who built the 1,000-acre Panola Plantation, which is now a series of subdivisions occupied by predominately African-American families. Lithonia was situated in the midst of one of the largest granite areas, leading to the development of large quarry companies that provided employment for African-American families. Shown above are the Pine Mountain No. 3 Lithonia Quarry workers. In 1856, the town of Lithonia was incorporated. Granite from Lithonia is used in buildings all over the country. Following the Civil War, African Americans migrated to the area. By the 1970s, there were over 2,200 black residents (48 percent of the population).

Today, Lithonia is a fast-growing area with sprawling subdivisions for middle- and upper-income African Americans.

In the 1960s, the Department of Transportation constructed and opened I-20, creating a major transportation hub for the area. (Courtesy of Patricia Wade Drozak, Georgia Department of Archives and History.)

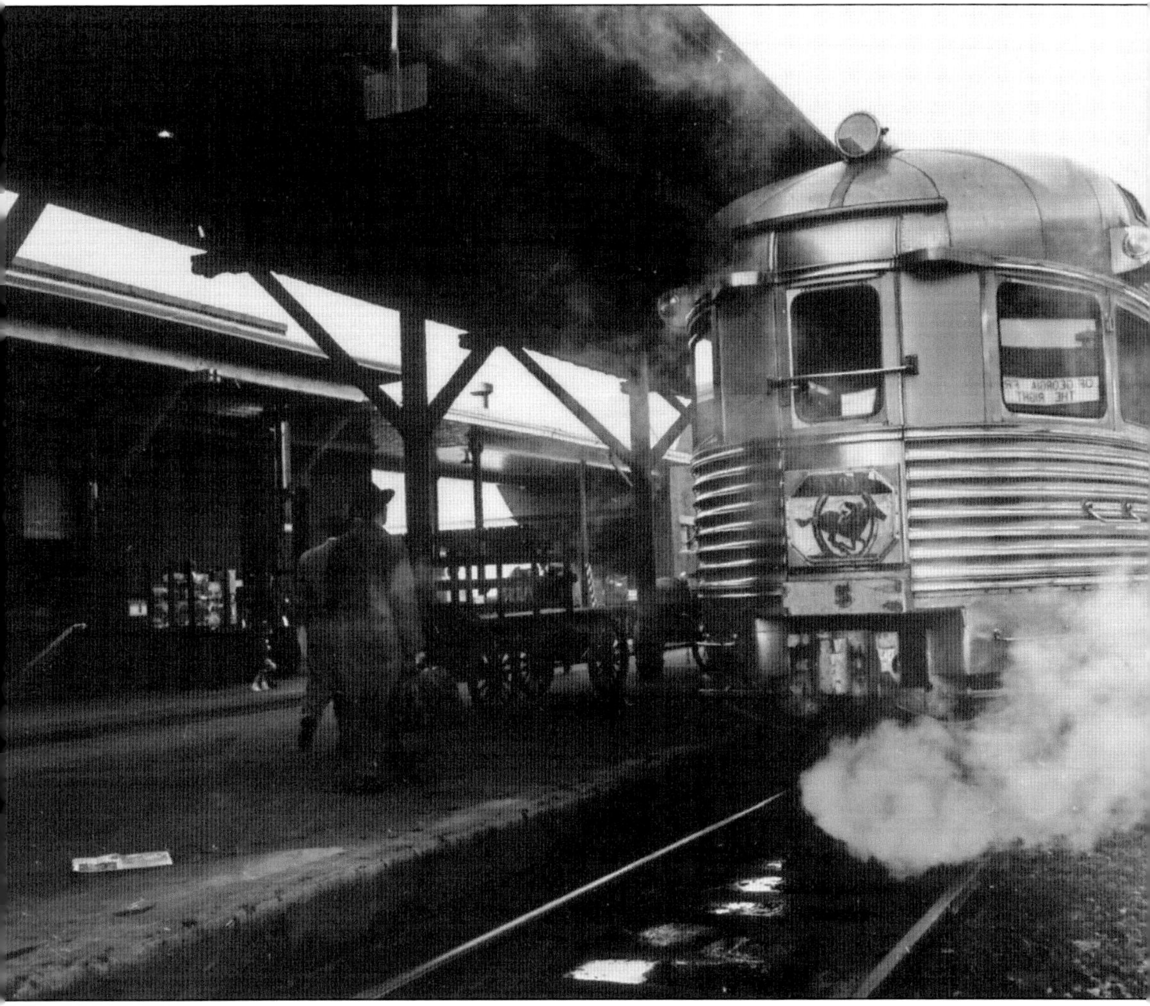

Initially, the Central of Georgia streamliner *Man O' War* made two daily roundtrips between Atlanta and Columbus. It was quite a success; the train carried a total of 300,000 in its first two years of operation. The *Man O' War*, with tavern-lounge "Fort Benning" on the rear, is pictured here prior to a late-1940s run.

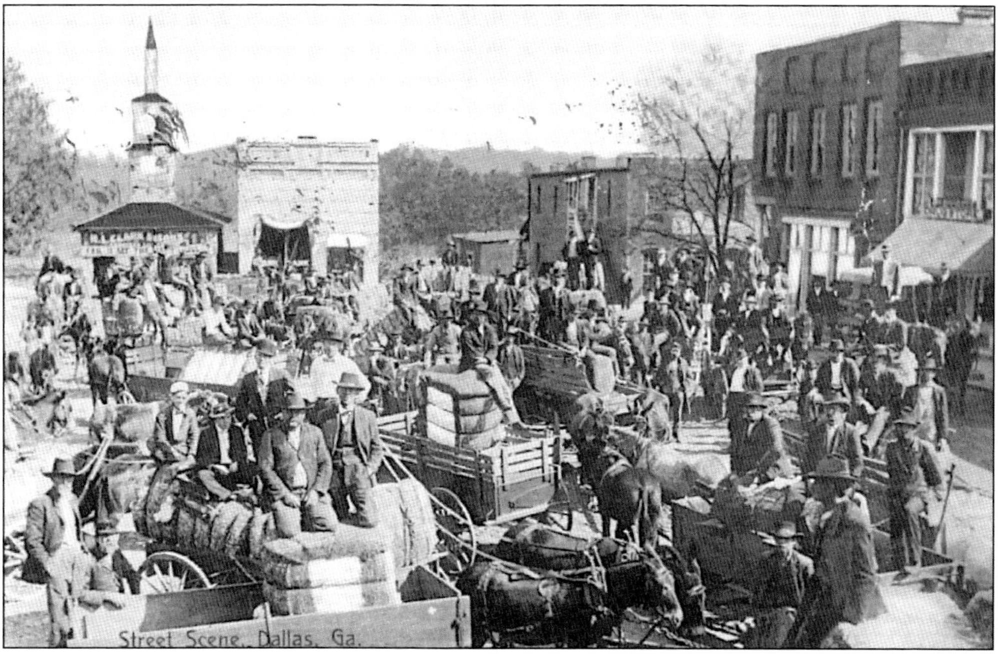

Evidently it is a Saturday, when farmers came to town to sell and trade. This street scene is representative of the early 1900s. On the town square we see the business of M.L. Clark and Sons and the bank building at center rear, and a drugstore at extreme right. It is obvious why the men are here; they are intent on the photographer. (Published by Hanna Drug Co., Dallas; card sent 1909.)

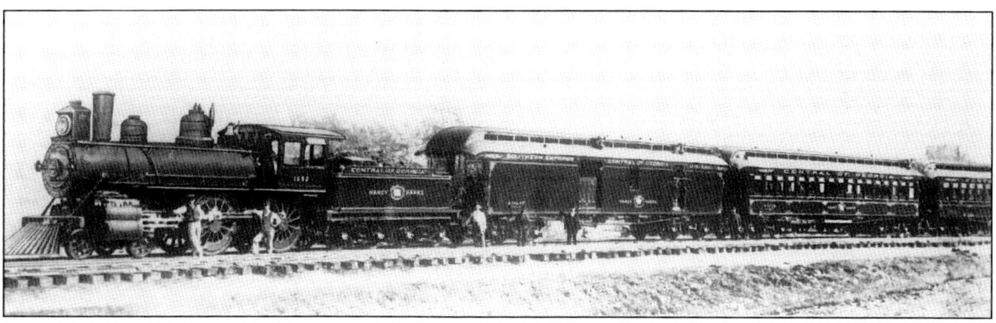

Like the *Nancy Hanks II*, the first *Nancy Hanks* ran between Atlanta and Savannah; in two back-to-back incarnations, it ran for a total of only ten months. Named after the racing horse that set a speed record for trotters in 1892, the Central of Georgia train was fast, too. Its quick pace even inspired a song: "Some folks say the *Nancy* can't run/ But stop, let me tell you what the *Nancy* done/ She left Atlanta at half past one and got to Savannah by the settin' of the sun/ The *Nancy*, she was so fast/ She burnt the wind and scorched the grass." This photograph dates from 1892 or 1893.

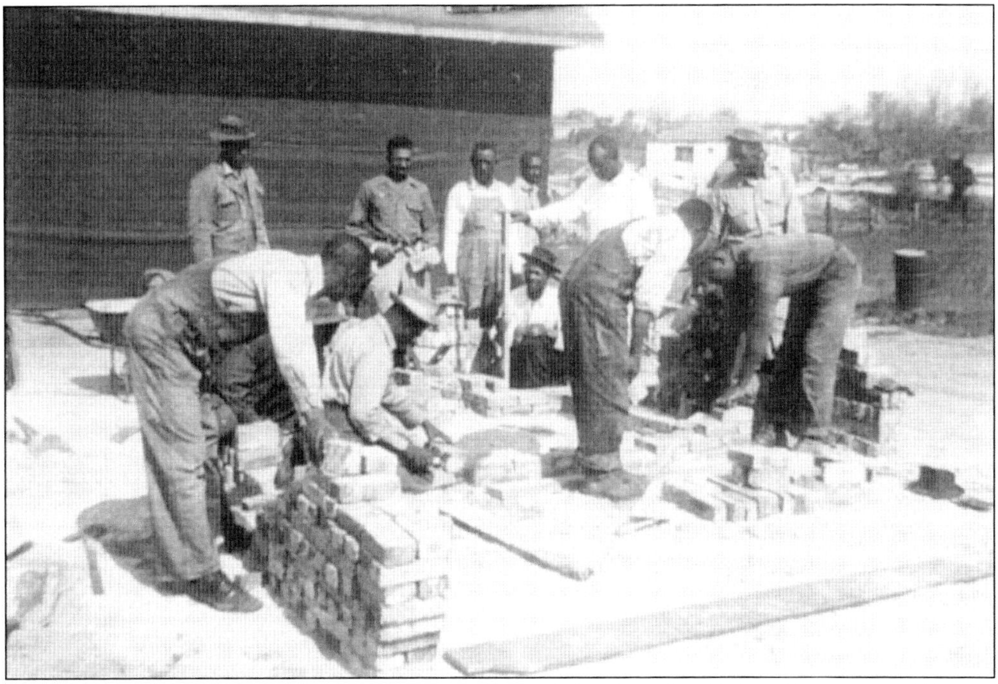

Pictured here is a bricklaying class at Bruce Street School in the 1940s. (Courtesy of Narvie Jordan Harris.)

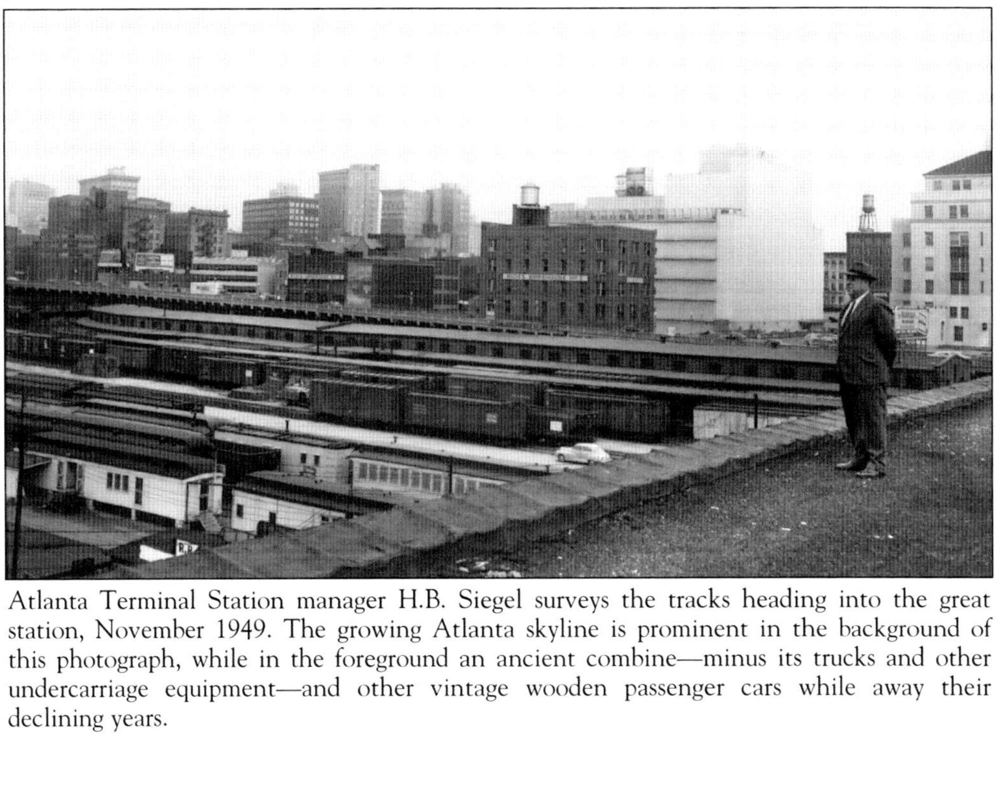

Atlanta Terminal Station manager H.B. Siegel surveys the tracks heading into the great station, November 1949. The growing Atlanta skyline is prominent in the background of this photograph, while in the foreground an ancient combine—minus its trucks and other undercarriage equipment—and other vintage wooden passenger cars while away their declining years.

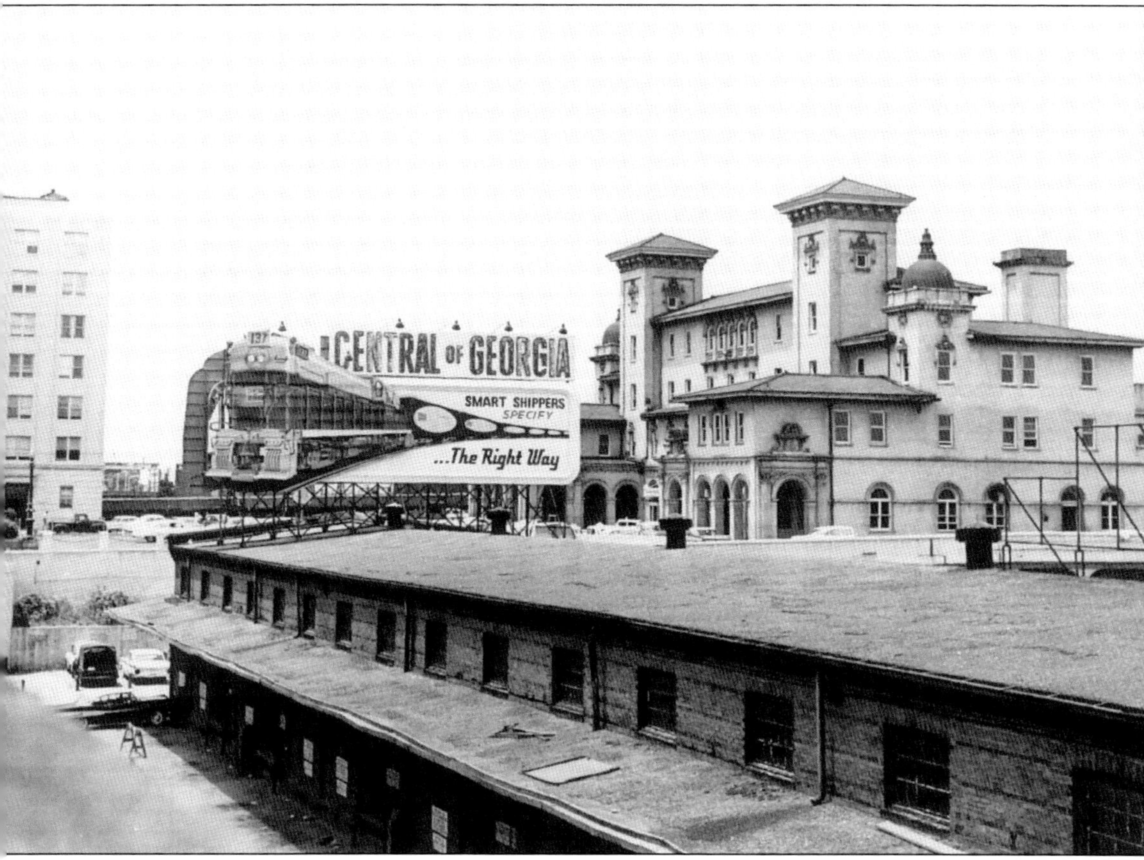

The P. Thornton Marye-designed Atlanta Terminal Station and a billboard advertising the Central of Georgia's freight service are seen here in a c. 1964 photograph. At left are the Southern Railway's 99 Spring Street offices, across Mitchell Street from the station. When Terminal Station was closed for good in June 1970, the *Nancy Hanks II* was relegated to a small ticket office and waiting lounge created for passengers in the Southern Railway building; Terminal Station's other remaining passenger trains—Southern Railway's *Crescent* and *Southerner*—were transferred to Southern's Brookwood Station on the north side of the city.

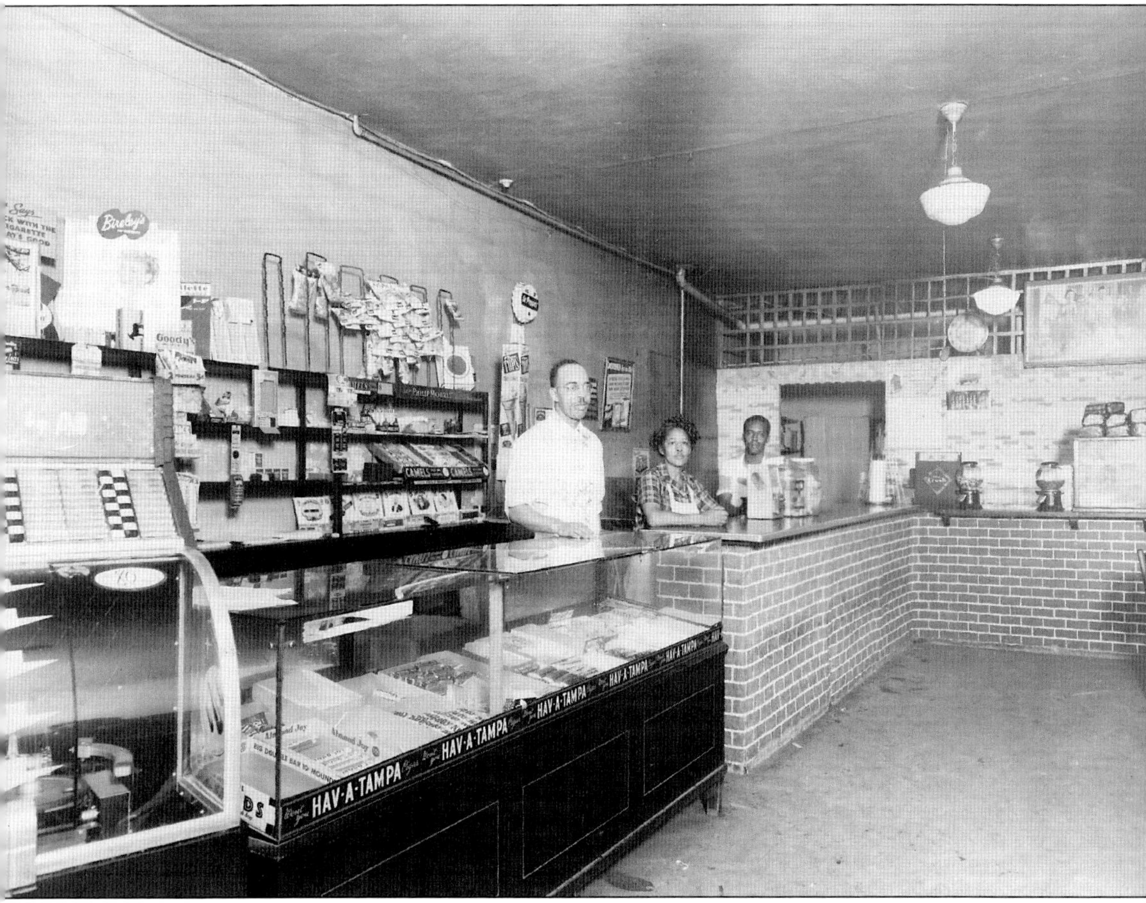

Atlanta Avenue was to African Americans in Decatur as Auburn Avenue was in Atlanta; it was a street where businesses flourished. According to oral history, it was once the Sandtown Indian Trail, an important Native American thoroughfare that ran from Stone Mountain to the Chattahoochee River. Some of the businesses on Atlanta Avenue included a dry cleaning firm owned by Archie Clark, restaurants operated by Eugene Jones, Clarence Clark, and Edward Levitt, the Ever Ready Cafe, Terrell and Steele Restaurant (Tom Steele), Edward Lee's Cafe, Otis Spates Rib Shack, Rogers Taxicab, Coopers Funeral Home, Star and Fisher Beauty Parlor, and Lena's Beauty Shop. Pictured here are Tom Steele, his wife, Ethel, and son Winfred Mills, (*c.* 1930) in his cafe. Splits were sold at both Tom Steele's and George Sterling's. At Tom Steele's, you could buy a split for 10¢, a Coke for 5¢, and a bag of chips for another nickel. Steele also served as a commissioner for the City of Decatur. George Sterling's Cafe was originally located on Marshall Street before moving to Atlanta Avenue. There, a split cost 15¢ (supposedly his splits were made of real meat and you could have lettuce and tomatoes in your sandwich). (Courtesy of Mollie Clark Mills.)

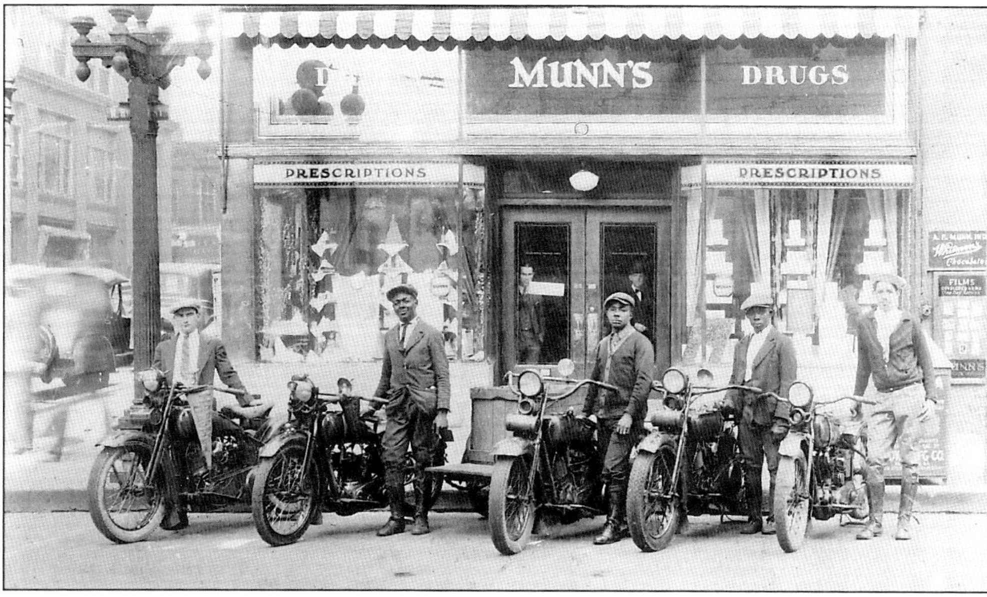

Delivery boys pose beside their motorcycles in front of Munn's Drugstore on Broad Street, c. 1920. (Courtesy Atlanta History Center.)

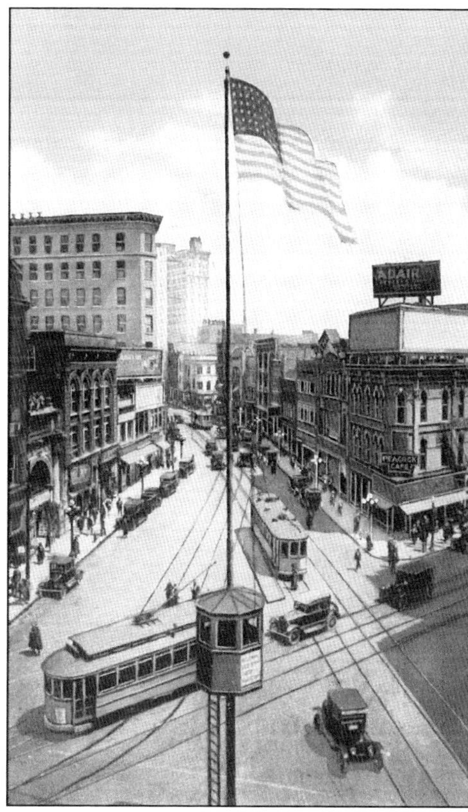

The Atlanta Convention Bureau informs us on this card that "Five Points is the radiating center of the Southeast . . . where more traffic to the square inch moves in safety than in any other city in the world." The police officer, seen in his elevated traffic control station, was undoubtedly kept busy. (Published by Imperial Post Card Co., Atlanta.)

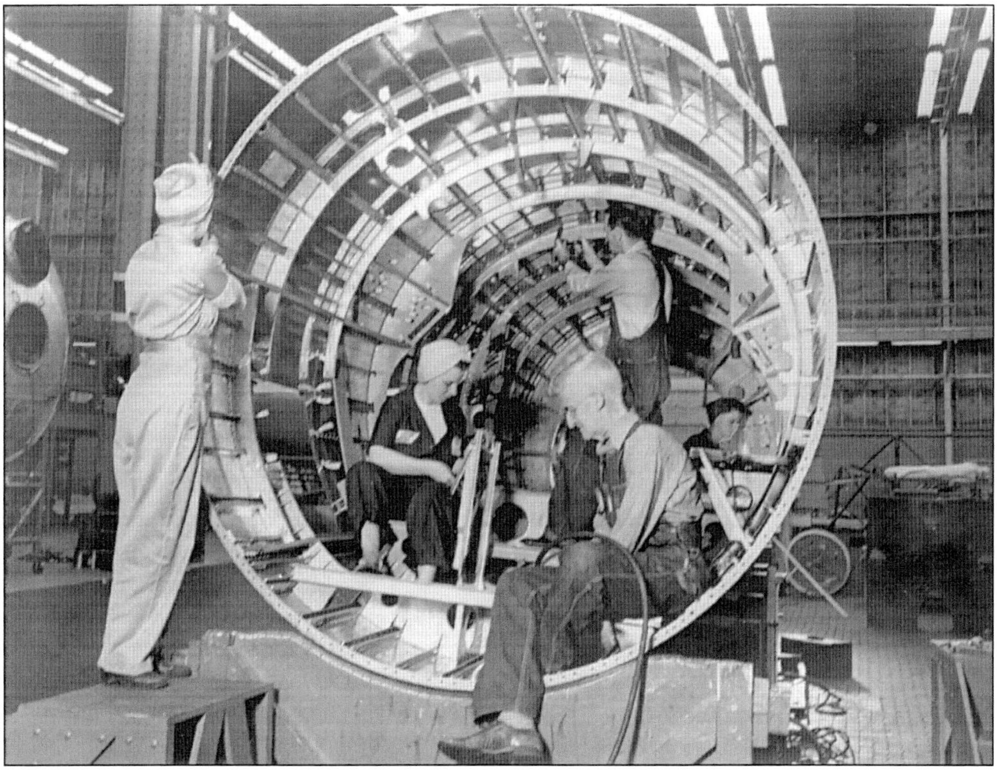

Bell Aircraft workers during World War II included women and older men, shown here working on a B-29, as staples of the production force. (Courtesy Bill Kinney collection.)

Two

To Serve and Protect

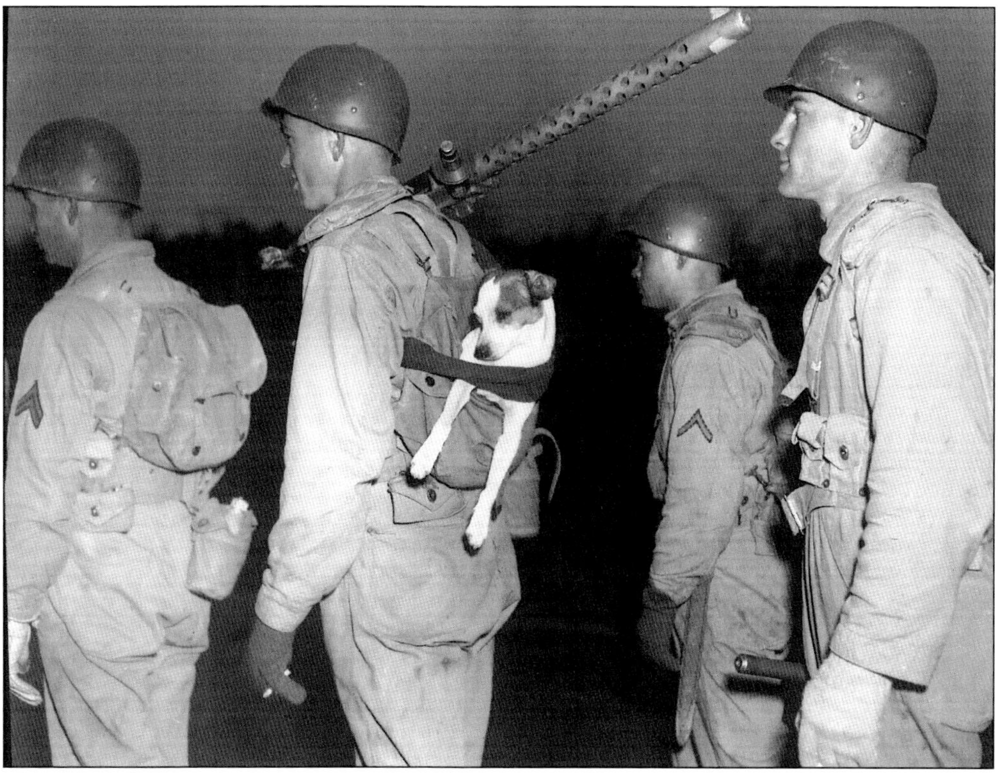

This scene from Georgia's Fort Benning, home of the U.S. Army Infantry School, was taken in the 1940s. The importance of Fort Benning, established in 1918, grew during World War II with the arrival of the First Infantry Division and the establishment of Officer Candidate School and airborne training. (Courtesy Atlanta History Center.)

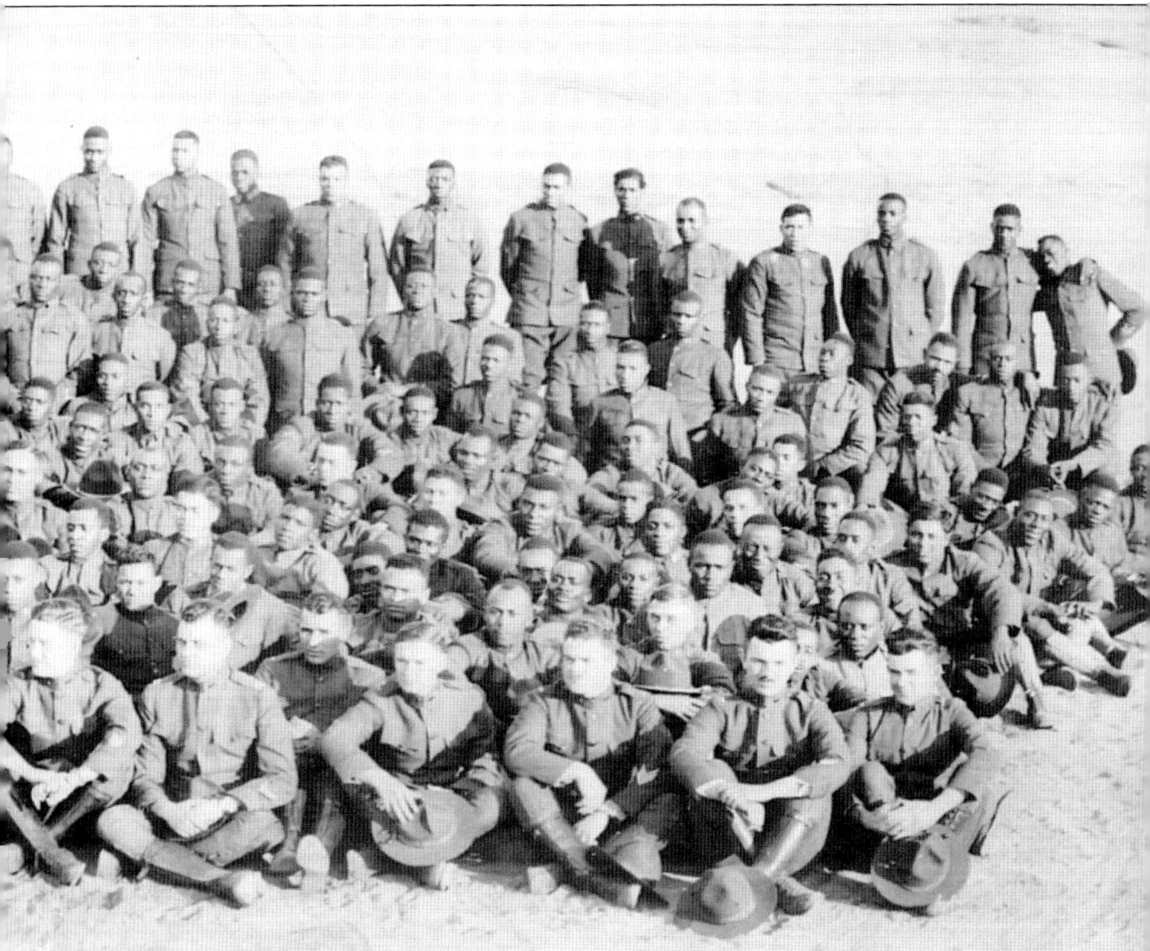

Pictured here are some of the African-American soldiers stationed at Camp Gordon, c. 1919. When the war against Germany was declared April 6, 1917, it was quickly recognized that this was to be a war for all the people of the United States. More than 400,000 black soldiers were called to the war. It was proven at Camp Gordon in DeKalb County that black and white men could be trained together without friction. The first call for "colored" selection came in September 1917, with approximately 9,000 men reporting. It was during WW I that soldier Henry Johnson became the first African American to receive the Croix de Guerre, for killing 4 Germans and wounding 22 with his bolo knife. Emmett J. Scott, former secretary to Booker T. Washington at Tuskegee and special assistant to Secretary of War, the Honorable Newton Baker, compiled an official history of African-American participation in WW I in his book *The American Negro in the World War*. The book documented not only soldiers, but also other war related organizations such as the YMCA, the YWCA, and the War Camp Community Service. Located near Camp Gordon was Johnsontown, an African-American settlement situated where Lenox Square shopping mall now sits. Today, the Chamblee/Doraville area is one of the most culturally diversified communities in Georgia, stretching along a 6-mile strip of Buford Highway between North Druid Hills and Gwinnett County. (Courtesy of Willis Jones/Digging It Up Archives.)

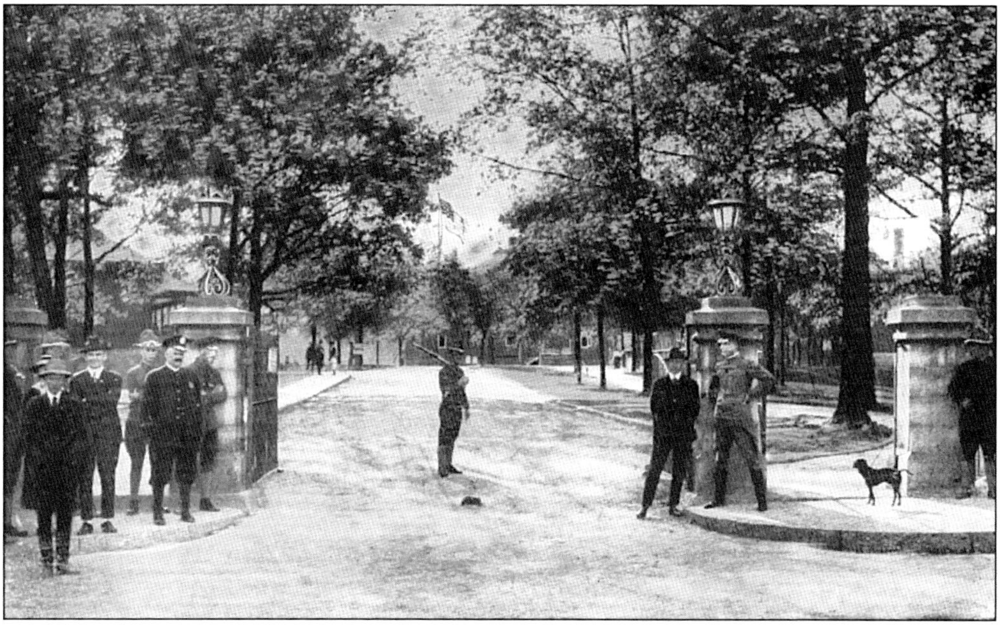

Established in 1867 on the present site of Spelman College, Fort McPherson was named for General James Birdseye McPherson, a Union commander killed in the Battle of Atlanta. In 1885 the military facilities were moved to the present site in the southeast Atlanta area. (Published by Imperial Post Card Co., Atlanta.)

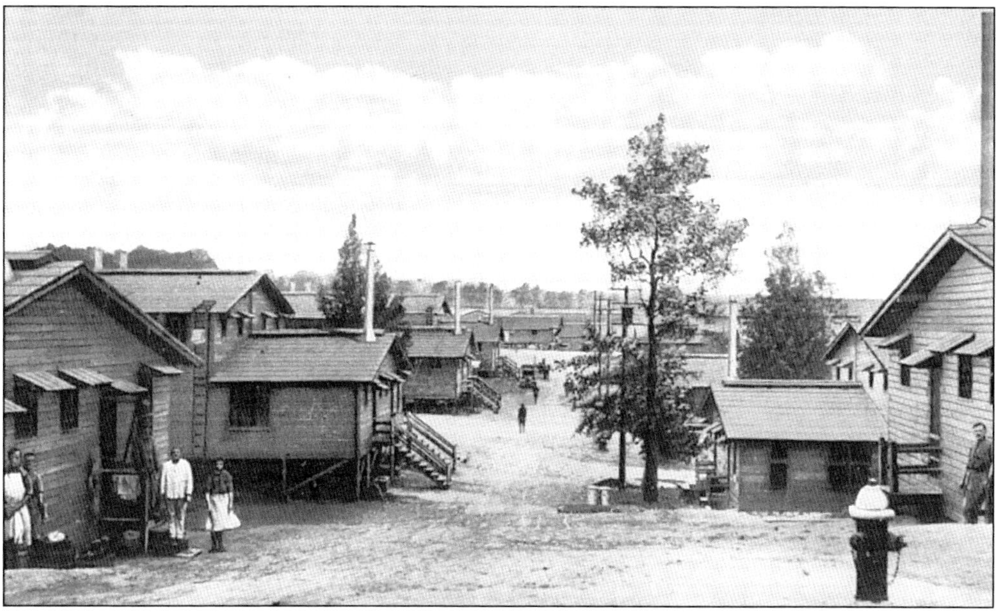

This typical scene illustrates both the village-like atmosphere of Camp Gordon and its impermanence. The lonely fire plug symbolizes the special 13 miles of water pipes that were installed to service the camp. Such installations ran up the cost of Camp Gordon to $6 million. (Published by I.F. Co., Atlanta.)

Georgia Military Institute Cadet Private James A. Blackshear is pictured in full dress uniform at the Marietta school in the late 1850s. Blackshear fought with his classmates in the Confederate army and survived the war, but died of tuberculosis in 1867. (Courtesy Marietta Museum of History collection.)

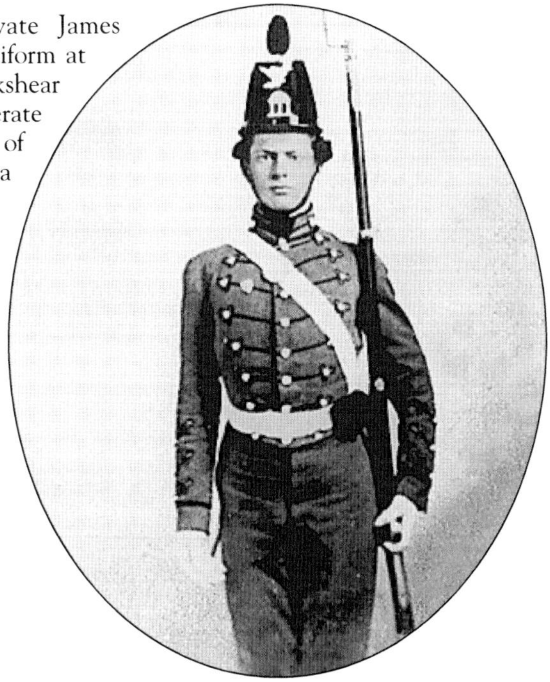

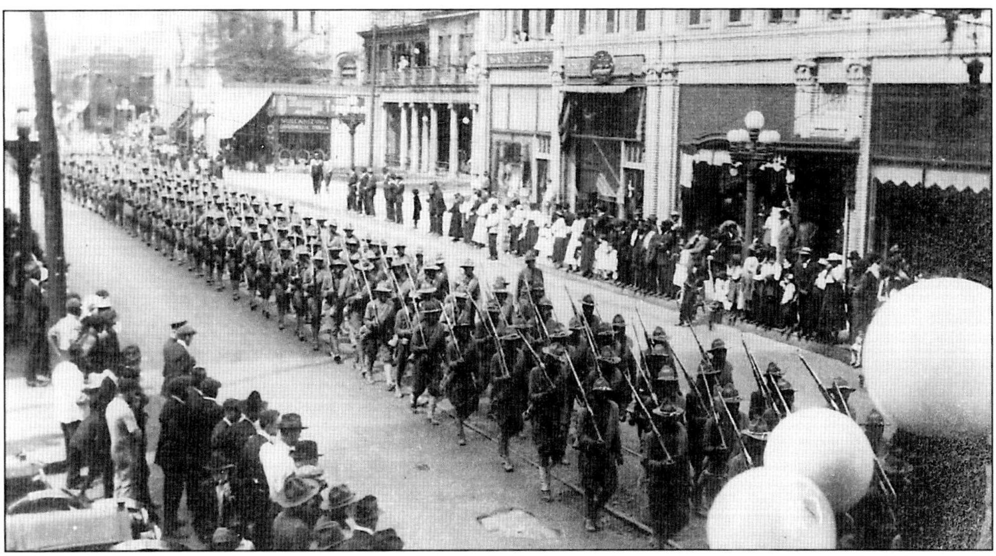

African-American soldiers from Camp Gordon in DeKalb County and auxiliary groups poured onto the streets of Atlanta in a gallant parade the day after the Germans signed an armistice. Camp Gordon was one of the largest training centers for Negro troops, housing over 9,000 blacks by 1917. Most of the black recruits were assigned to engineer or labor service battalions. The end of the war was a major relief for the troops segregated in their service for their country. Mayor Candler called for a victory parade on November 12, 1918, and the troops marched down Peachtree Street near 10th Street to Whitehall Street as this photograph shows. (Courtesy Digging It Up Archives.)

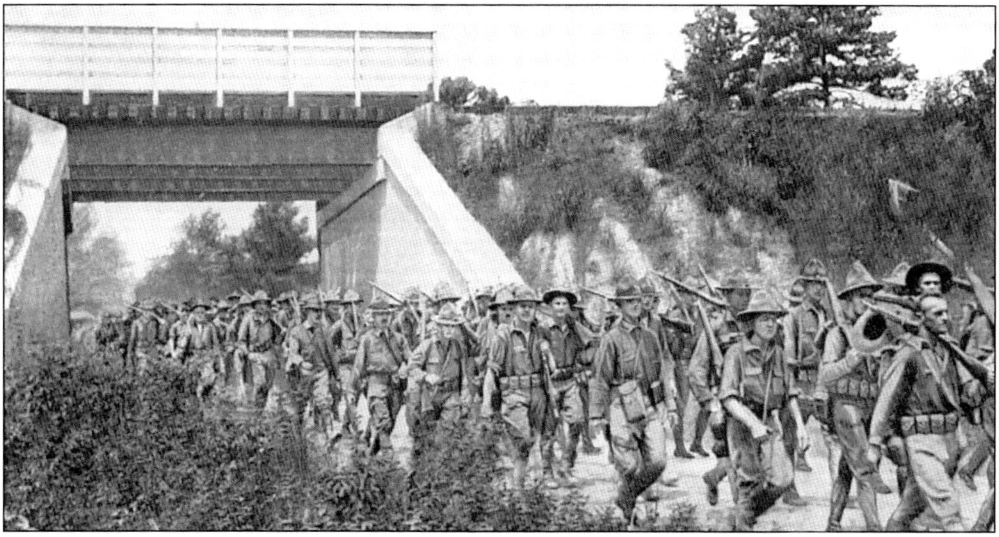

In the summer of 1917 the nearby town of Chamblee experienced an economic boom with 40 new stores opening. The sender of this card comments: "I went out to Camp Gordon last Sunday and saw thousands of soldiers. Sixty thousand live there . . . One hundred French soldiers were there—all have been wounded fighting in France." (Published by I.F. Co., Atlanta.)

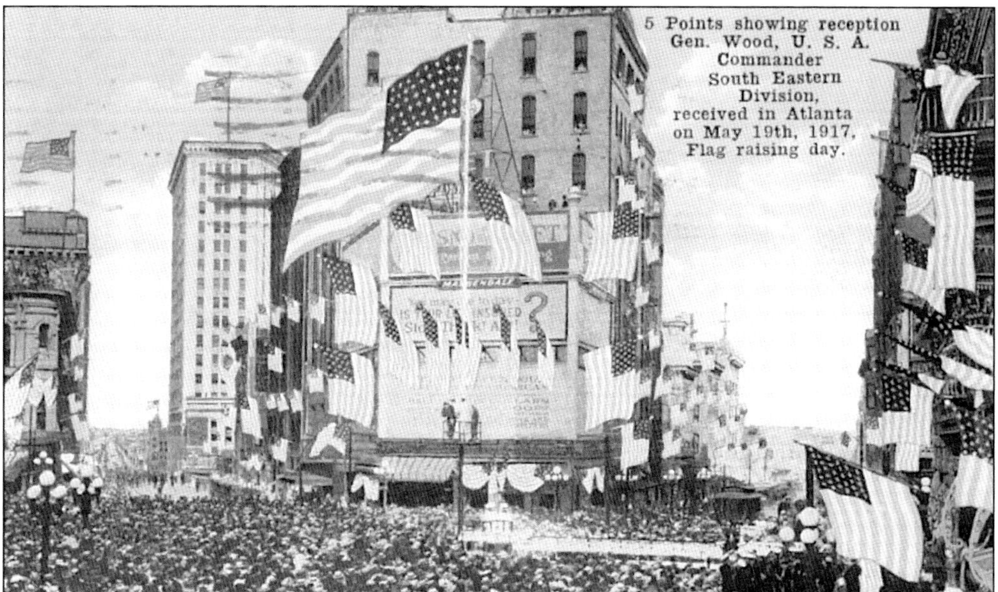

Patriotic Atlanta is shown here in its fervor to greet General Leonard Wood. Many military and civilian groups marched in the parade, including the entire student body of Georgia Tech. The Atlanta Constitution said, in part: "History was made at Five Points Saturday afternoon when the greatest parade Atlanta ever saw passed in review . . . It was an Atlanta chapter in the greatest volume of history the world has ever known . . . being written in blood and fire on the battlefields of Europe today." (Published by the Imperial Post Card Co., Atlanta; card sent 1917.)

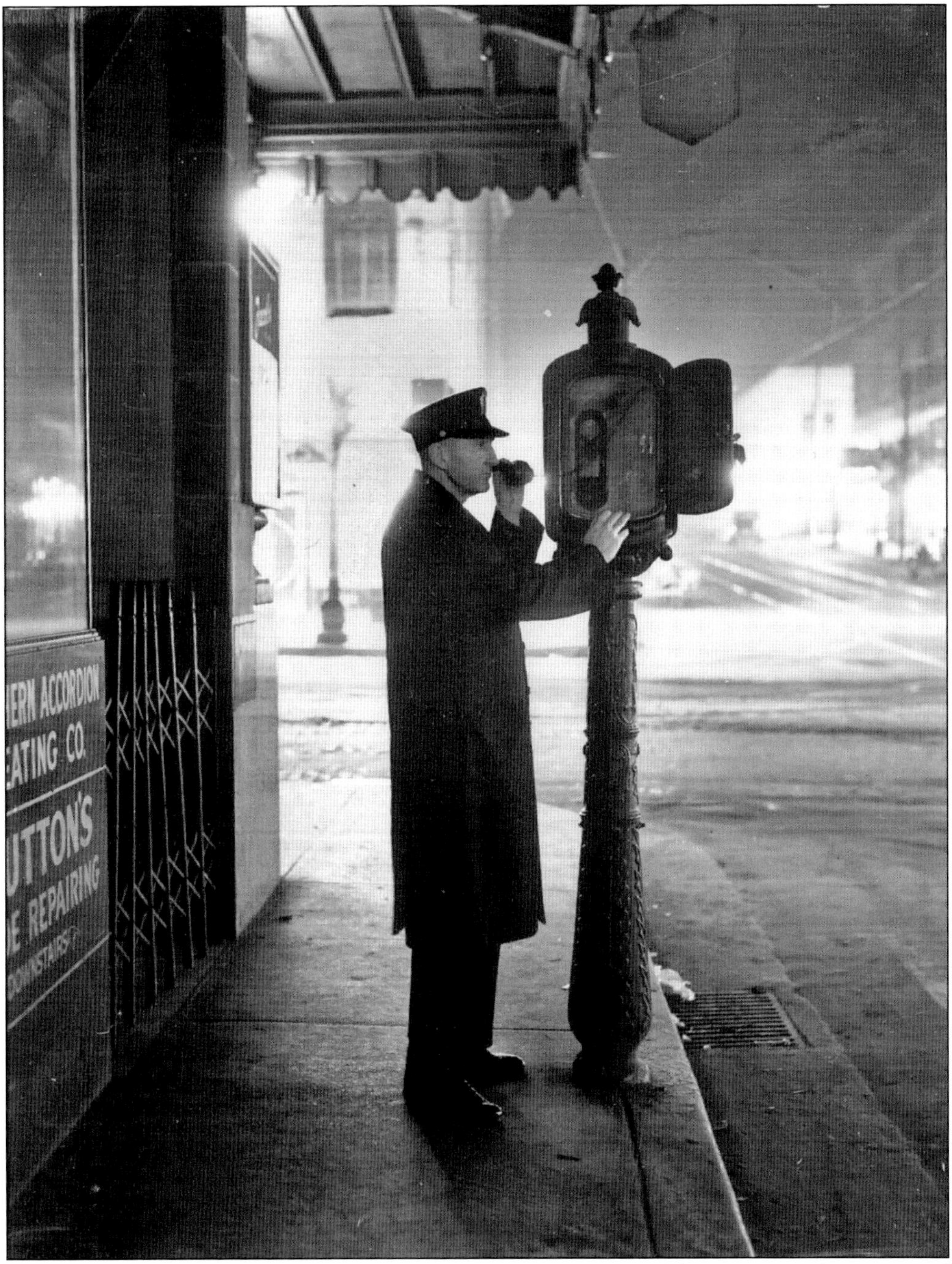

A city policeman checks in at a call box located on Lower Alabama Street (now part of Underground Atlanta). The construction of viaducts over downtown rail lines to alleviate traffic led to a one-floor elevation of the street level and the virtual abandonment of the original ground-floor storefronts beneath. (Photograph by Kenneth Rogers. Courtesy Atlanta History Center.)

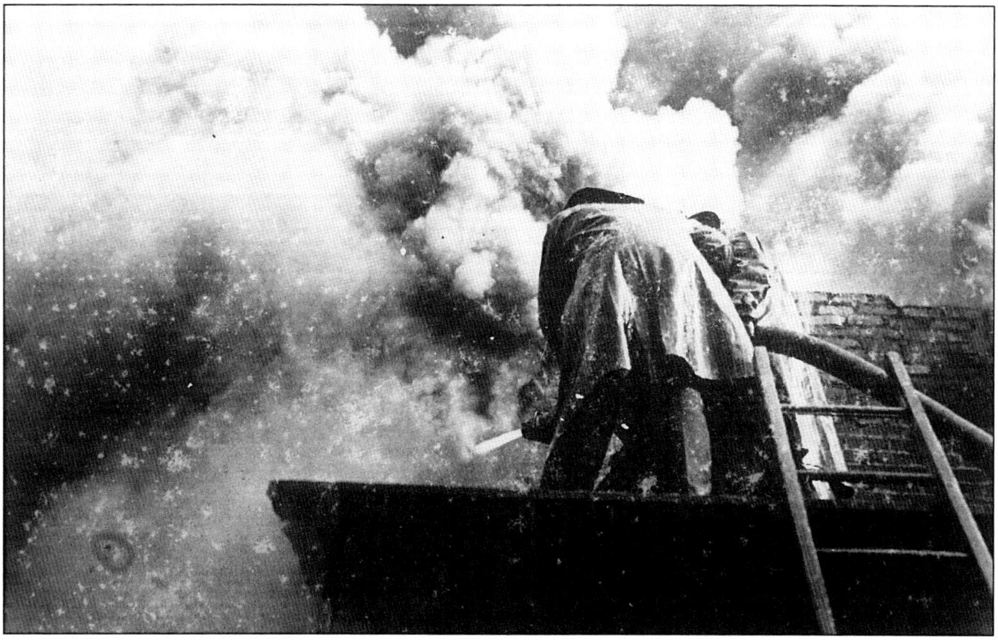

With the addition of professional staff photographers, such as Francis Price, publishers increased the number of action scenes in newspapers. In February 1914, the entire Atlanta Fire Department battled a blaze in the McKenzie Building at Peachtree and Forsyth Streets. Causing an estimated $150,000 damage, the fire burned for a number of hours and drew a Sunday afternoon crowd of 25,000 onlookers. The city's fire department was organized in 1882, but faulty water lines, poor fire code enforcement, and flammable building materials hampered efforts to fight fires in the early years of this century. (Courtesy Atlanta History Center.)

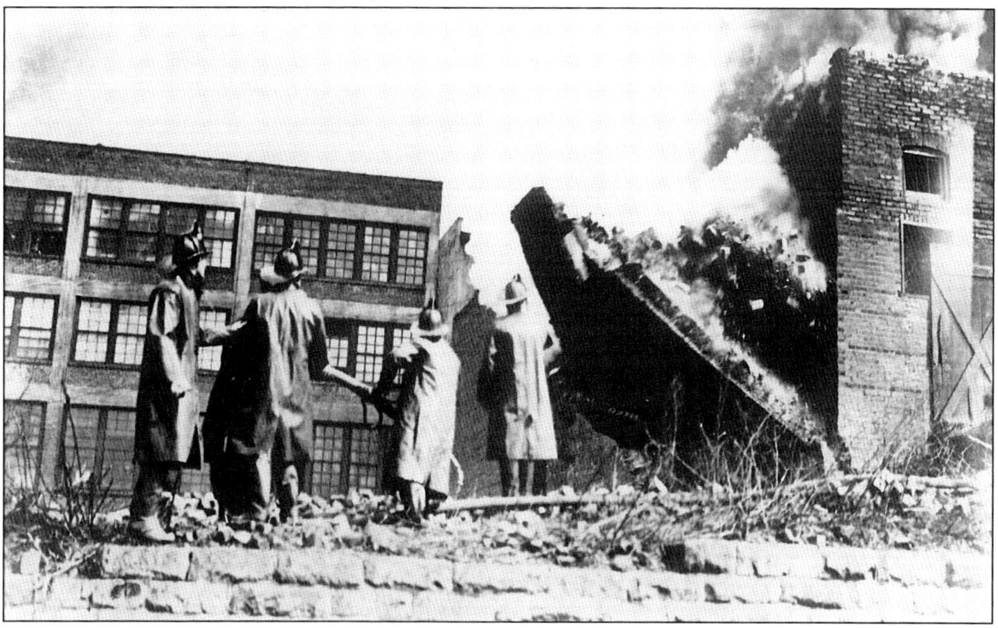

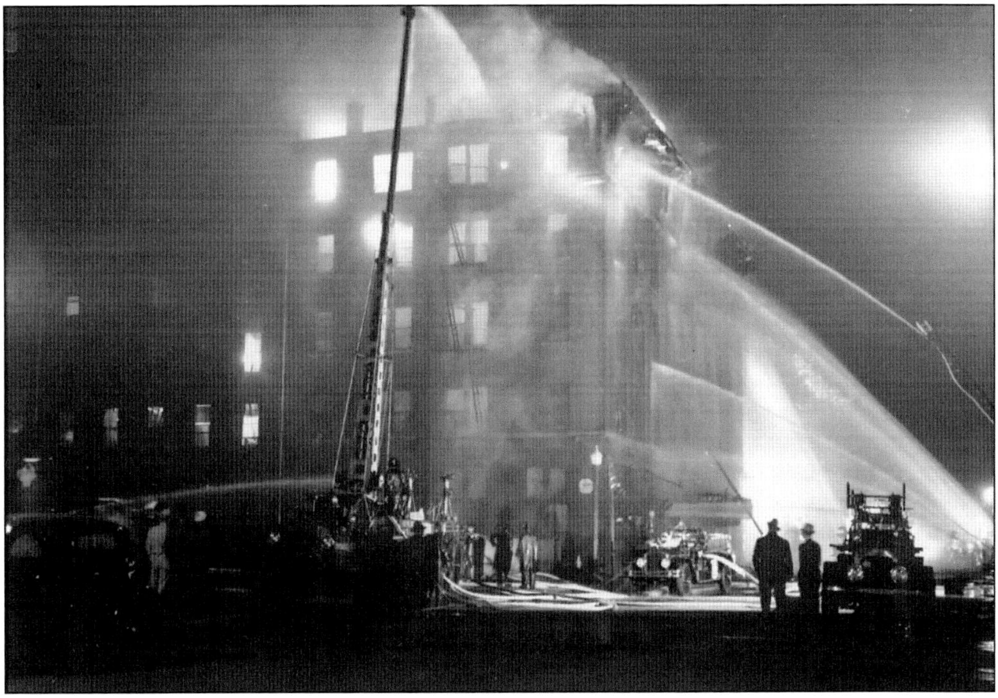

Pictured here is a scene from the Terminal Hotel fire on May 16, 1938. The five-story structure, located at Spring and Mitchell Streets, across the street from Atlanta's rail station, was engulfed in flames minutes after the fire alarm sounded. The roof collapsed shortly after firemen arrived, hindering rescue efforts. Thirty-four people died in the blaze, making it Atlanta's worst, until the Winecoff Hotel fire of 1946. (Courtesy Atlanta History Center.)

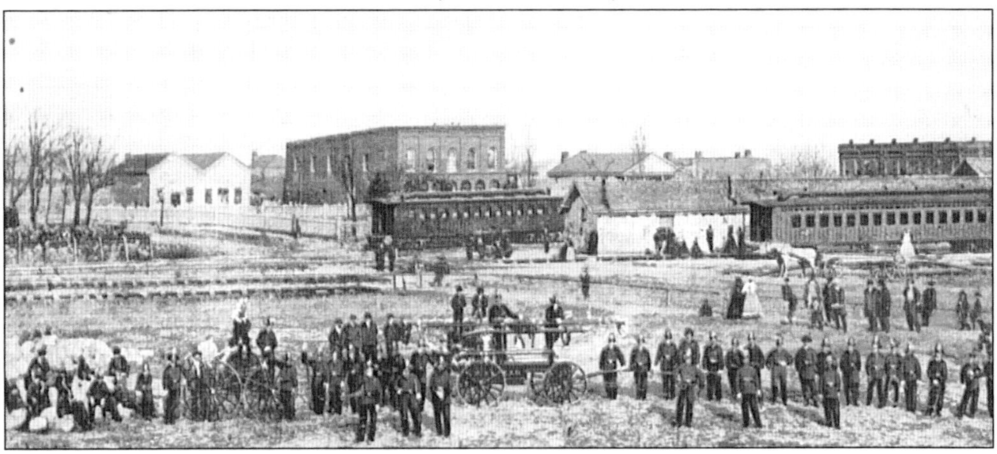

This well-known photograph was put on a postcard about 1907. Here we see the Atlantic Volunteer Fire Department lined up in front of the passenger depot and the Atlanta Hotel. At left we see the famous hand-engine "Blue Dick," and at center the hook-and-ladder truck "Old Reliable." The Fire Company No. 1 was chartered in 1850 and was located at Broad (then Market) Street and the Macon and Western railroad tracks. (Published by Cole Book Co., Atlanta; card sent 1909.)

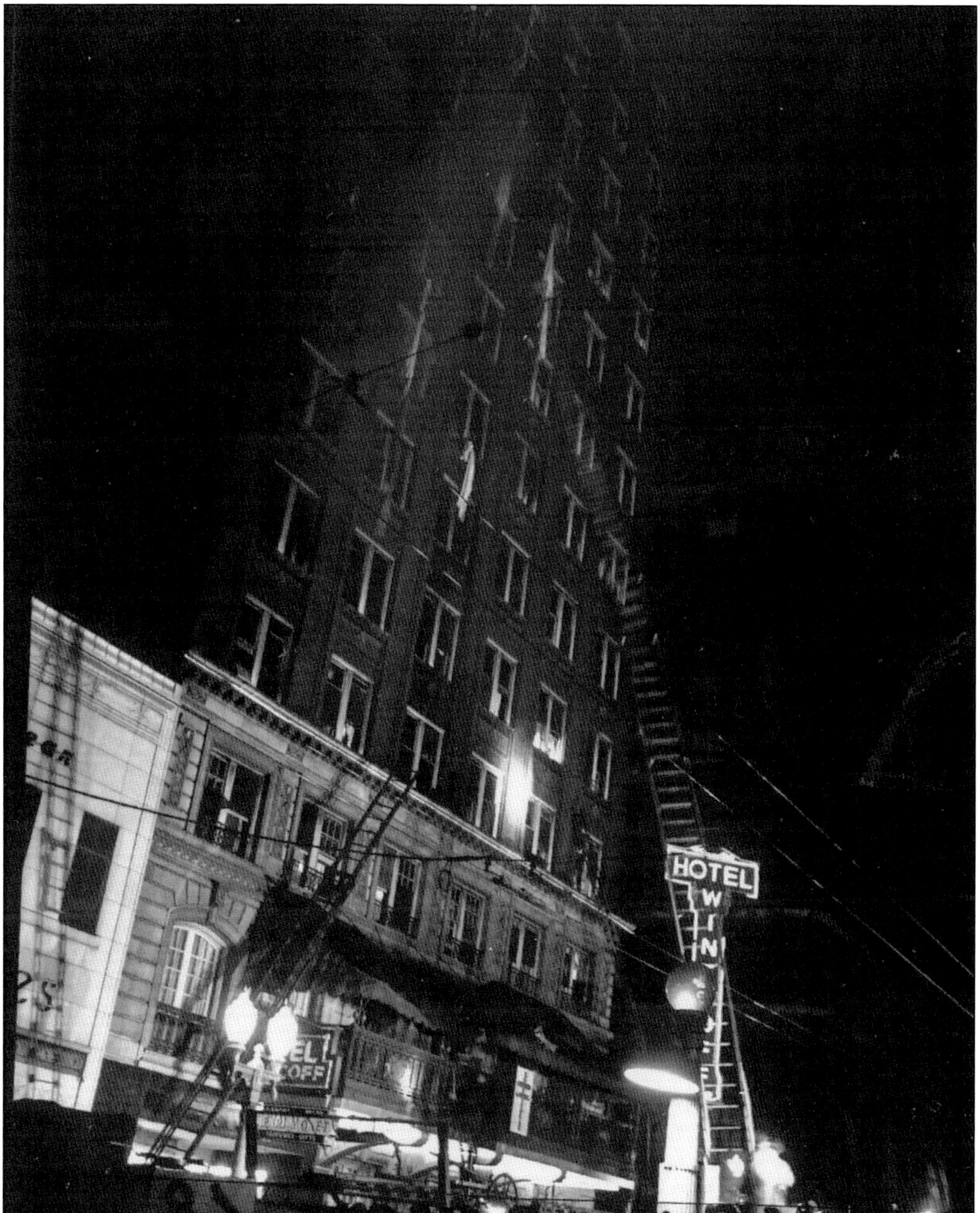

On December 7, 1946, Atlanta's Winecoff Hotel—then the city's tallest—caught fire, killing 119 people. Built in 1913, the hotel had neither fire escapes nor a sprinkler system; the city's new fire code did not apply to older buildings. The Winecoff disaster still bears the dubious distinction of being the worst hotel fire in American history. (Courtesy Atlanta History Center.)

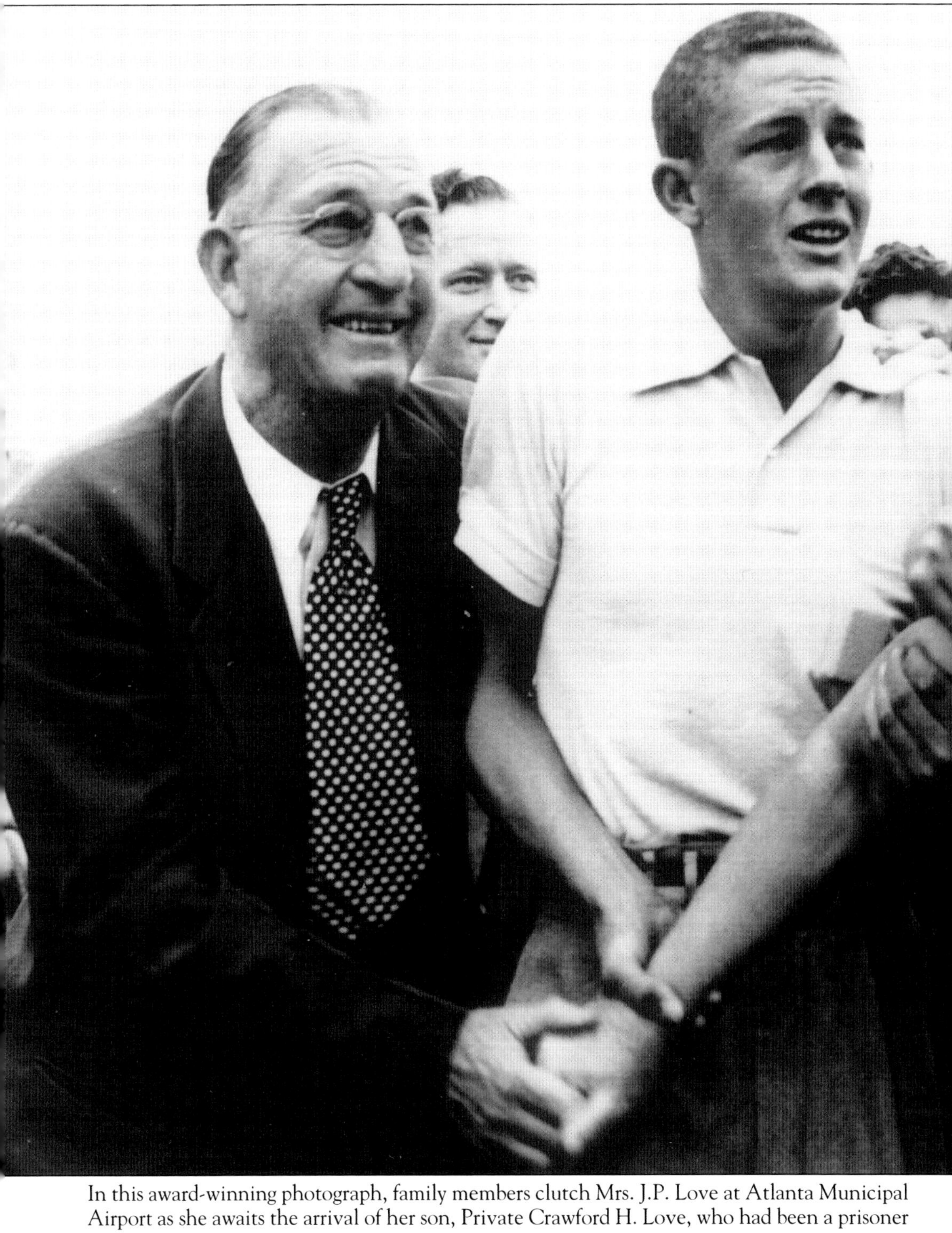

In this award-winning photograph, family members clutch Mrs. J.P. Love at Atlanta Municipal Airport as she awaits the arrival of her son, Private Crawford H. Love, who had been a prisoner

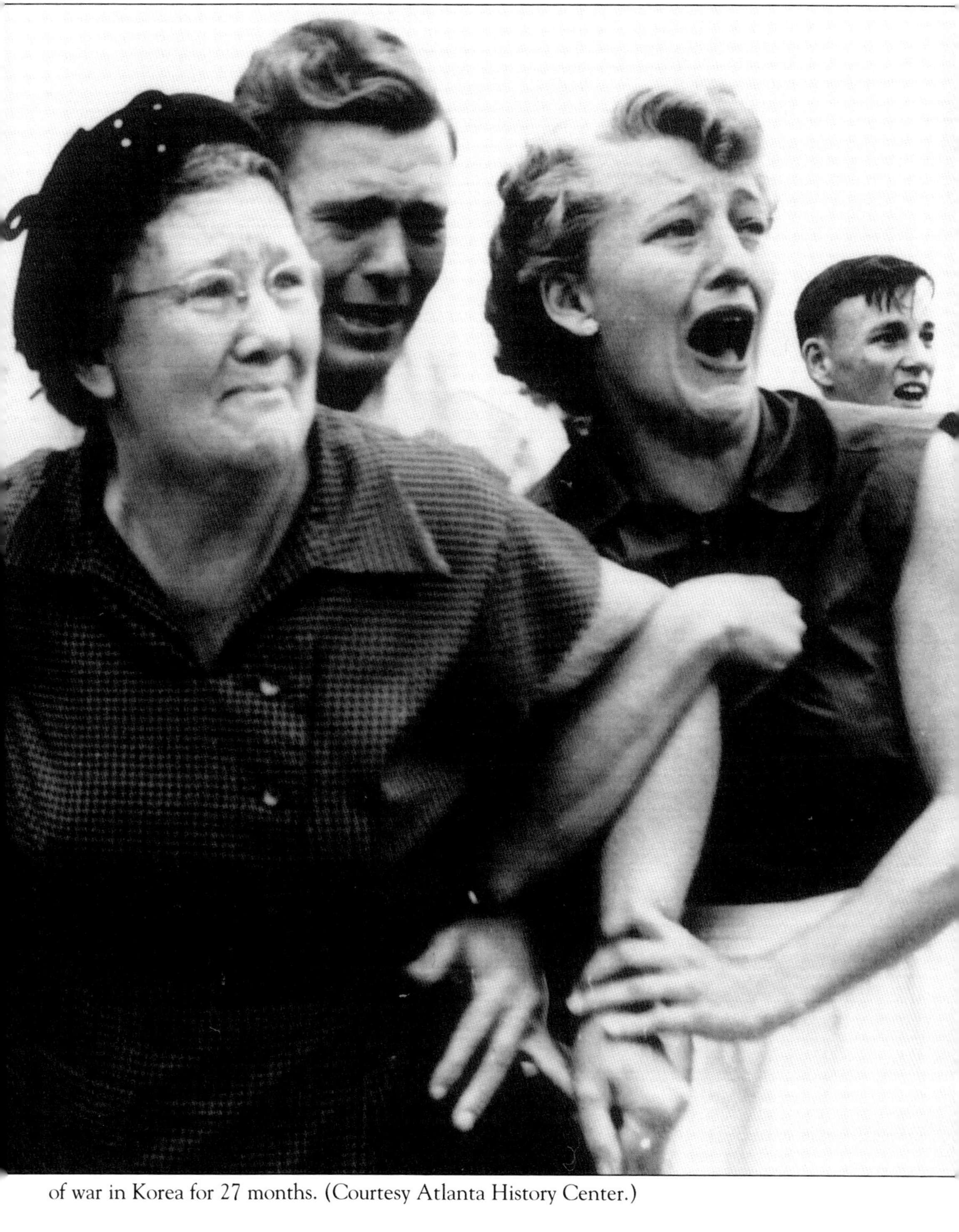

of war in Korea for 27 months. (Courtesy Atlanta History Center.)

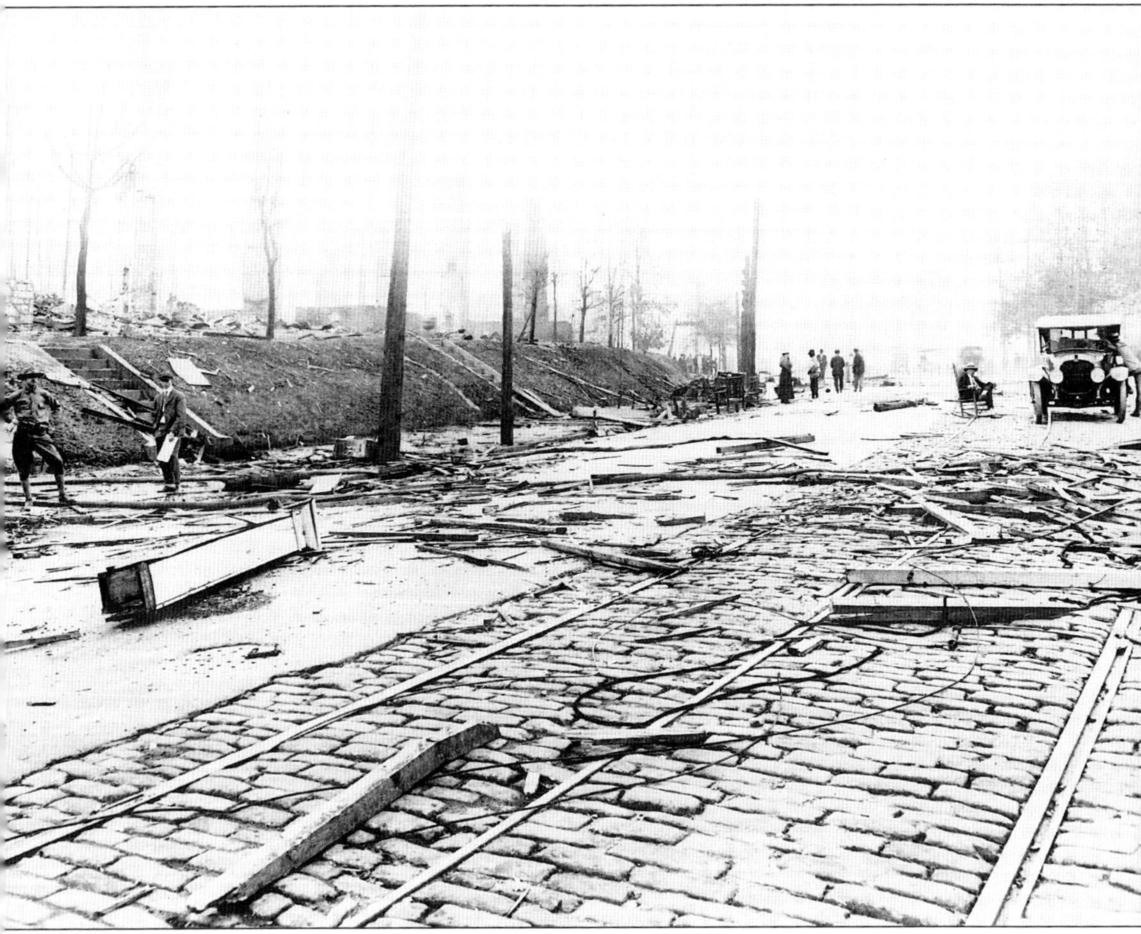

The lone man seated at right surveys the destruction of the Great Atlanta Fire of May 1917 from the comfort of possibly all he has left—his rocking chair. Erupting on the morning of the 21st, the fire burned out of control for nearly 12 hours until a fire break was created by dynamiting dozens of homes along Ponce de Leon Avenue. Nearly 50 city blocks were destroyed at a 1917 cost of more than $5 million. Amazingly, there were no deaths reported in the conflagration. (Courtesy Atlanta History Center.)

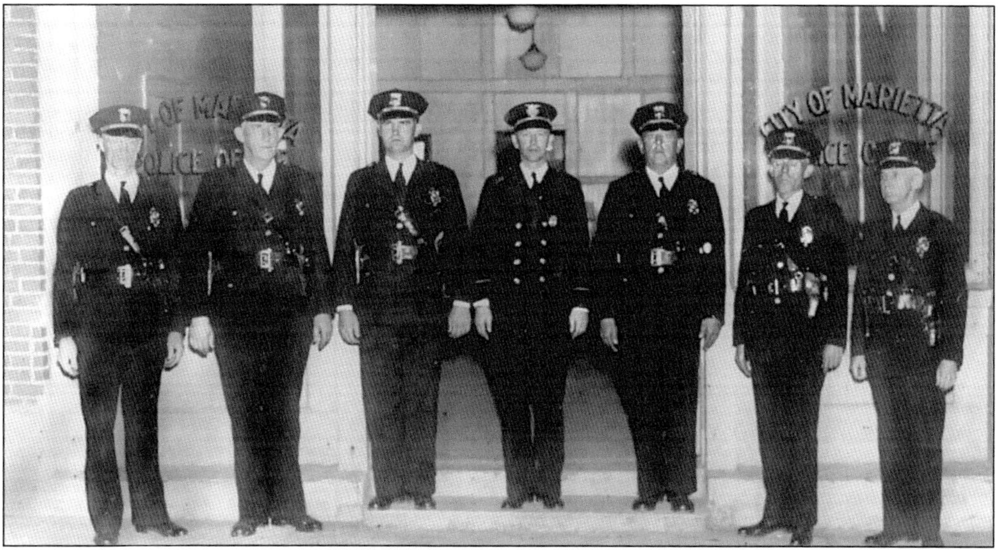

Marietta's entire police department posed for this picture in front of the Atlanta Street headquarters in 1938. This scene includes from left to right: unidentified, unidentified, Harold P. Griggs, Chief W.J. Black Jr., Harry Scoggins, unidentified, and Floyd Jolley. Griggs became department chief in 1939, and served until 1947 when he left police service. Ten years later, he joined the Cobb County Police Department and served as chief investigator until his retirement in 1964. (Gretchen Griggs Vaughan Collection.)

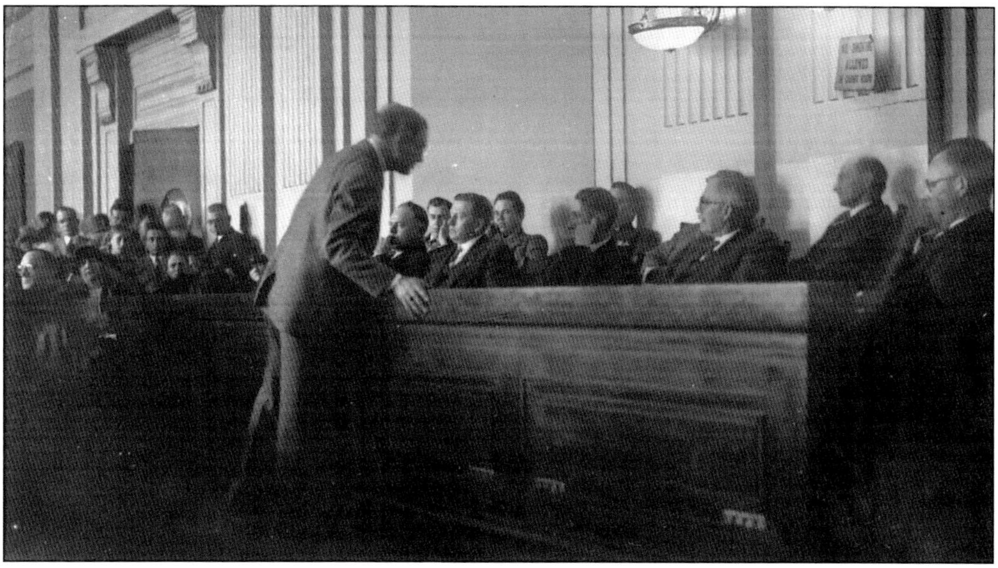

On the night of October 20, 1938, Willard Smith, a drugstore clerk, was killed in an attempted robbery. The ensuing trial of his murderers—George Harsh and Richard Gallogly, two Oglethorpe University students from socially prominent families—captured the imagination of the South. Ultimately, Harsh was convicted and Gallogly, following two mistrials, pled guilty to save his friend from the electric chair. The defense attorney appeals to the jury in an image taken before the prohibition of courtroom photography. (Courtesy Atlanta History Center.)

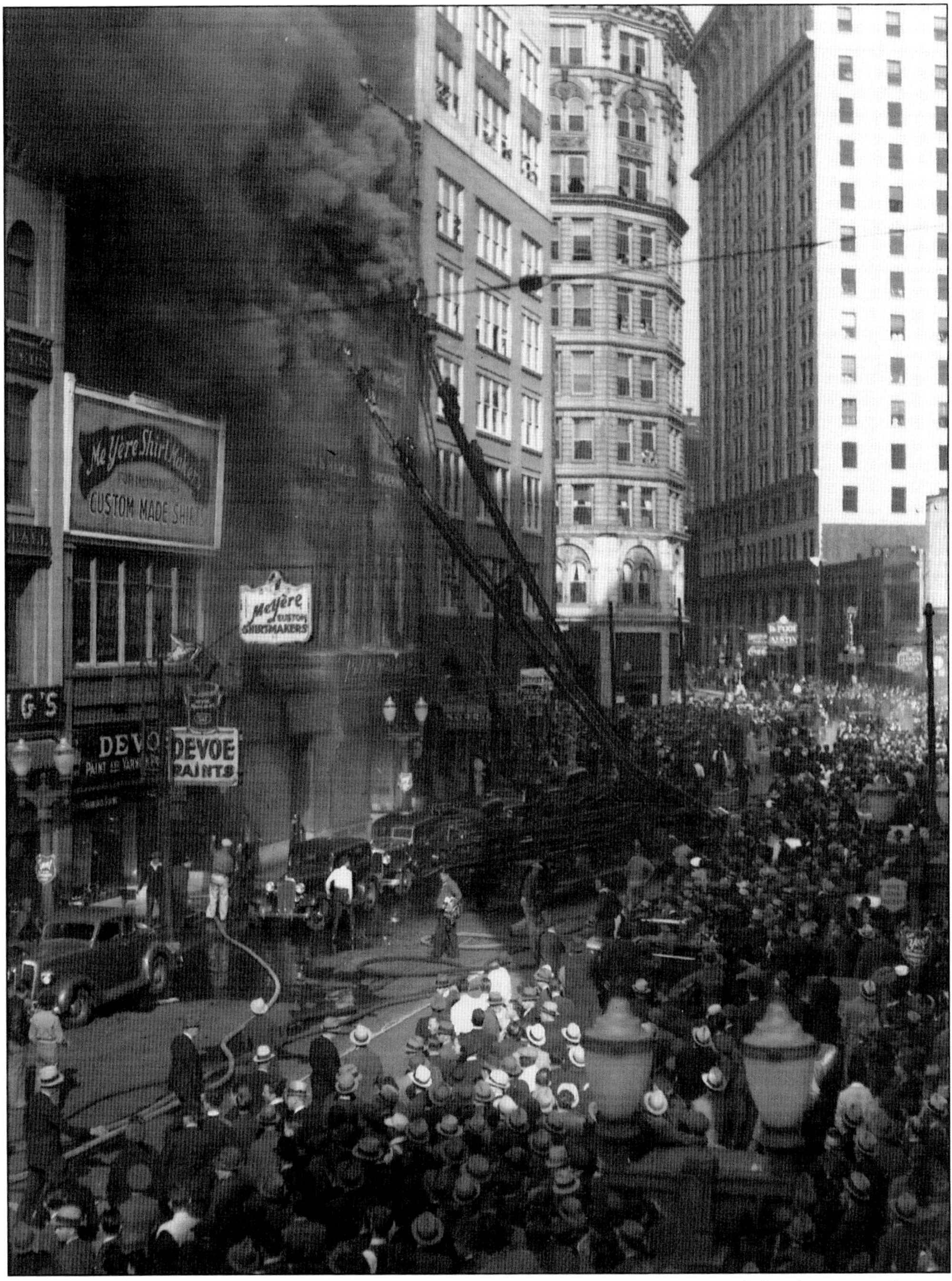

In November 1936, thousands of bystanders witnessed the destruction of the five-story home of the Cable Piano Company on Broad Street. A probe into the fire emphasized the city's need for more aerial ladders, masks, and equipment, but many were convinced that the "hysterical army" of spectators had caused much of the tragedy. (Courtesy Atlanta History Center.)

Three

SIGHTS AND SCENES

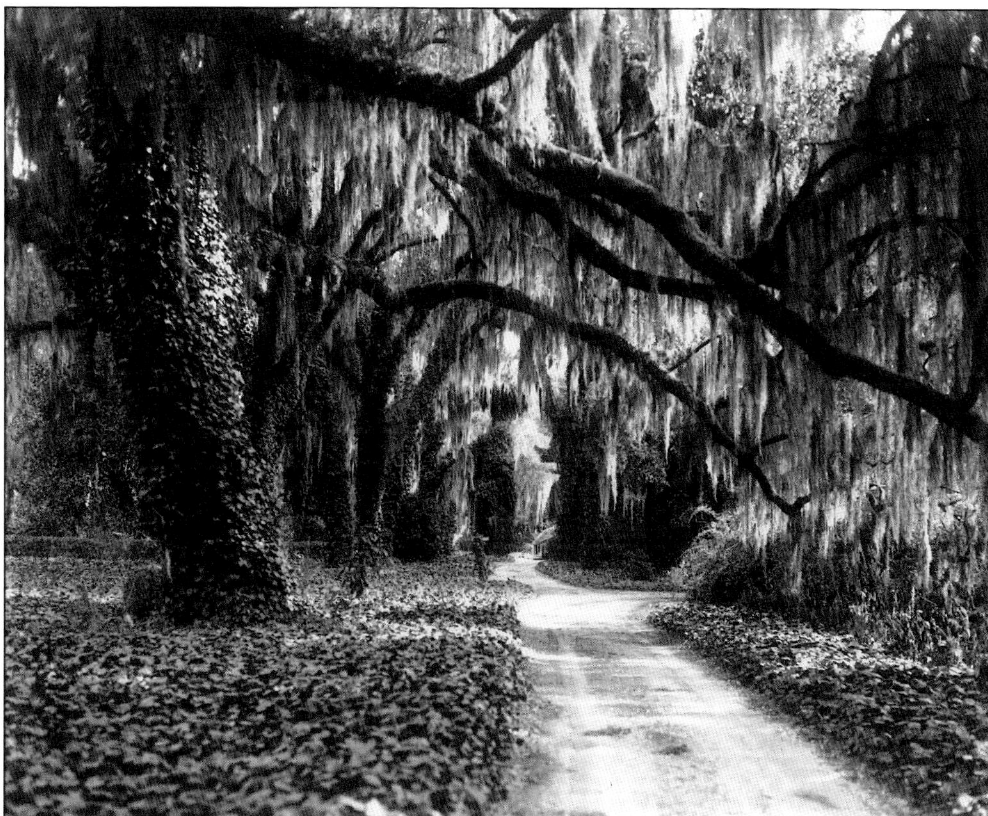

Beyond Kenneth Rogers' work as a newspaper photographer, he was well known for his nature shots of the north Georgia mountains, the coastal islands and marshes, and the south Georgia swamps and pine woods. Many Atlantans were familiar with these scenes through a series of illustrated desk calendars published by Rich's department store in the 1950s. (Courtesy Atlanta History Center.)

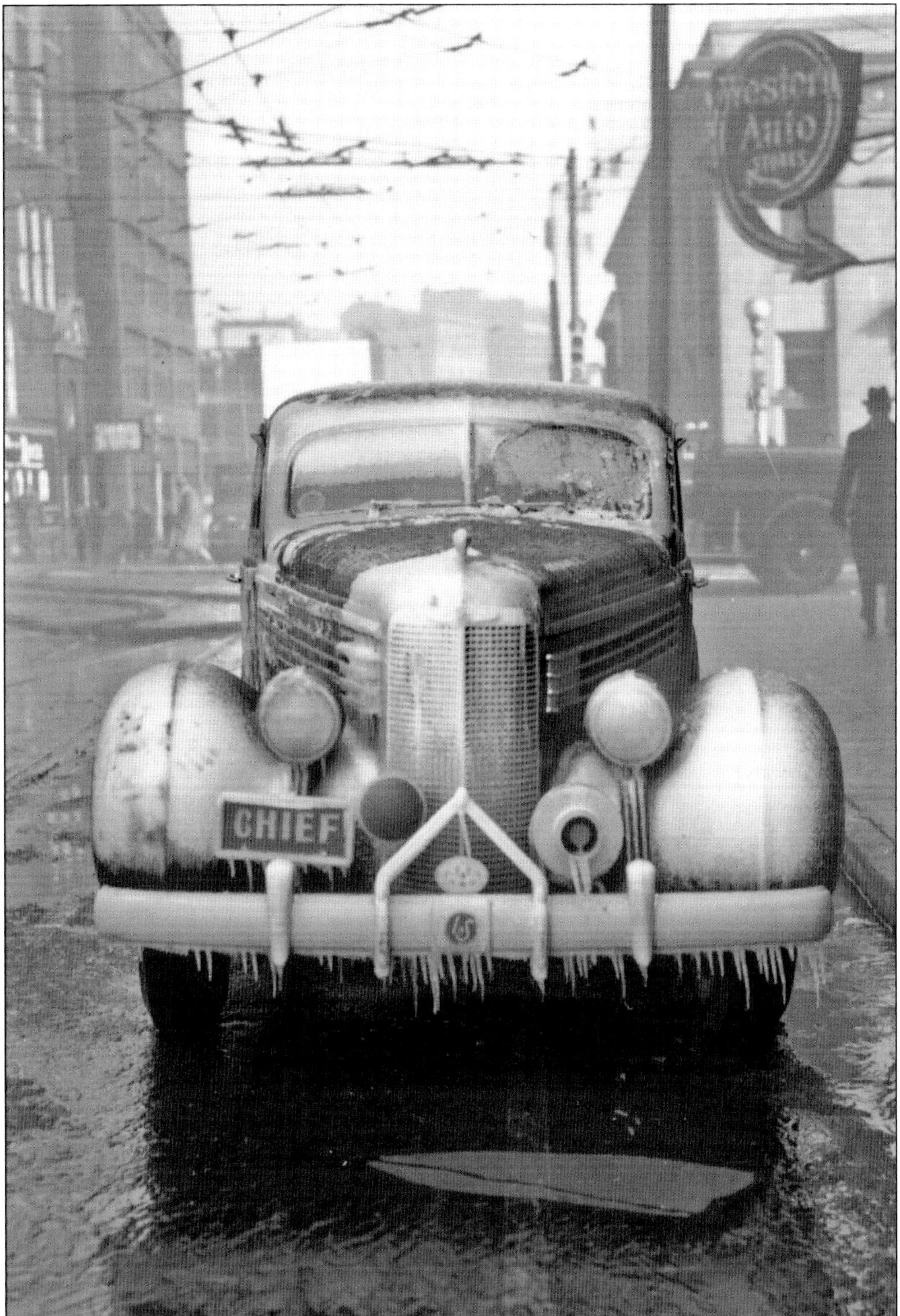
Auto
CHIEF

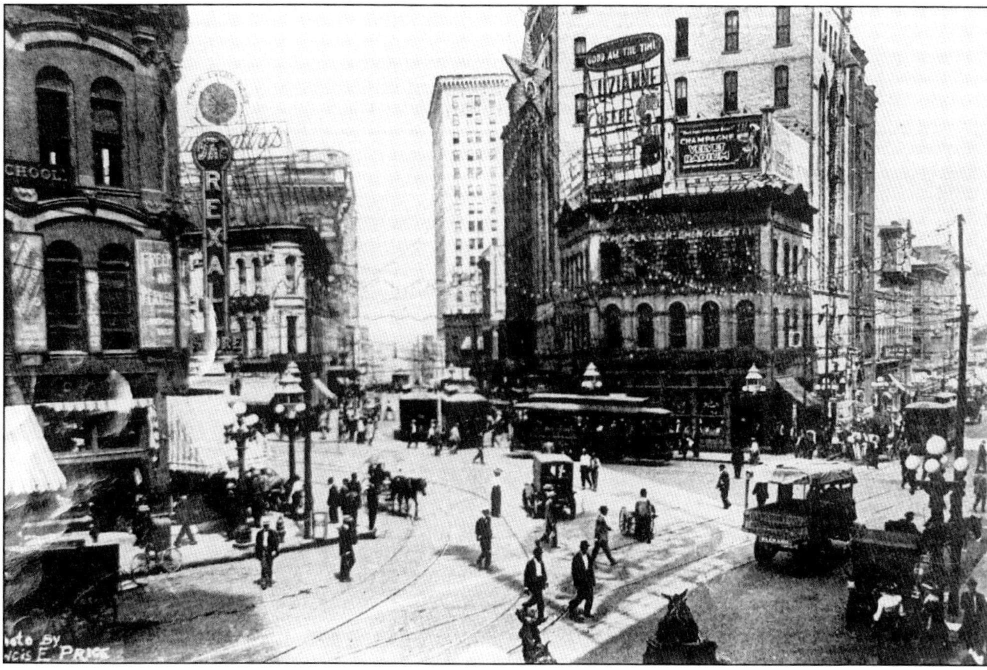

The business and cultural center of early Atlanta was Five Points—the convergence of Peachtree, Edgewood, Decatur, and Marietta Streets in downtown Atlanta. Looking east along Edgewood Avenue, this scene includes street decorations for the Shriners' 1914 national convention. (Courtesy Atlanta History Center.)

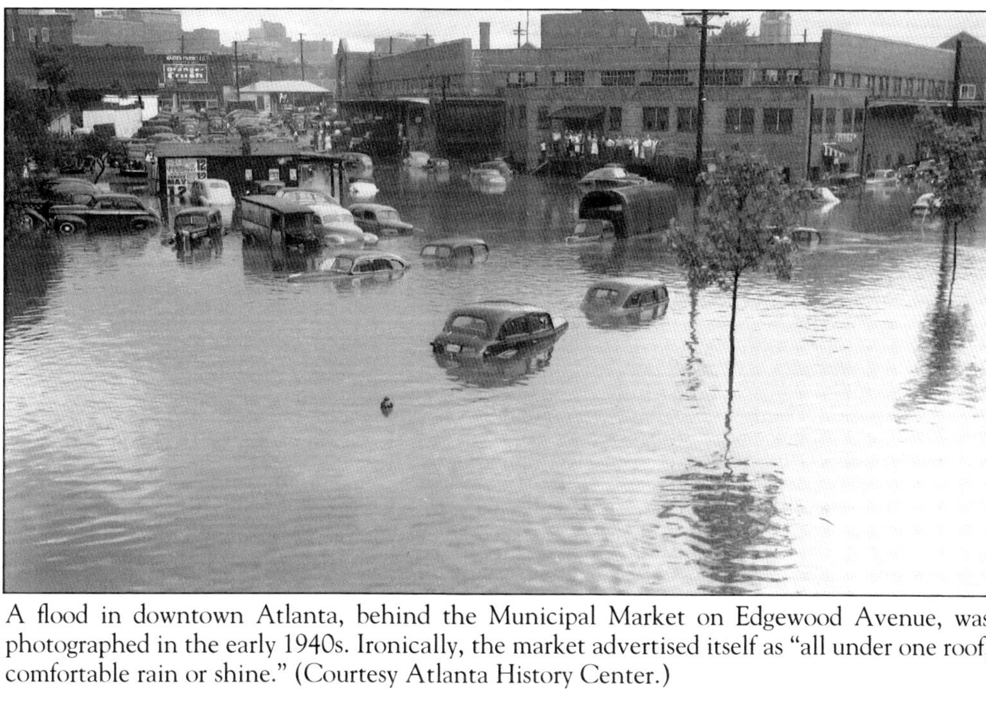

A flood in downtown Atlanta, behind the Municipal Market on Edgewood Avenue, was photographed in the early 1940s. Ironically, the market advertised itself as "all under one roof, comfortable rain or shine." (Courtesy Atlanta History Center.)

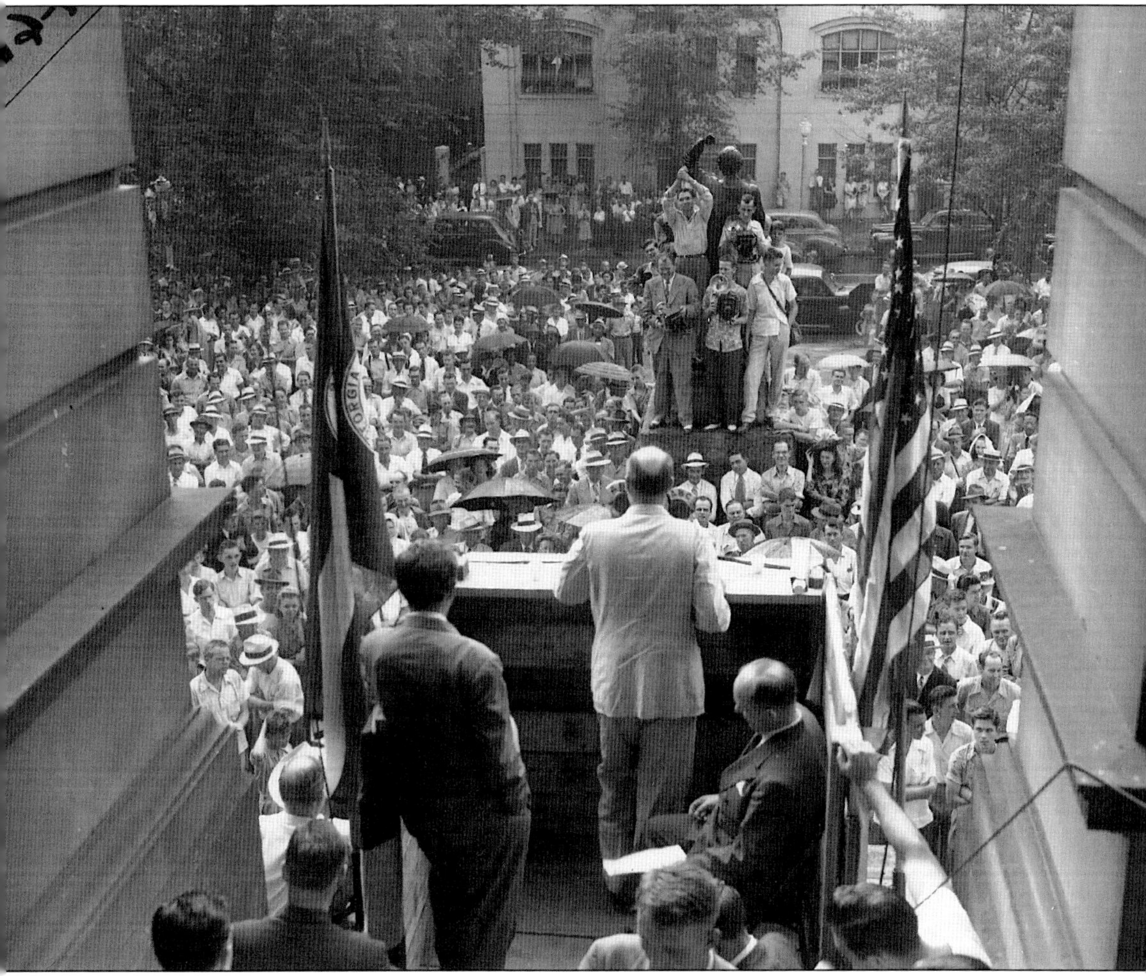

The steps of Georgia's capitol have long been a favorite pulpit from which politicians and pundits preach their messages to the people. At this July 1946 rally, Drew Pearson, a syndicated Washington columnist and radio commentator, delivered a nationally broadcast speech denouncing the Ku Klux Klan to a crowd of 2,000 people (and a pack of photojournalists, including Marion Johnson and Kenneth Rogers). (Courtesy Atlanta History Center.)

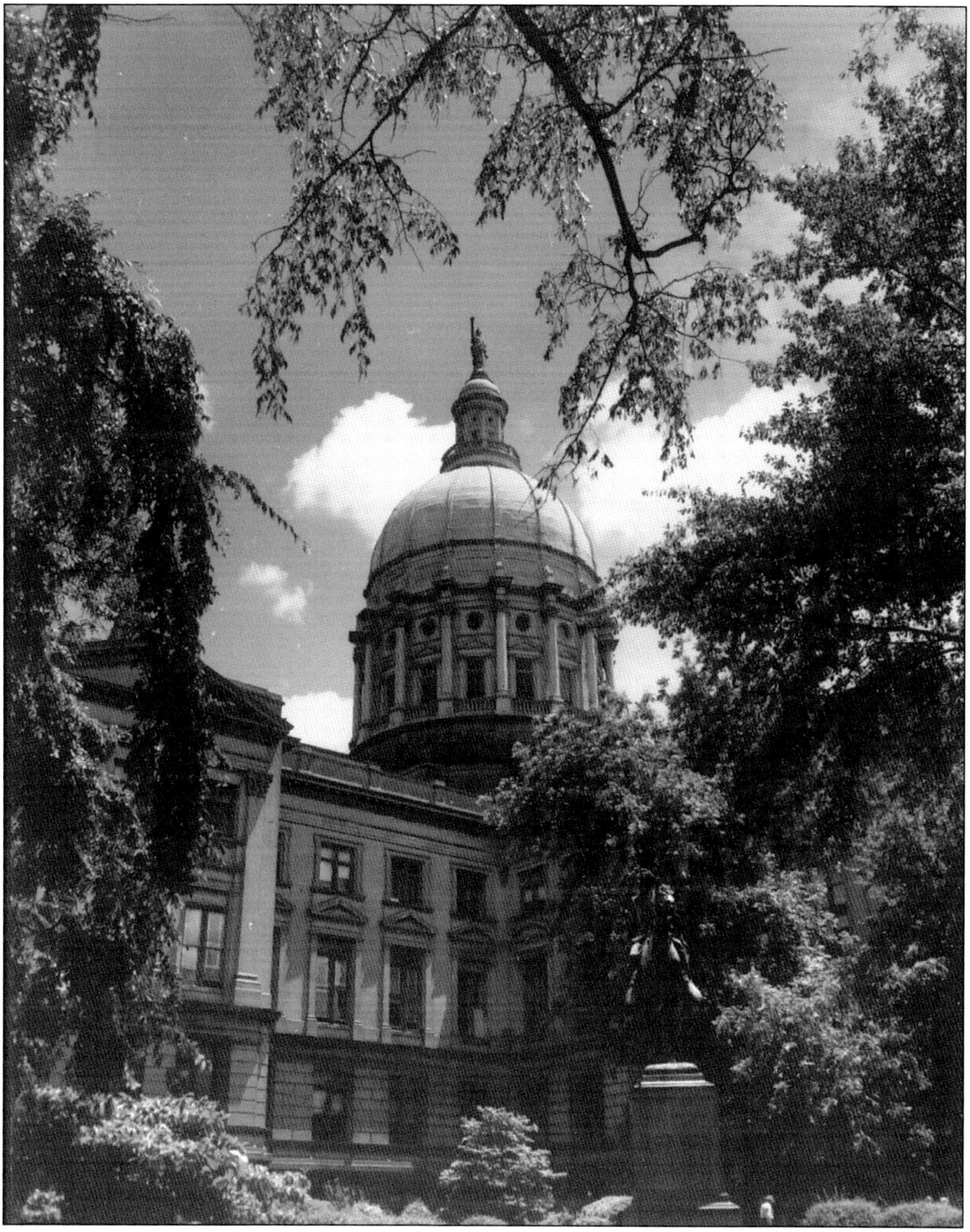

This scene depicting Georgia's capitol demonstrates why Atlanta is so often called the "City in the Forest."

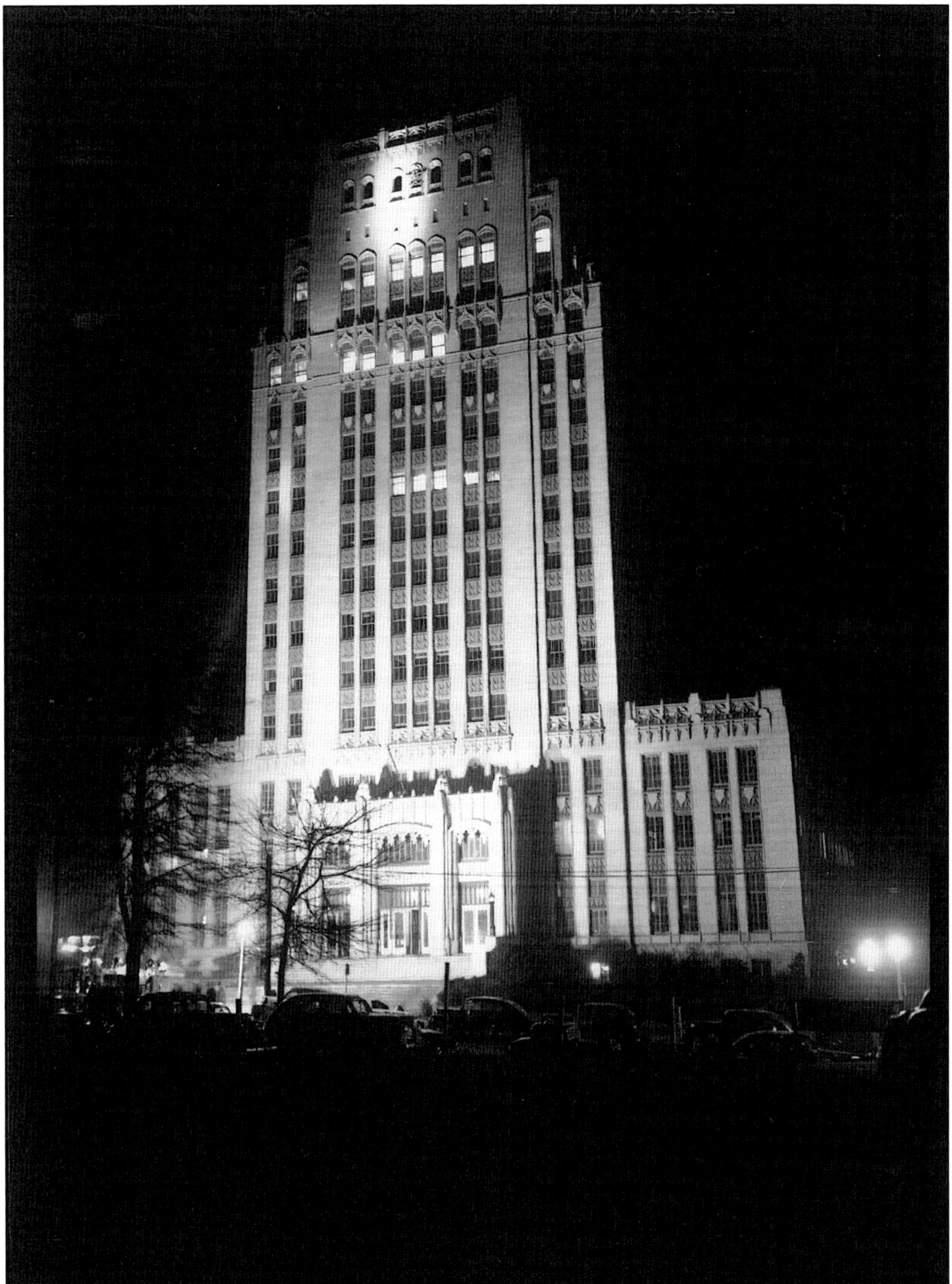

Completed in 1930, Atlanta's City Hall combines Art Deco style with Gothic accents. The building stands on Mitchell Street on the former site of the John Neal house, the location of General William T. Sherman's headquarters during the Civil War. (Courtesy Atlanta History Center.)

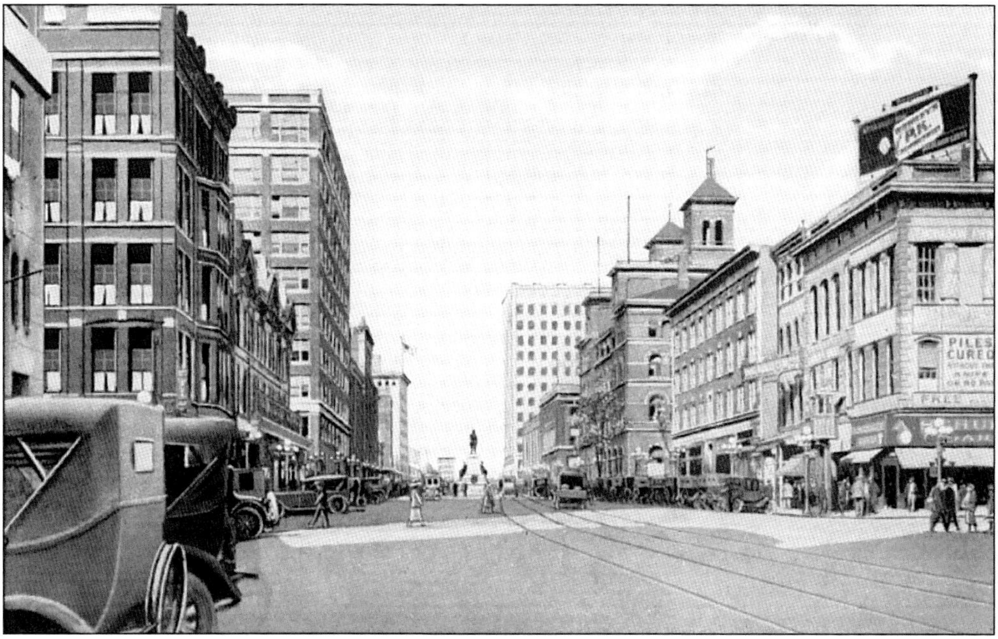

There are several historic points of reference in this picture. The old U.S. post office/city hall is seen at right center; the Henry Grady statue stands silhouetted against the sky at center; and the automobiles are indicative of the 1920s. Women's dresses are noticeably shorter. An interesting advertisement on the building on the right reads, "Piles Cured without the Knife or No Pay." (Published by Imperial Post Card Co., Atlanta.)

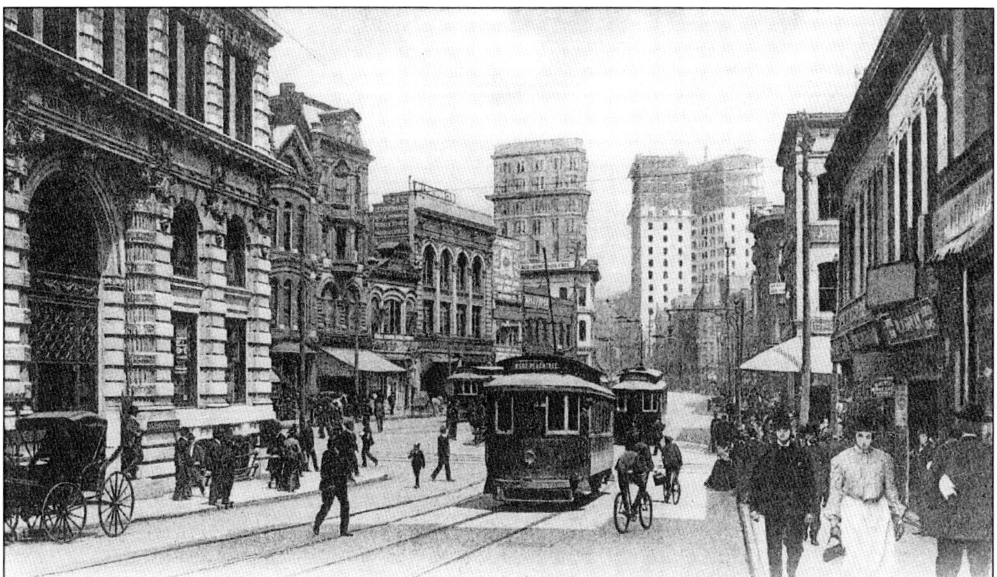

In the immediate Five Points area is the Fourth National Bank (left), and construction is under way on the Candler Building's double edifice (right center). The date is probably 1905. (No publishing information available.)

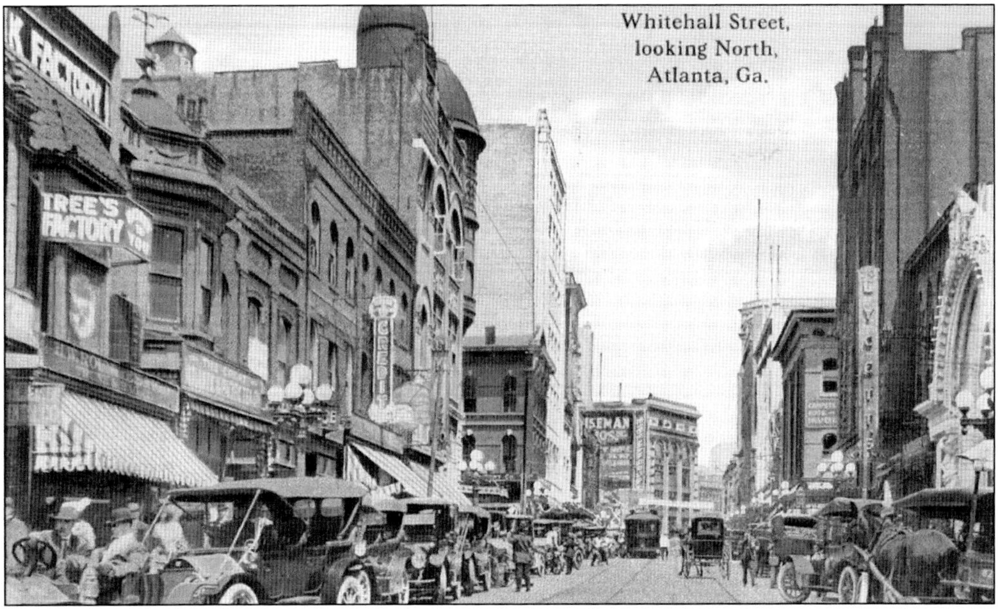

This picture was probably taken from Mitchell Street, looking north toward Five Points. The first two buildings on the left are Tree's Factory and the Great Atlantic and Pacific Tea Company. On the right is the marquee of a theater, Lycett's, then the corner of a building displaying a sign for "Carpets, Rugs, and Drapery." Early automobiles are crowded at the curb. (Published by I.F. Co., Atlanta; card sent 1919.)

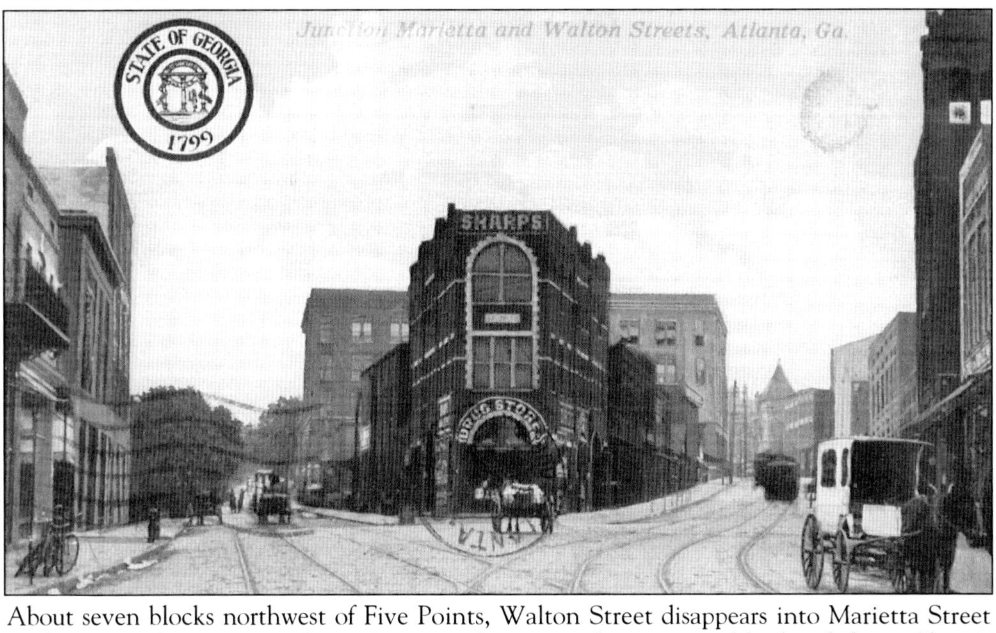

About seven blocks northwest of Five Points, Walton Street disappears into Marietta Street at this triangular junction. An early view of a seemingly quiet neighborhood shows Sharp's Drugstore in the apex of the triangle, with a delivery wagon on the right and typical vehicular transport. (Published by Witt Bros., Atlanta; card sent 1918.)

The unusual triangular building in the center of the card on the right, the English-American or Flatiron Building, was erected in 1897 and has become one of the famous landmarks of Atlanta. Located at the intersection of Broad and Peachtree Streets at Luckie Street, it is one of several triangular intersections dominating the business district. (Published by I.F. Co., Atlanta; card sent 1916.)

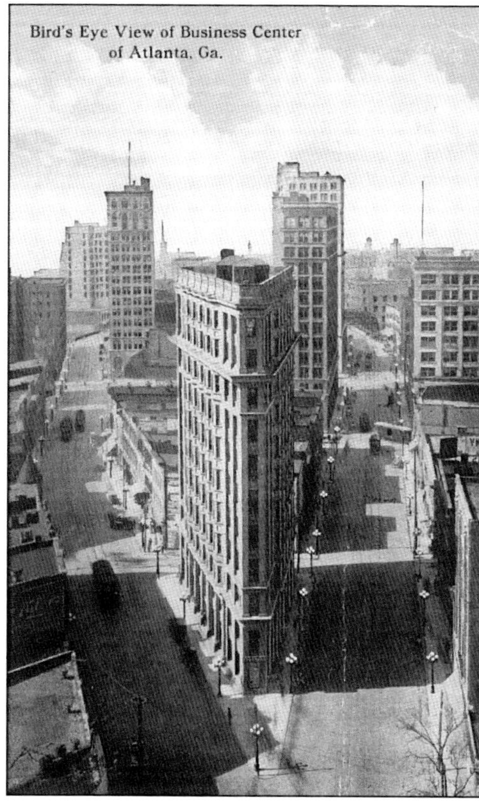

Depicted below is "La Reve," home of Amos G. Rhodes, at 1516 Peachtree Street NW. The 23-room mansion, built in 1900, had a series of Tiffany stained-glass windows showing The Rise and Fall of the Confederacy and contained numerous portraits of Georgia statesmen. In 1930 it became the repository of the Georgia Department of Archives and History. Later the mansion became the Peachtree Branch of the Archives, and the stained–glass windows were removed to the new archives building on Capitol Avenue.

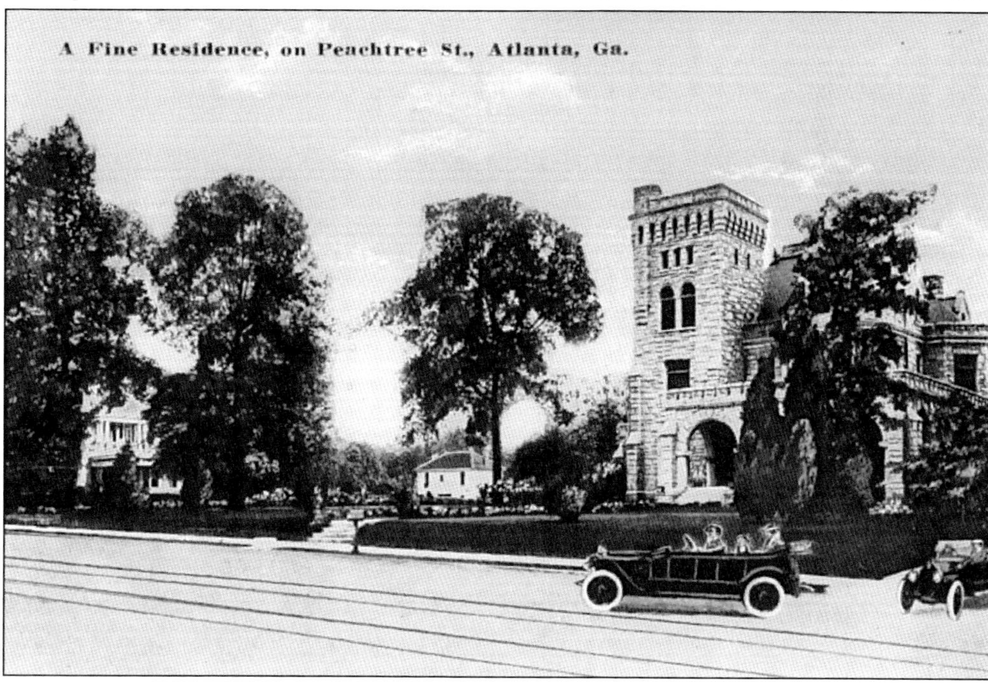

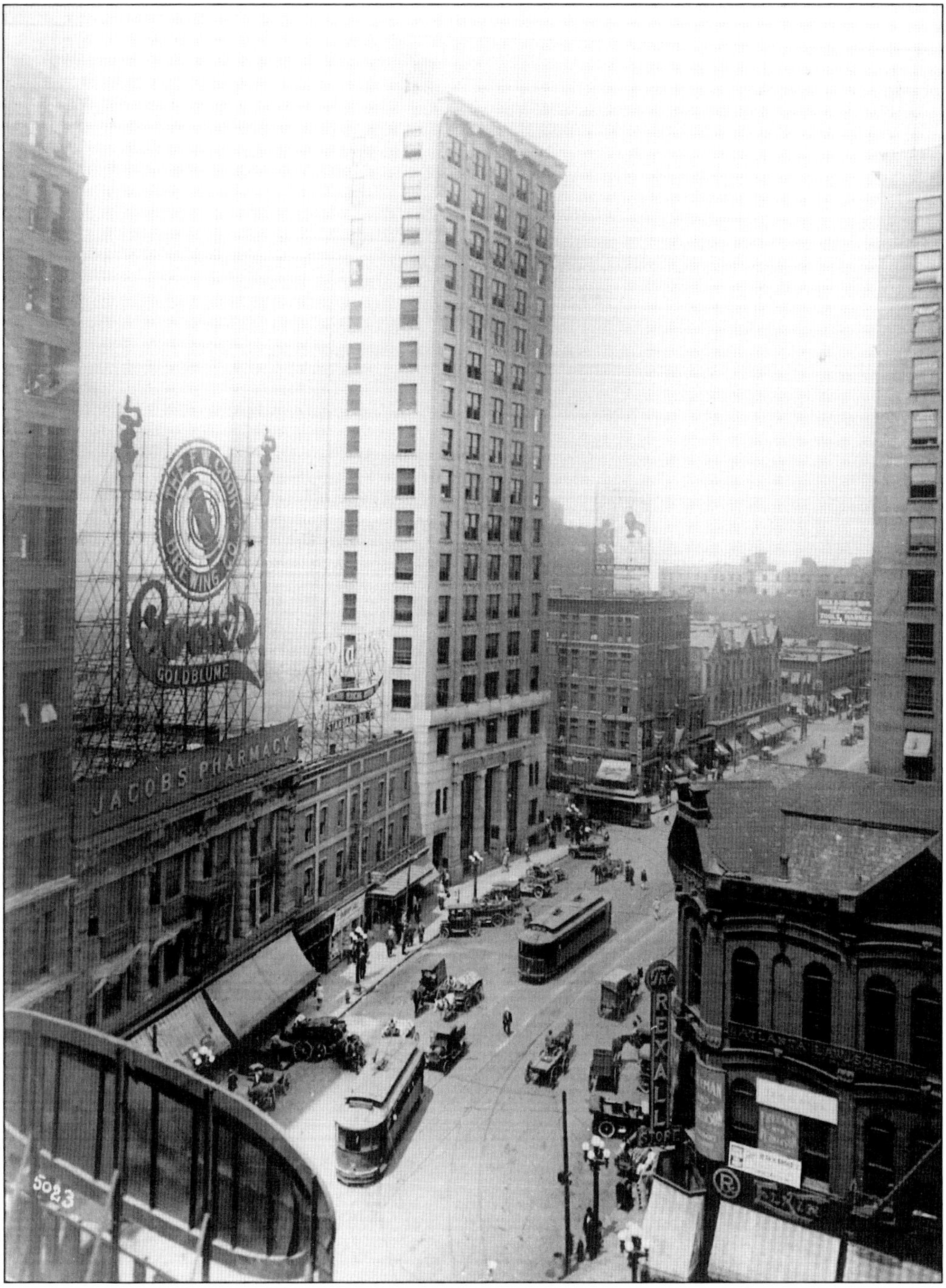

Jacob's Pharmacy (lower left), *c.* 1915, stood on Marietta Street at the northwest corner of Five Points, in the heart of Atlanta's business district. It was here in 1886 that the first sale of Coca-Cola took place at Willis Venable's soda fountain. (Courtesy Atlanta History Center.)

Constructed in 1913 at Edgewood Avenue and Exchange Place, the Hurt Building commemorates Joel Hurt (1850–1926), one of Atlanta's pioneer entrepreneurs of civic betterment. His substantial projects include the Atlanta Home Insurance Company, the East Atlanta Land Company, and the building of Inman Park through his establishment of the first electric streetcars in the city. In 1908, he sold 1,500 acres of his landscaped properties to initiate the development of Druid Hills. The Hurt Building, extended in 1927, became the largest office building in the South. (Published by I.F. Co., Atlanta.)

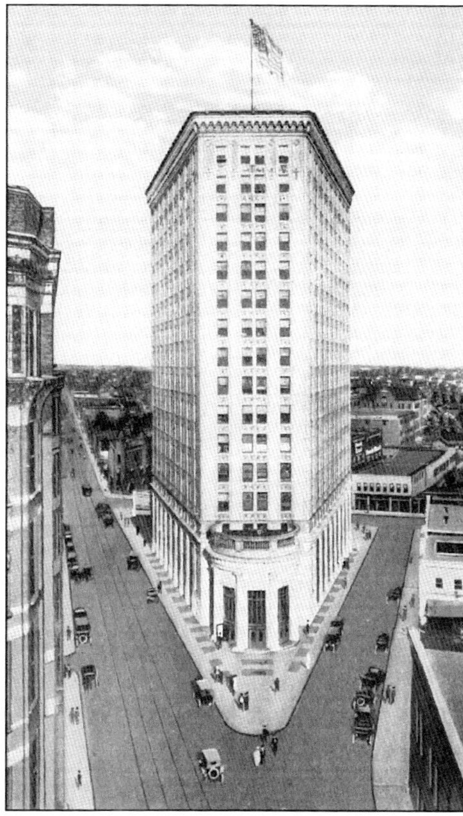

This card depicts the intersection of Whitehall and Hunter streets. Note the building shown on the right with an advertisement for "Carpets, Rugs, and Drapery." The white building on the left is undergoing renovation. In the distant center, the Eiseman Bros. building stands prominently. The sign includes "Clothing, Shoes, Furnishings, Hats" from the readable portion. Cars come in many models, and pedestrians are numerous. The time is *c.* 1920. (Published by Imperial Fruit Co., Atlanta.)

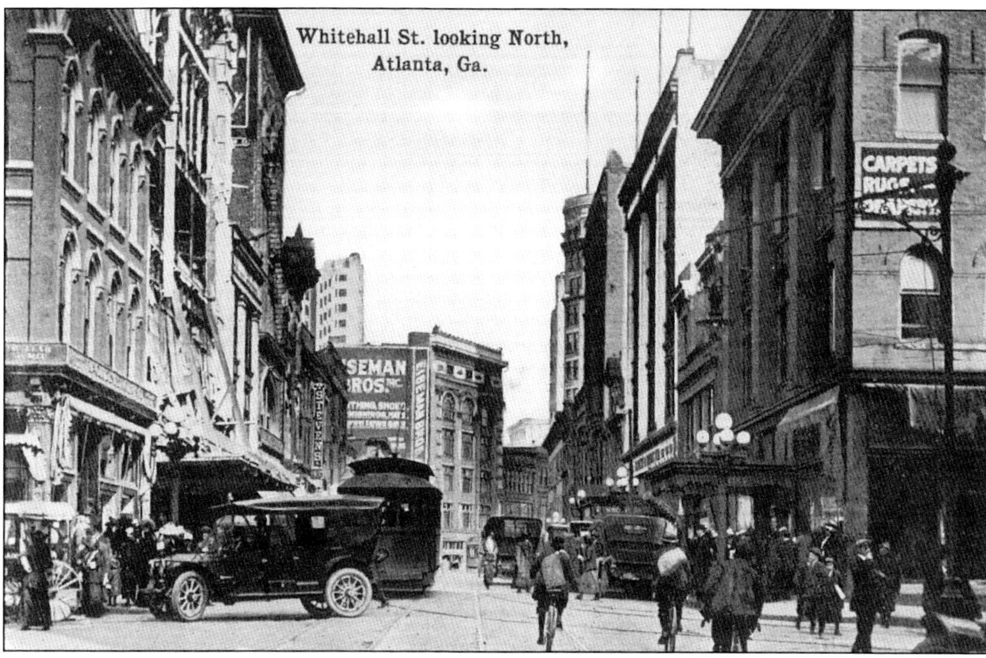

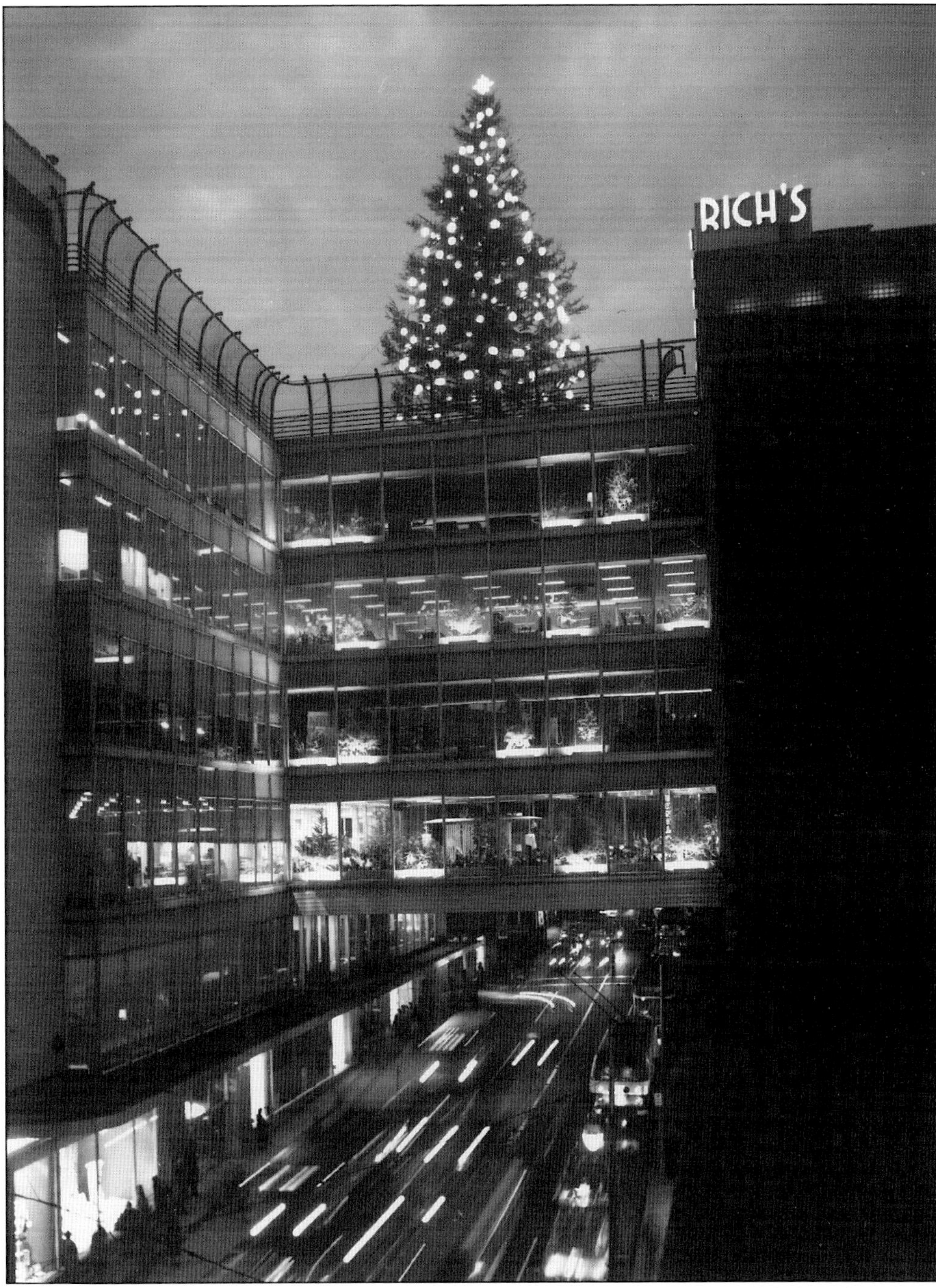

In 1948, Rich's downtown department store began a longstanding and beloved Atlanta tradition with its Thanksgiving-night lighting and holiday display of a giant Christmas tree atop the "crystal bridge." With the demolition of the Broad Street Rich's in 1994, the tree lighting moved to Underground Atlanta. (Courtesy Atlanta History Center.)

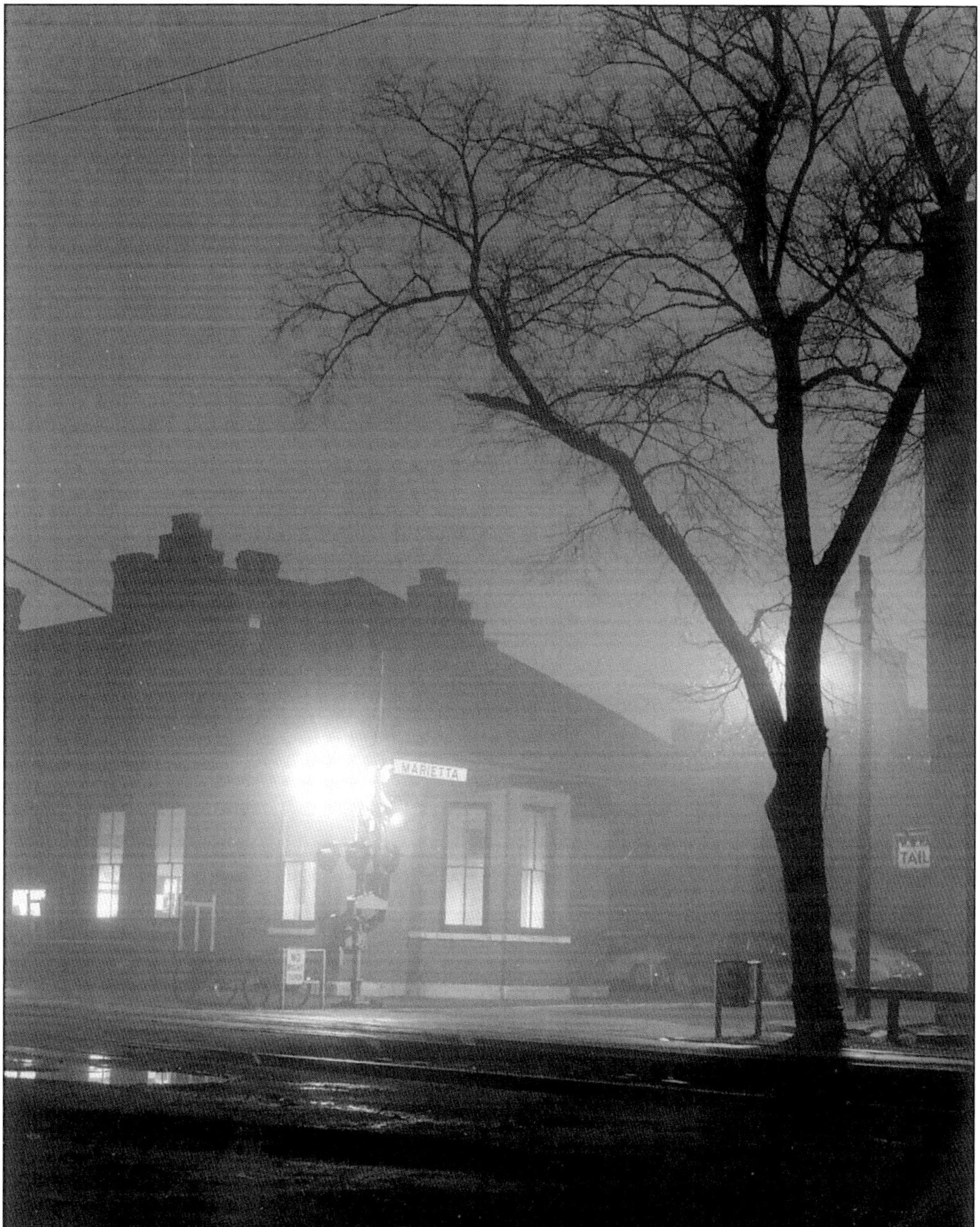

This view of the Marietta train station looks north on a foggy night. (Photograph by Joe McTyre.)

Marietta's railroad passenger depot was built in 1898 and used by rail passengers until 1969. The building now serves as the Marietta Welcome Center and Visitors Bureau. (Photograph by Joe McTyre.)

Four

Community

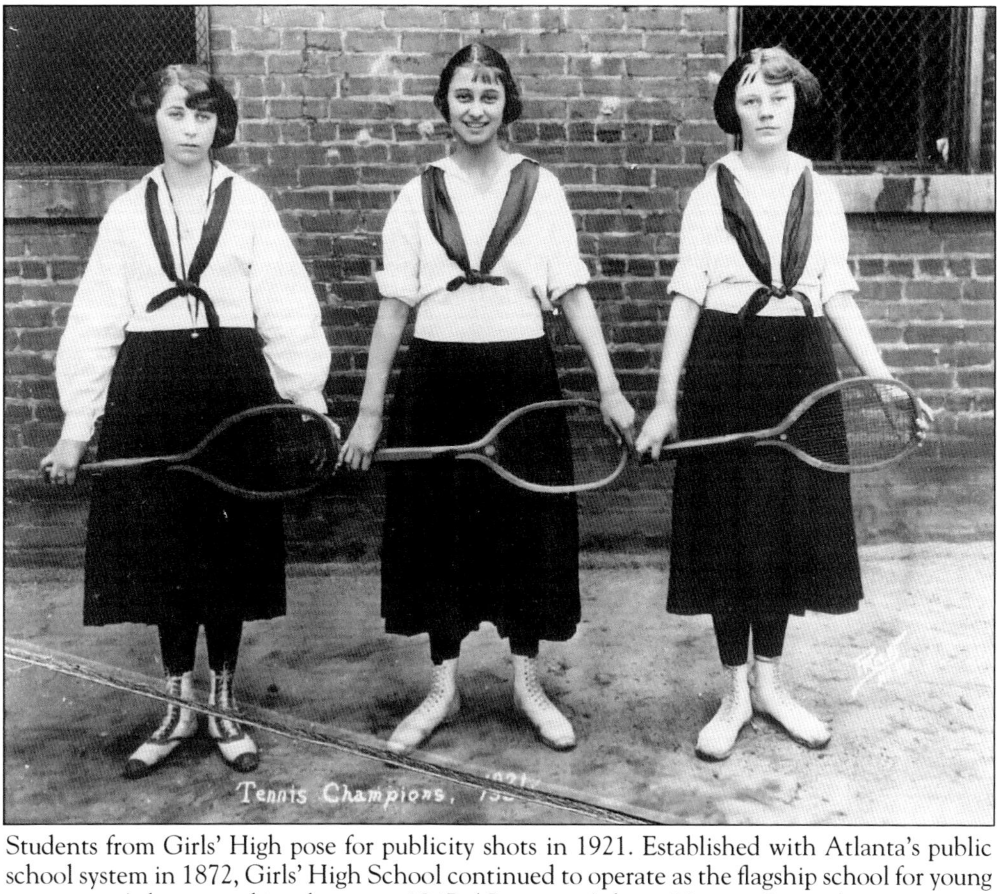

Students from Girls' High pose for publicity shots in 1921. Established with Atlanta's public school system in 1872, Girls' High School continued to operate as the flagship school for young women in Atlanta until its closure in 1947. (Courtesy Atlanta History Center.)

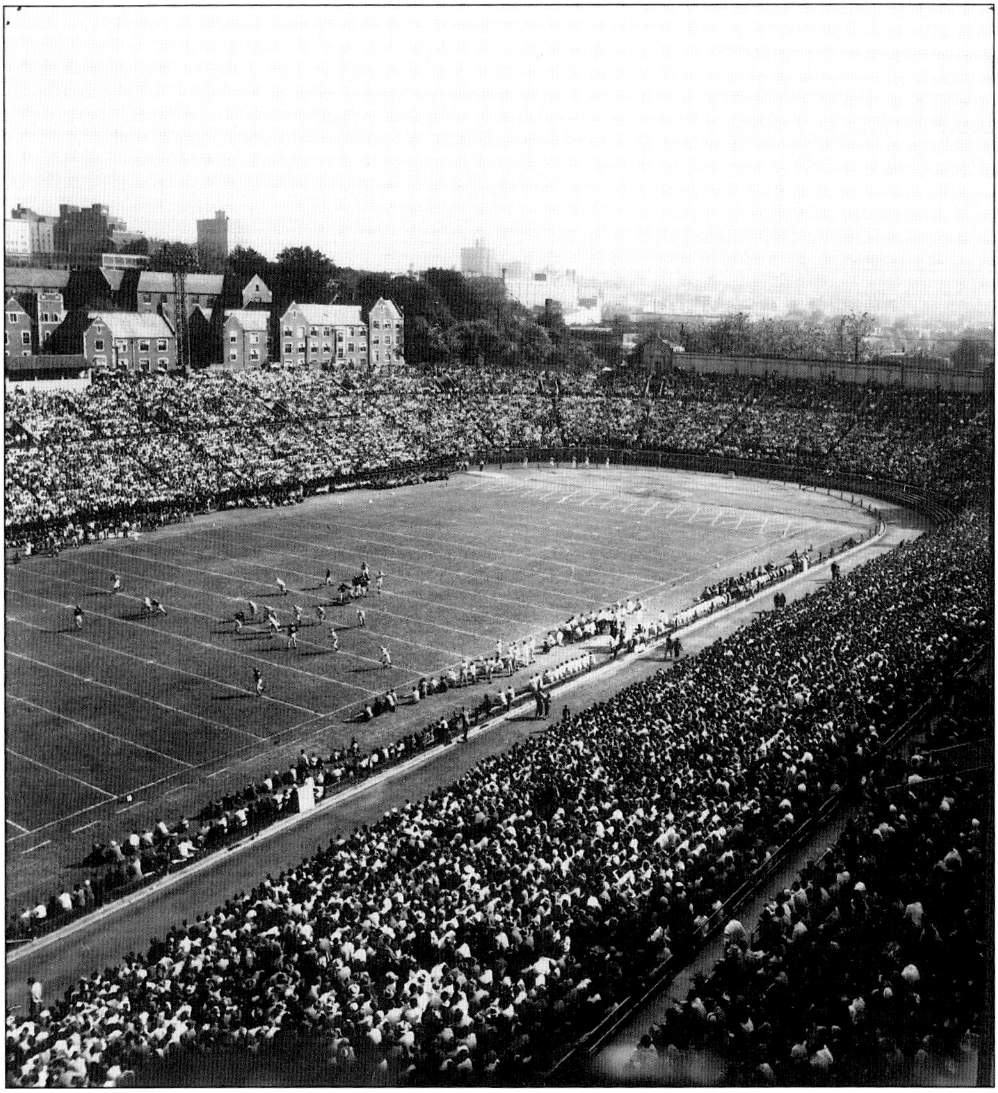

For many, Georgia Tech football is an essential part of Atlanta life, and 1952 was a standout year for the Ramblin' Wreck. The team finished the season 11-0 and defeated Ole Miss in the Sugar Bowl, but lost the national championship vote to Notre Dame. This scene is from the 1952 homecoming game against Vanderbilt, won by Georgia Tech, 30-0. (Courtesy Atlanta History Center.)

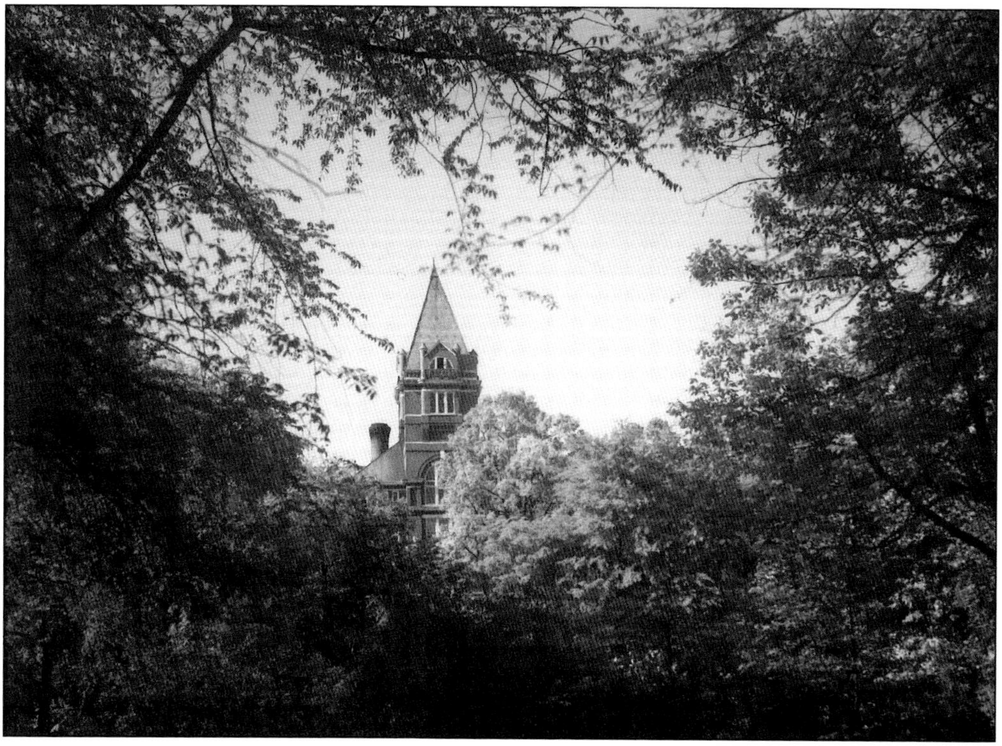

Constructed in 1889, Georgia Tech's Administration Building (above) is the campus's oldest building and a symbol of the university. The Georgia Institute of Technology opened in 1888, with 130 students and offering one course—mechanical engineering. (Courtesy Atlanta History Center.)

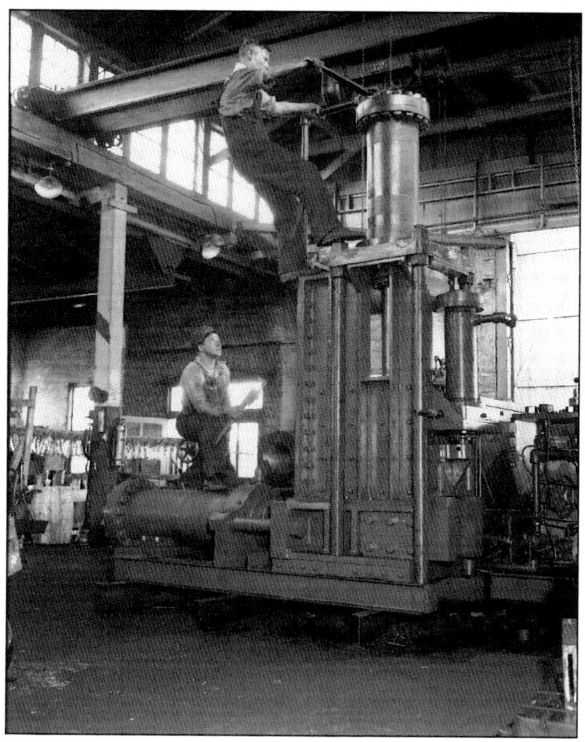

Begun as the Georgia Electric Light Company in 1884, the Georgia Power Company underwent expansion under the New Deal's Rural Electrification Administration. Power lines were extended throughout the state, and hydroelectric dams, such as the Crisp County Hydroelectric Plant near Cordele, were constructed or purchased to meet the state's growing electrical demands. (Courtesy Atlanta History Center.)

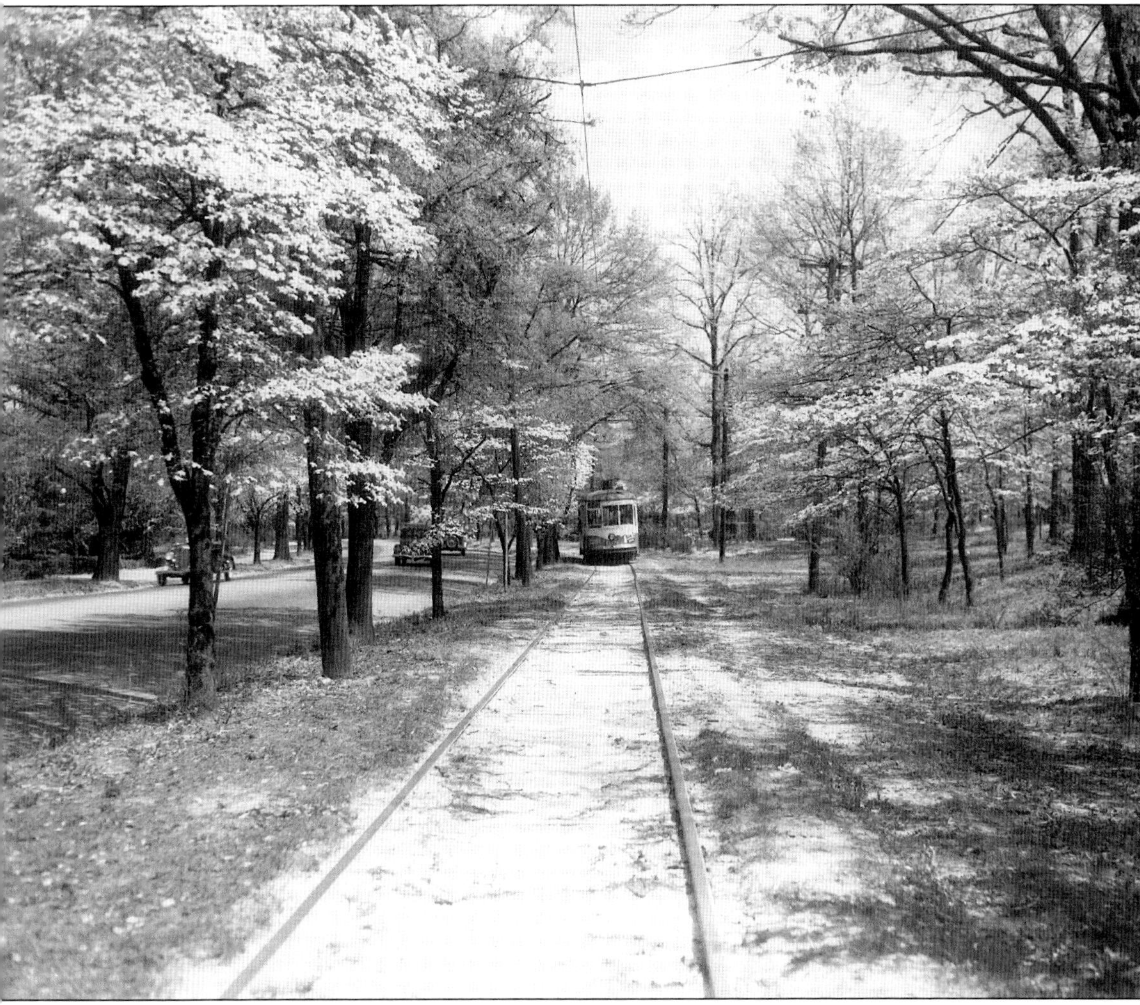

Trolley line running along Ponce de Leon Avenue in the Druid Hills neighborhood, 1930s. (Photograph by Kenneth Rogers.)

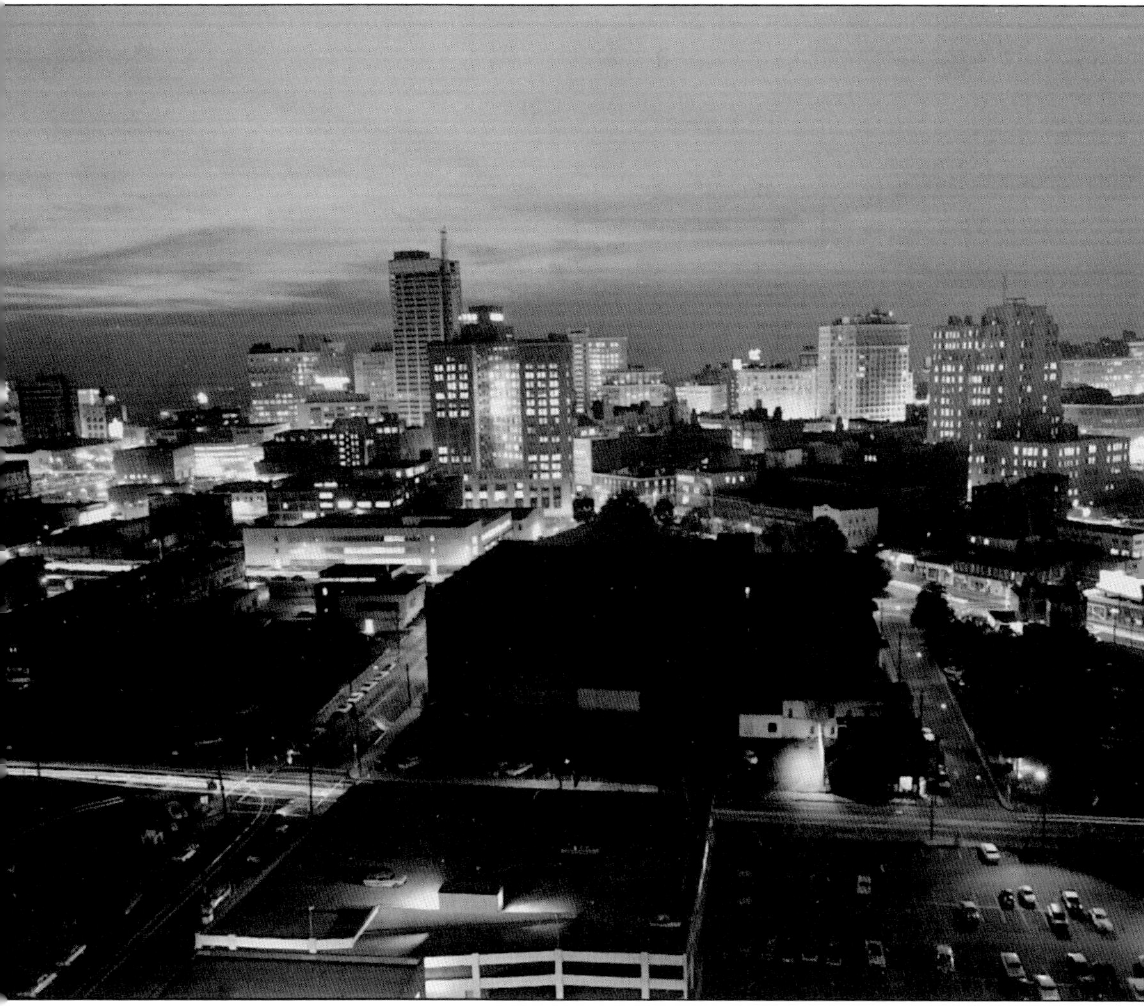

Atlanta at night, late 1950s. (Photograph by Kenneth Rogers.)

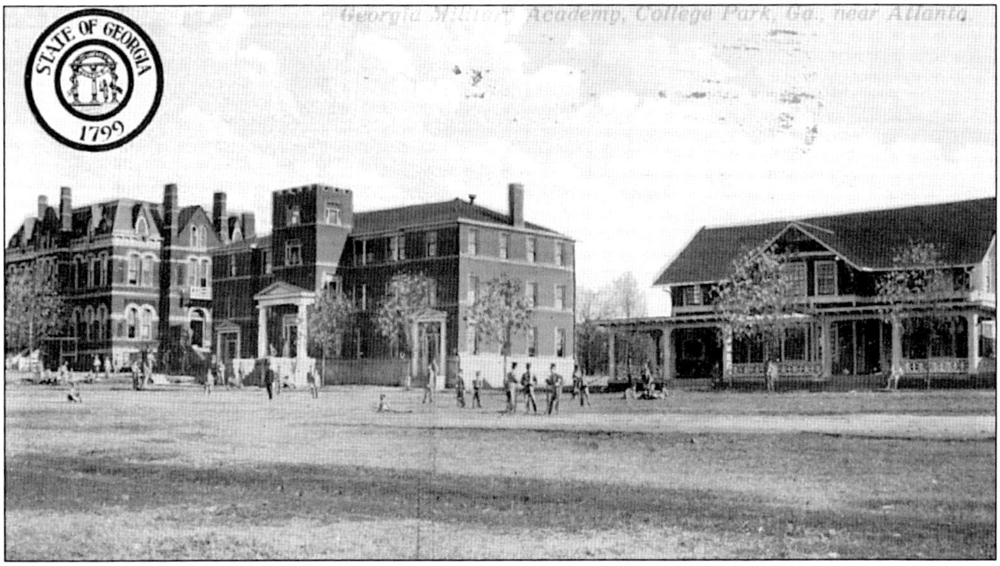

Founded in 1900 by Col. John C. Woodward, the Georgia Military Academy has achieved a superior rating given by the United States War Department through the years for its standards of military training. It occupied 12 buildings on a 30-acre campus in College Park. For years the public enjoyed the Sunday afternoon parades, watching the cadets in their blue-gray coats and white trousers. (Published by Witt Bros., Atlanta; card sent 1911.)

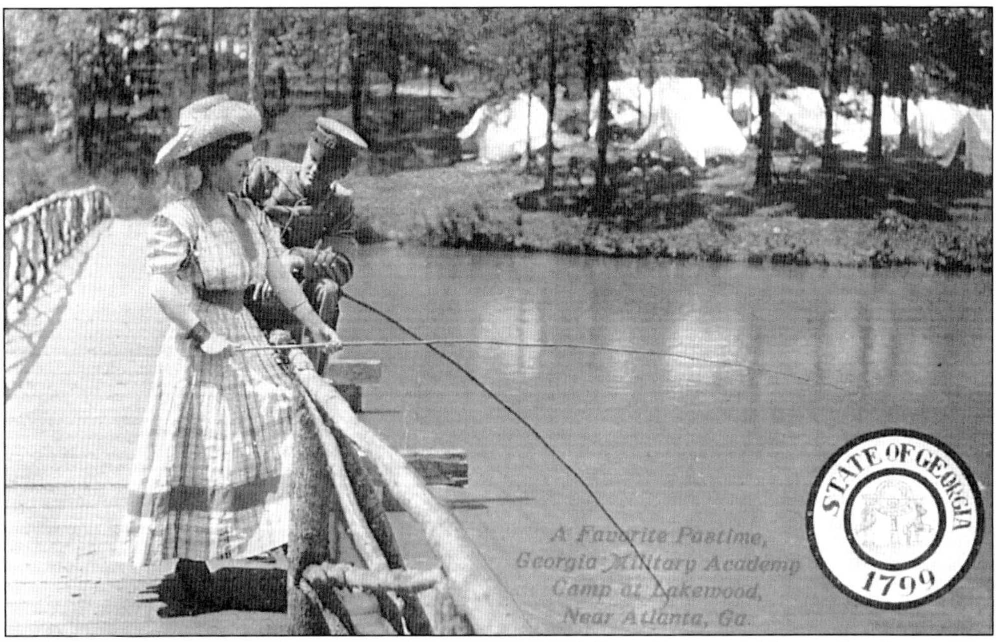

A charming scene around 1912 reveals one aspect of life at Georgia Military Academy. The camp at Lakewood is shown in the background. In the mid-1960s the school dropped its military focus and became coeducational. It was renamed Woodward Academy in honor of its founder and now occupies 30 buildings on its 65 acres. (Published by Witt Bros., Atlanta.)

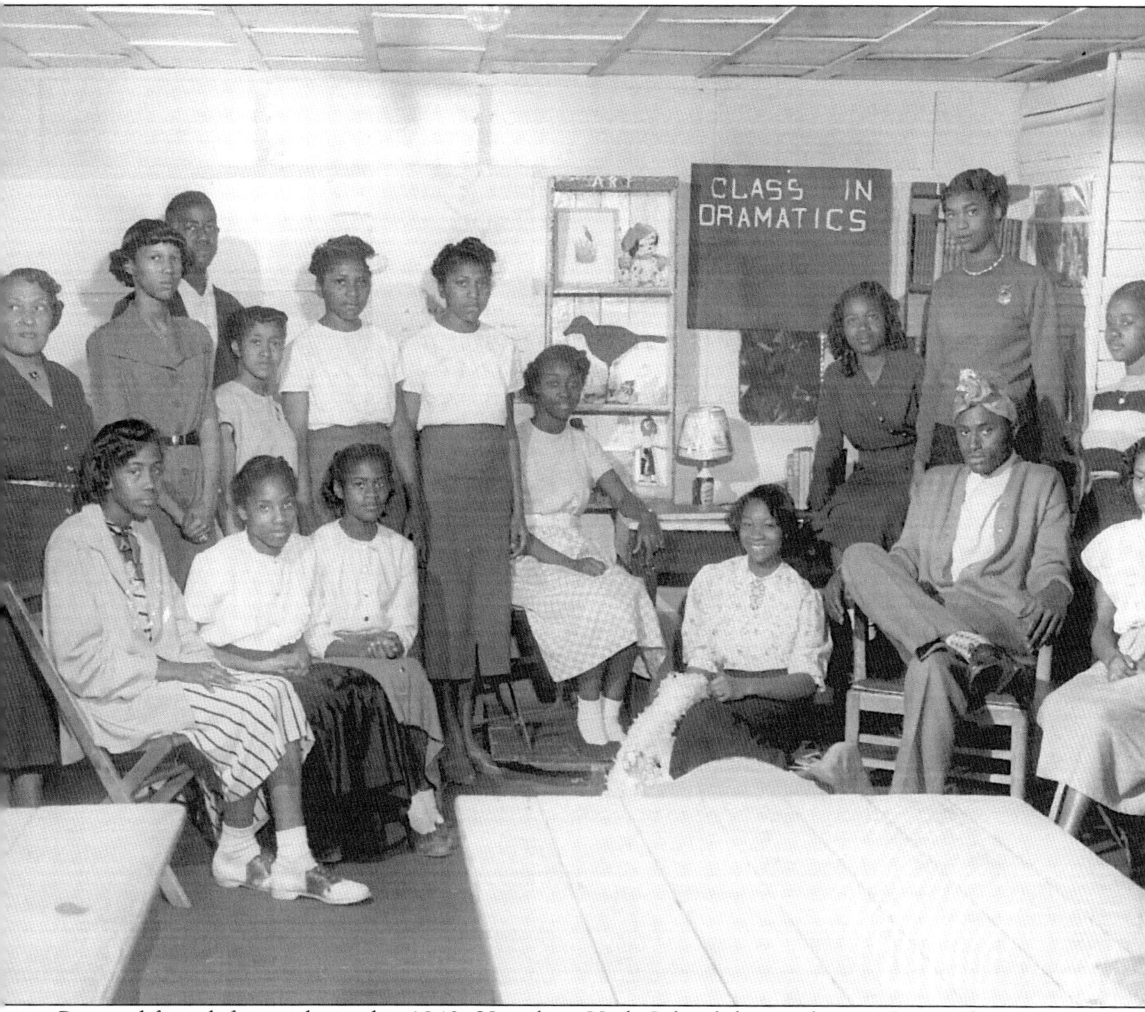

Pictured from left to right in this 1940s Hamilton High School drama class are Joyce Thomas, Sylvia Mosely, Menona Hammond, and Mr. Luther Stripling (in fancy turban). Drama, along with art and music (shown overleaf), were offerings that allowed an important vehicle for creative expression.

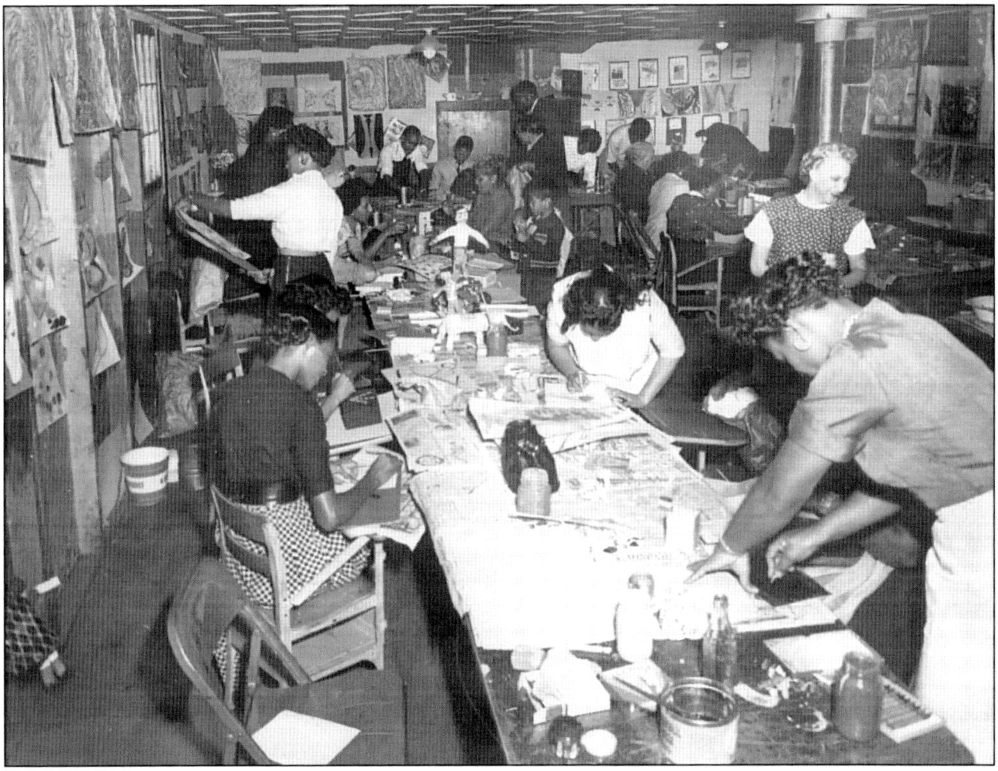

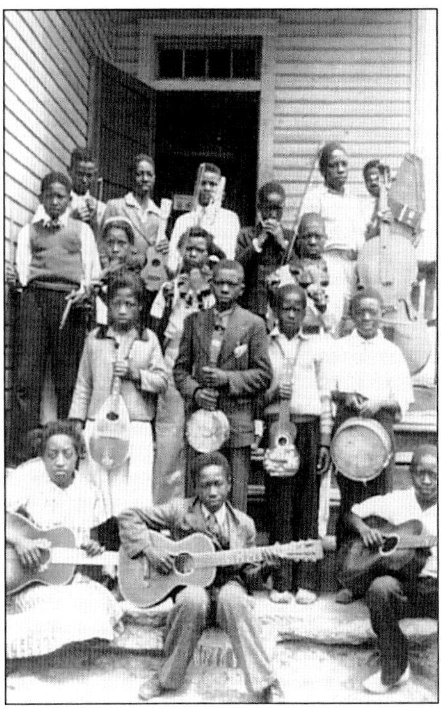

Teachers are being instructed how to enhance classroom instruction (conserving materials, creating materials, etc.) during the Binney Smith Crayola Art Workshop for Teachers in 1952.

Stone Mountain school band members pose outside of the school, c. 1930s.

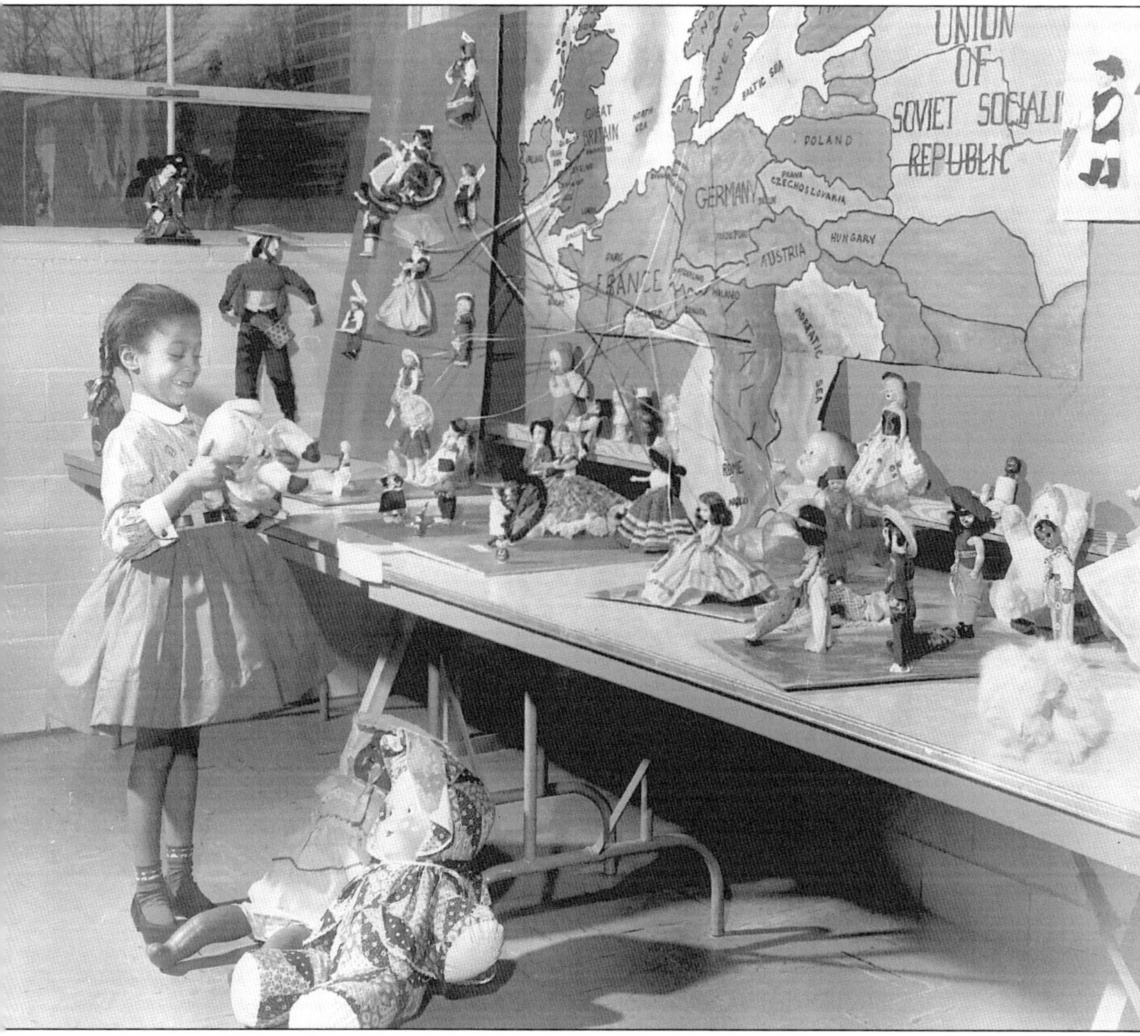

Daryll Harris is the daughter of Mrs. Narvie Harris. In January, the Doll Show was a community activity to build aesthetic appreciation. Students exhibited their dolls in various categories: large, small, beautiful, ugly, bridal, Barbie, etc.

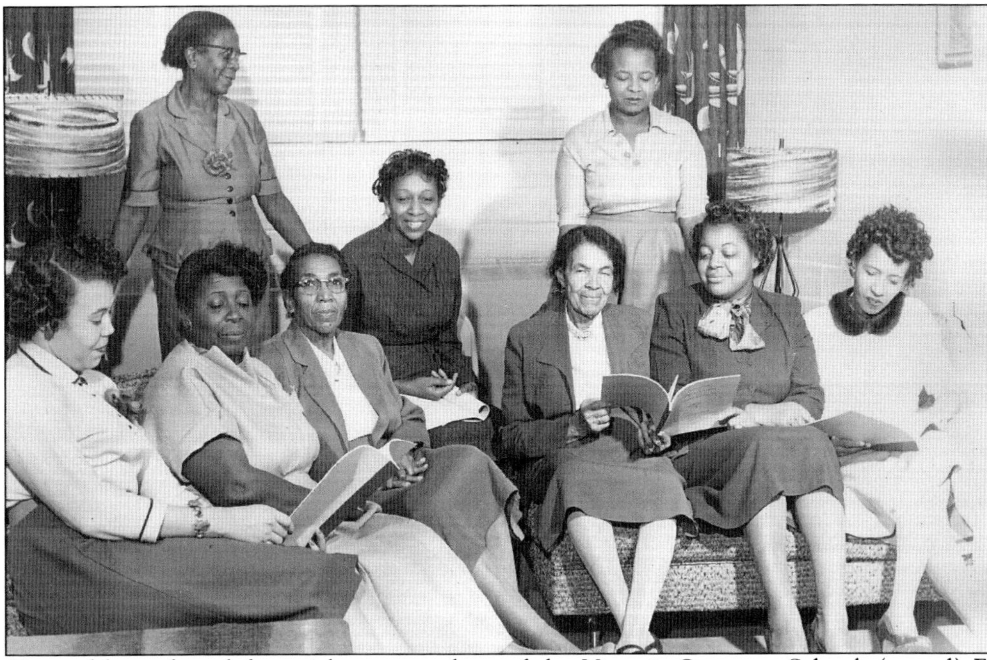

Pictured here, from left to right, are teachers of the Victoria Simmons School: (seated) E. Mallory, Frances Maddox, Lula Harper, Narvie Harris, Ora Woods, Z. Stafford, and Ruby McClendon; (standing) Fannie Dobbs and Jondelle Johnson. Jondelle Johnson would become a journalist and columnist for the *Atlanta Voice* and executive director of the Atlanta branch of the NAACP, where she served for 17 years until her death in April 1998.

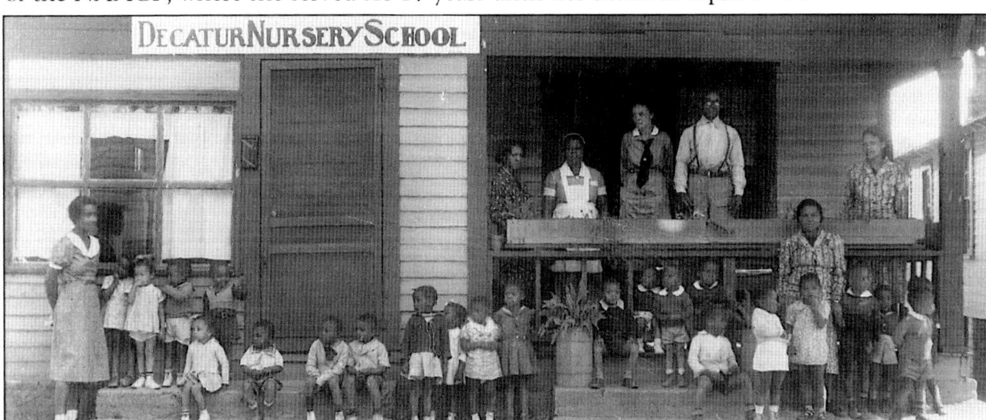

Now known as Trinity Avenue, the original Herring Street was the home of several important institutions within the Beacon Hill community of Decatur. By the 1920s several structures were demolished, including the St. James Presbyterian Church and the Odds Fellow Hall (which was located at the site of the present DeKalb County Court House). The office of Dr. Ross S. Douthard, Decatur's first African-American physician, was located in the building. Other buildings and businesses on the street included the Decatur Mission Kindergarten, Herring Street School (on the corner of Electric Avenue), Pearson Mason's Restaurant, and Pearl Crew, the first African-American dentist and nurse in Decatur. (Courtesy of Ross Douthard Jr.)

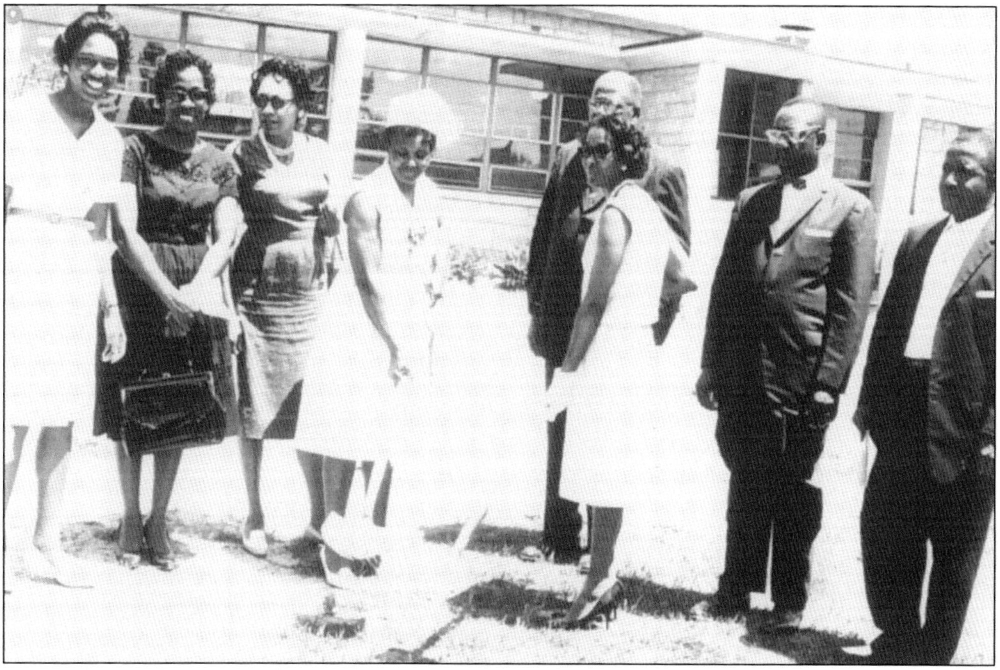

In the above photograph, local residents are seen participating in the groundbreaking for a new Bruce High School. Coy E. Flagg served as the principal for many years. Flagg joined the school in 1944. Other schools in the area included Rock Chapel, Stoneview, Lithonia High, and Salem Junior High School. (Courtesy of Narvie Jordan Harris.)

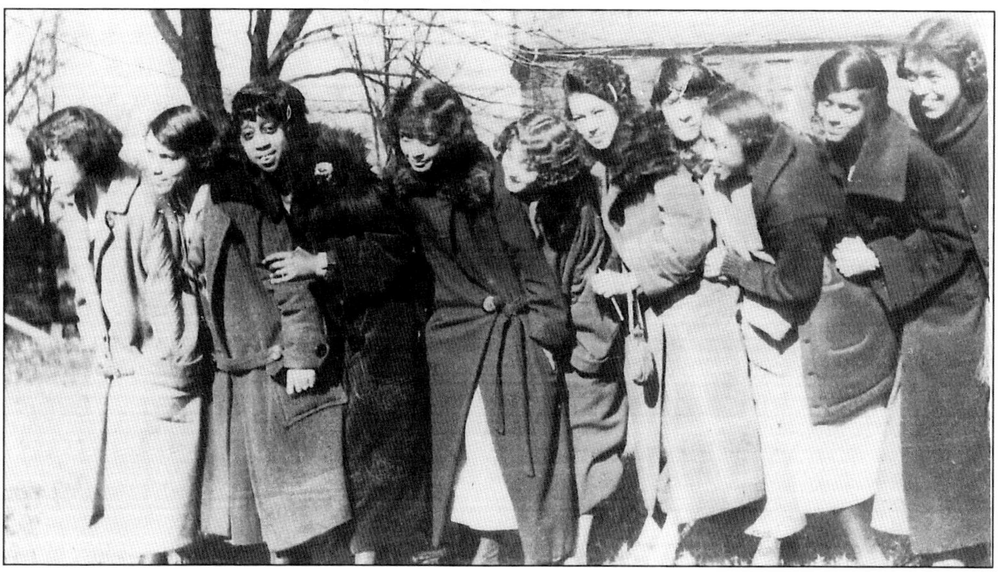

Pictured here are the charter members of Delta Sigma Theta Sorority at Atlanta University, c. 1923. From left to right are: Lula Brown, Florence Phelps, Hazel Shanks, Louise Holmes, Mattie Owens, Sarah Brimmer, Ruth Wheeler, Doris Pace, Altona Trent Johns, and Minnie Perry.

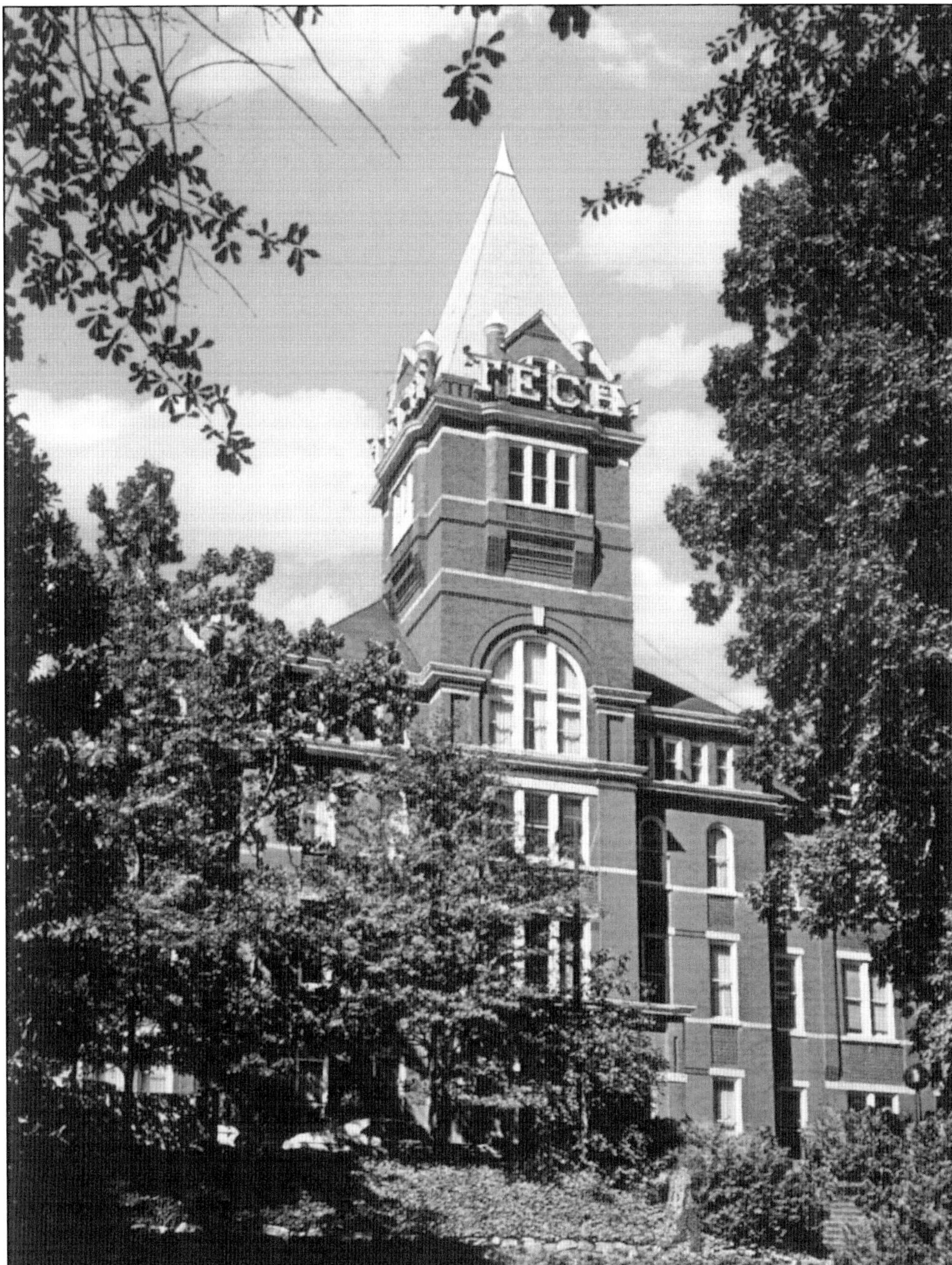

Pictured above is the Georgia Institute of Technology's Famous Tech Tower. This administration building was one of five erected in 1888; it dominates the campus with its spire emblazoned on all four faces with the word TECH. Georgia Tech offers Bachelor's degrees in nine departments, including engineering, architecture, chemistry, and industrial management. Both military and naval units of ROTC are maintained here. (Published by Aerial Photography Services, Atlanta.)

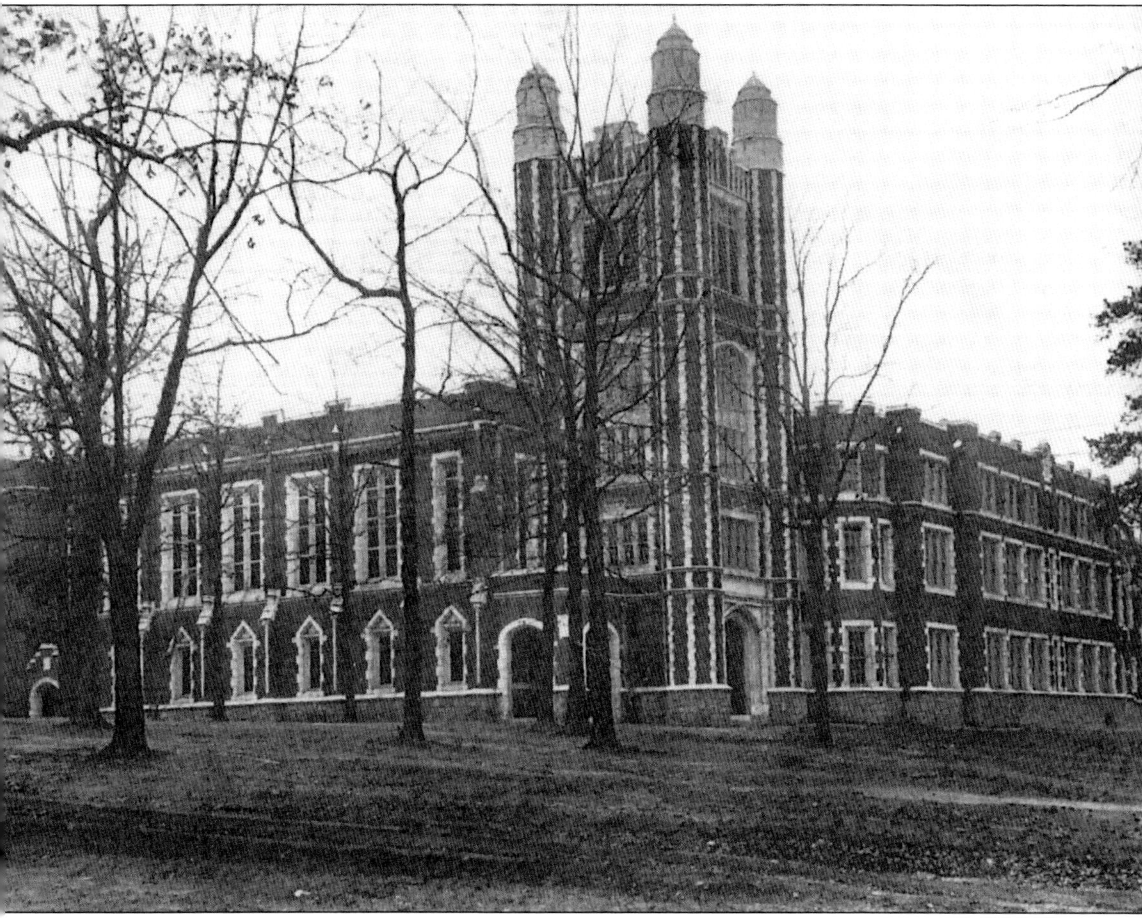

Clark University was situated in the "South Atlanta" area. It was bounded by McDonough Boulevard and Jonesboro Road. Founded in 1869 by the Freedman's Aid Society of the Methodist Episcopal Church, the University's first location was at Whitehall and McDaniel Street. Bishop Henry W. Warren secured a tract of land of between 400 and 500 acres in South Atlanta, and the school was moved in 1872. A large portion of the funds for the school were contributed by Mrs. Augusta Clark Cole, the daughter of Bishop D.W. Clark, who died in 1872. The school was named in the memory of the Clark family.

Some of the most visually well-crafted architecture in Atlanta was found on the South Atlanta campus of Clark University, including Crogman Chapel and Leete Hall. Crogman Chapel accommodated eight hundred persons. Crogman also contained a gymnasium, administrative offices, and classrooms, including science and biology labs. In 1920, the foundations were laid for Leete Hall (seen here), a structure costing over $200,000. It was dedicated February 15, 1922. The building is now used as the George Washington Carver High School.

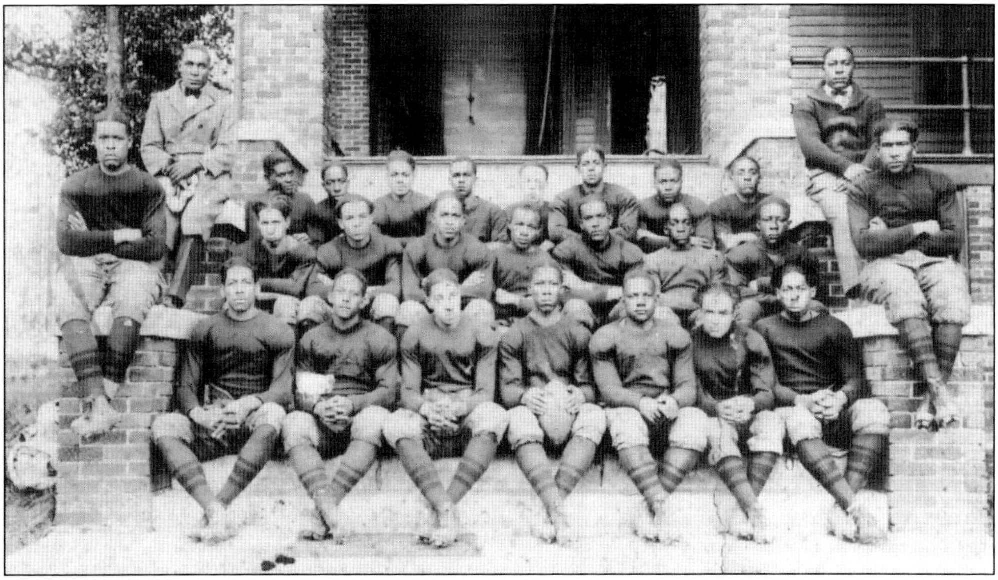

The 1928 Clark Panthers football team was known as the Black Battalion of Death. They were the winners of the first Turkey Day game between Clark and Morris Brown on November 28, 1929, before a crowd of eight thousand fans at the Ponce de Leon Ballpark. The team was coached by Samuel Taylor from 1925 to 1931.

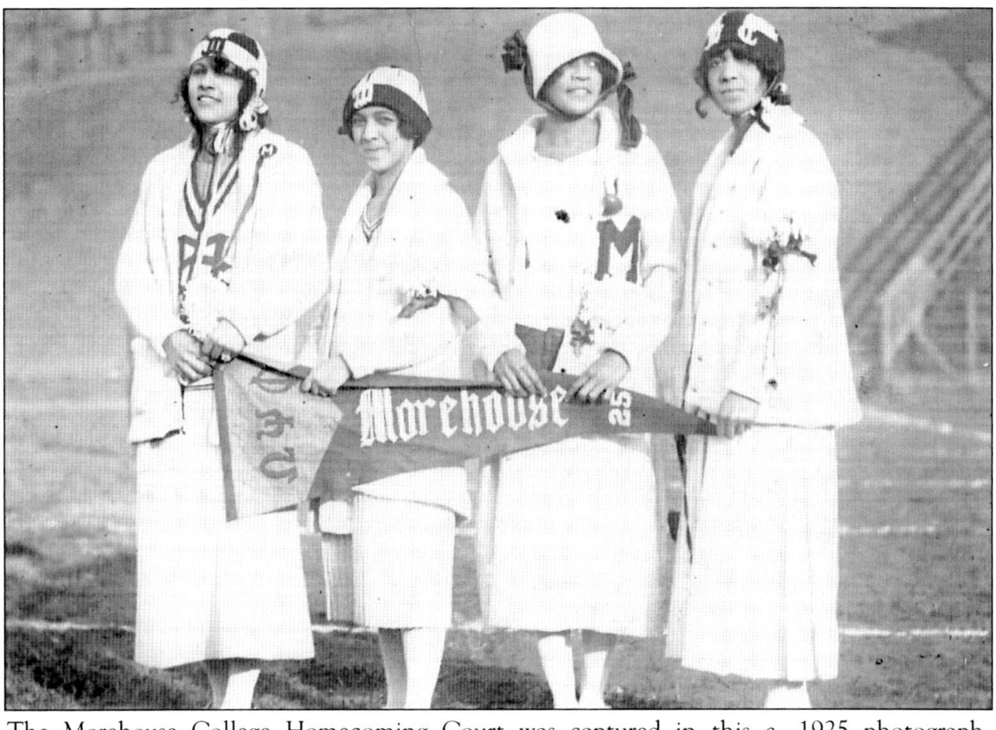

The Morehouse College Homecoming Court was captured in this *c.* 1925 photograph. (Courtesy Digging It Up Archives.)

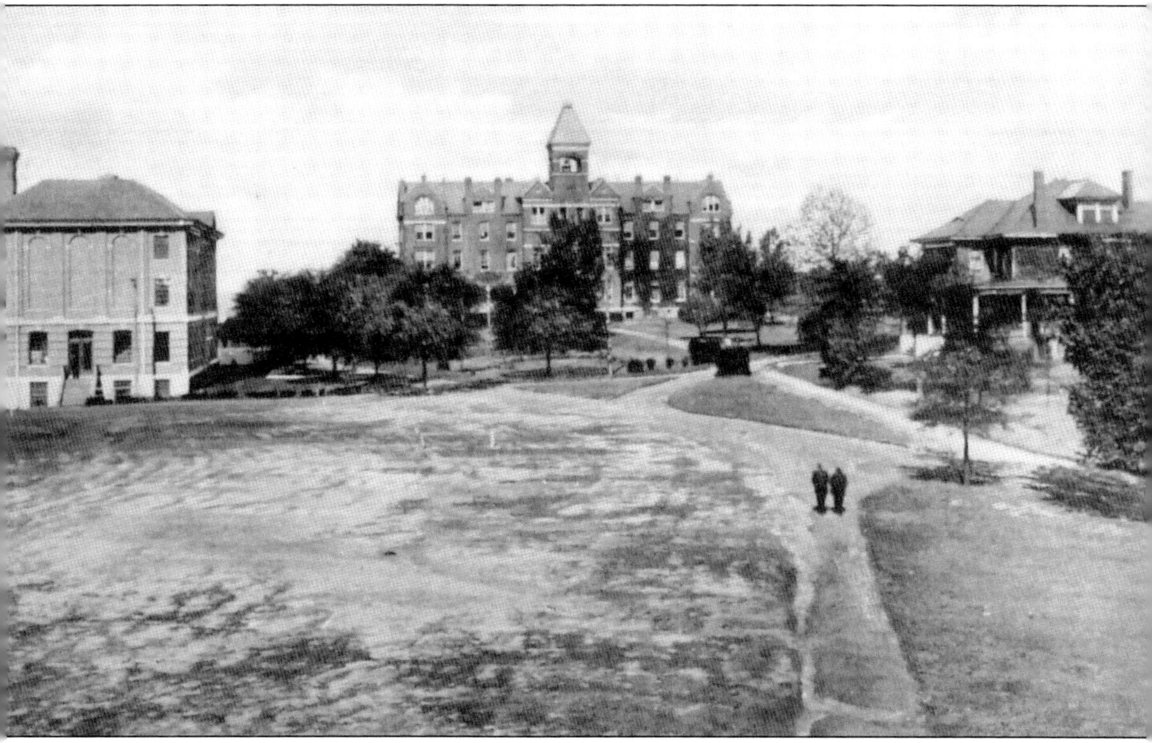

This postcard view of the Morehouse College campus features Sale Hall, Graves Hall, and the president's residence during the decade of the 1920s. This decade characterized successful academic life, cultural events, student activities, and faculty growth, according to E.A. Jones, author of *Candle in the Dark—A History of Morehouse College*. During the twenties, the enrollment in all of the departments (Academy, College and School of Religion) averaged about 450 students. Many great scholars joined the faculty during this decade, including a young Benjamin E. Mays, who taught mathematics, psychology, and philosophy. The school began its annual Shakespearean plays, published the school paper *The Athenaeum*, and enjoyed musical renderings from Professor Kemper Harreld and the Glee Club and the orchestra, which often featured renowned concert artists such as Roland Hayes and pianist Hazel Harrison.

A significant achievement of Morehouse during this decade was the creation of the Atlanta School of Social Work, born in the sociology classrooms of Professor Gary Moore and conceived in the intense interest of the Hopes, especially Mrs. Lugenia Burns Hope, who had already founded the Neighborhood Union and was serving as its president. (Courtesy Digging It Up Archives.)

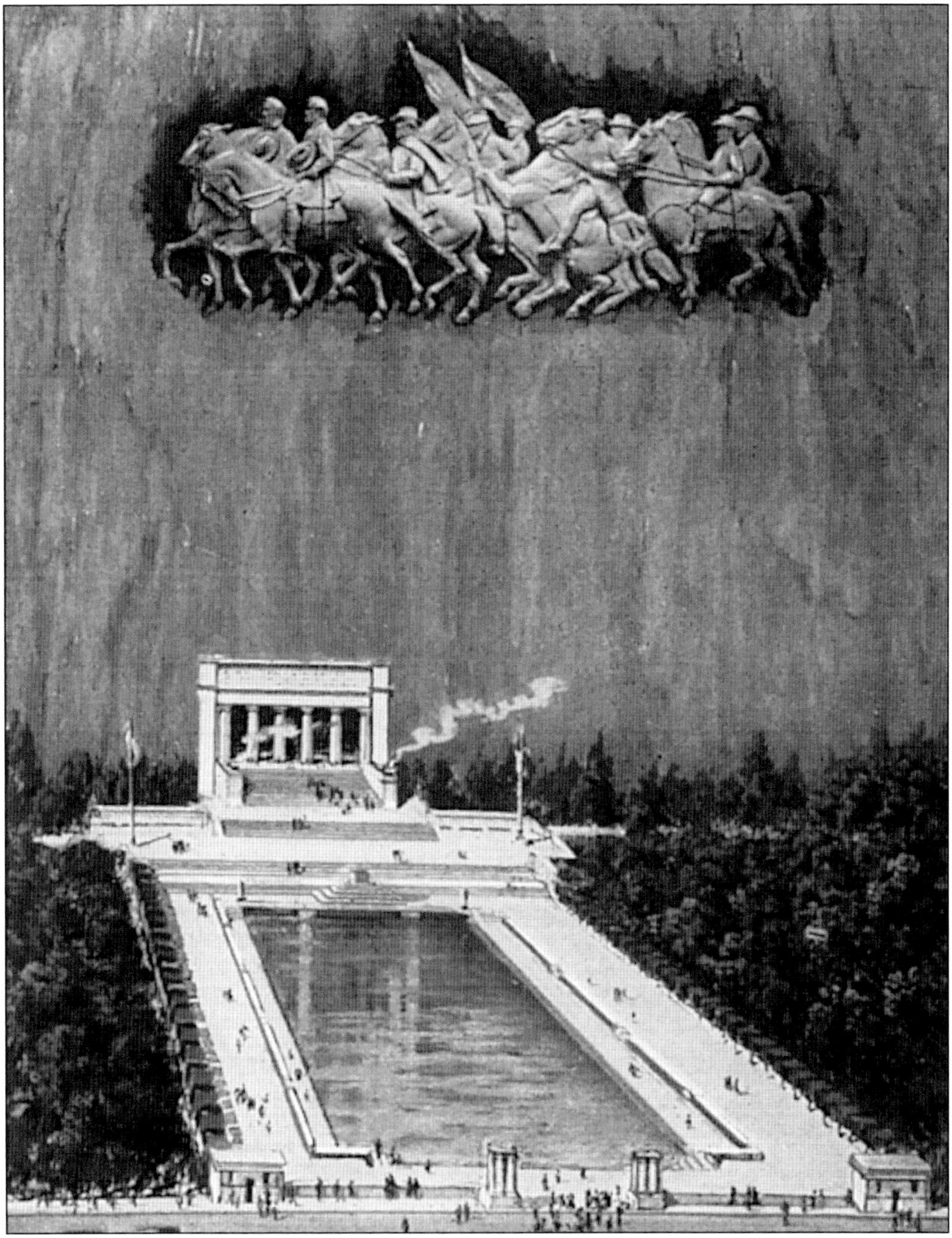

In 1912 Mrs. C. Helen Plane, widow of a Confederate officer and president of the Atlanta chapter of United Daughters of the Confederacy, suggested that a sculpture of Robert E. Lee be placed at Stone Mountain. In 1915 the Stone Mountain Memorial Association invited noted sculptor Gutzon Borglum to come and view these possibilities. Borglum suggested a much larger epic memorial to be carved on the mountain in full relief, which would be visible for miles. He envisioned "great characters in action, mounted. . . ." (Published by Imperial Post Card Co., Atlanta.)

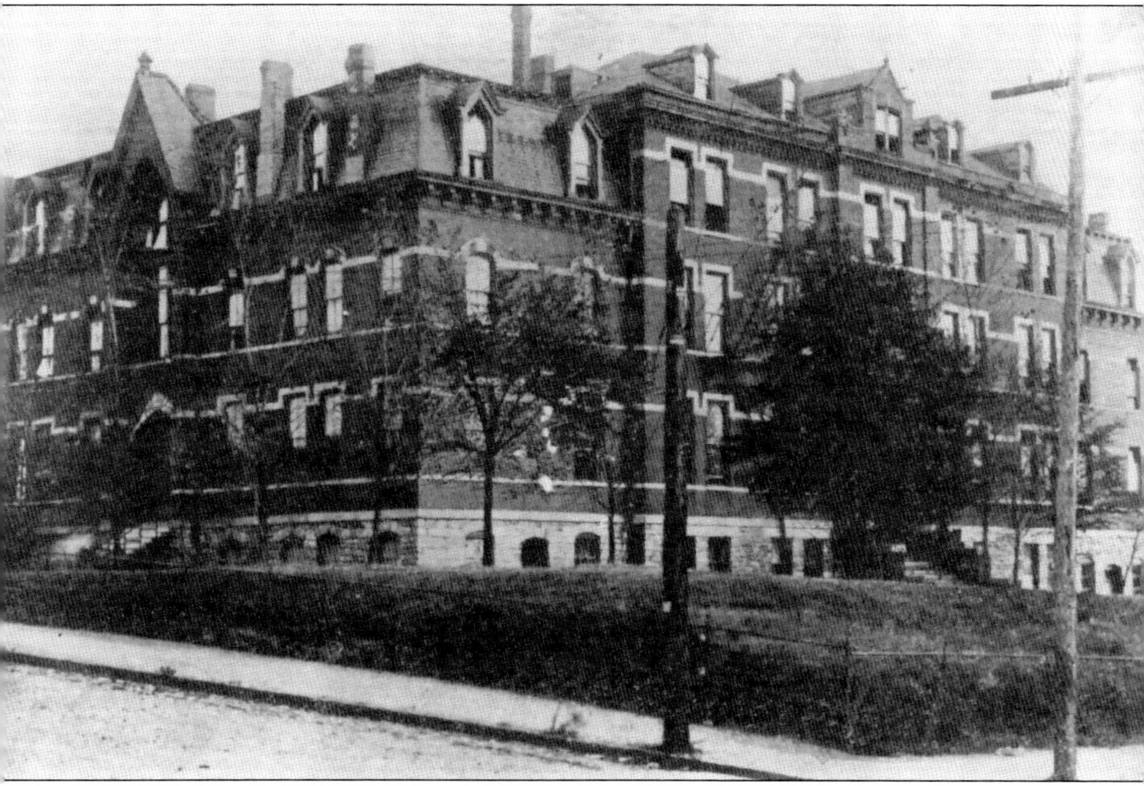

Founded in 1881, Morris Brown University was established by the African Methodist Episcopal Church in the basement of Big Bethel AME Church. By 1920, the campus had grown, and it offered elementary, high school, and normal schools, as well as a nursing school, a seminary, and satellite schools in Cuthbert and Savannah, Georgia. In Atlanta, the administration and classroom building (seen here) was located on the corner of Houston Street and Boulevard. Other buildings on the picturesque campus included Flipper Hall, a five-story brick building with a fifty-eight-room boys dormitory. Wylie Hall was turned into a classroom building. In addition, the Fair Haven Hospital on Irwin Street was organized in 1916, during the administration of President Fountain. (Courtesy Digging It Up Archives.)

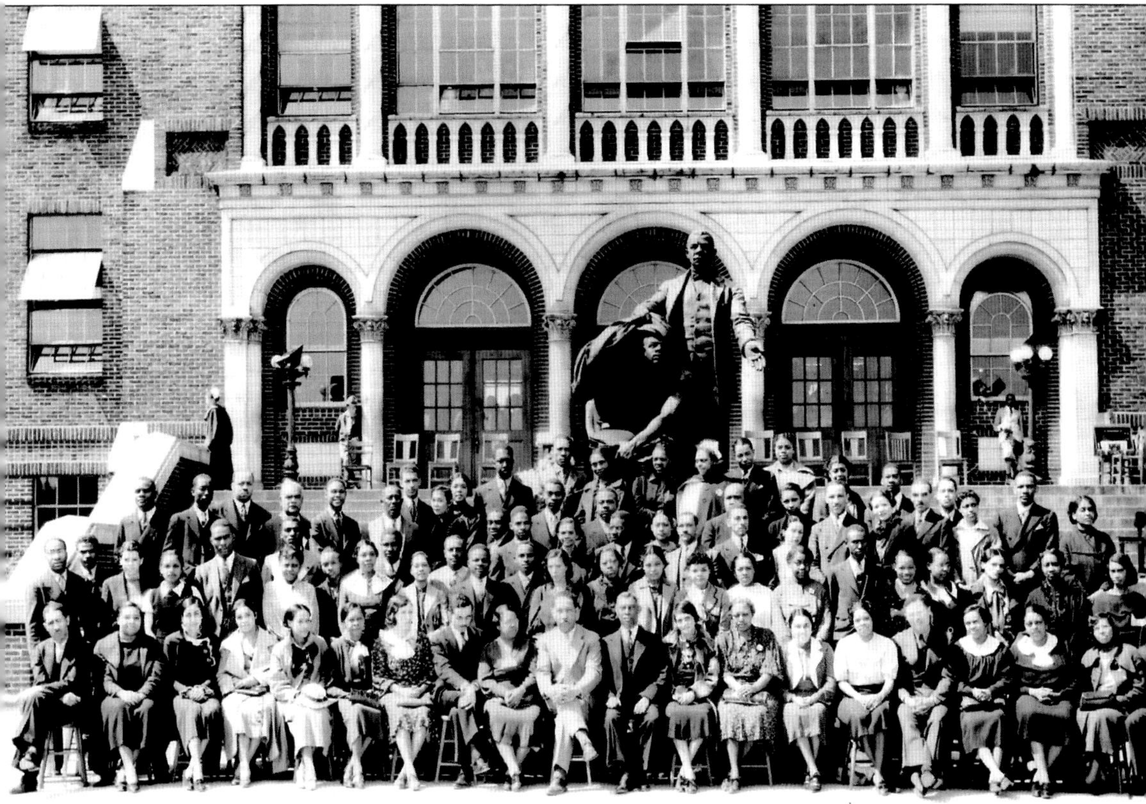

Members of the faculty posed for this photograph following the dedication of the statue of Booker T. Washington in front of the high school named for him in 1924. The first class graduated in 1927 and consisted of about one hundred fifty students. In 1928, Lena Horne enrolled at Washington High School and became one of thousands who would pass through its doors, including Martin Luther King Jr. Seated directly in the center, beginning tenth from left, are: Assistant Principal Professor Charles N. Cornell; Principal Professor Charles Harper; and English teacher Mrs. Louie D. Shivery, author of the school's Alma Mater. (Courtesy Digging It Up Archives.)

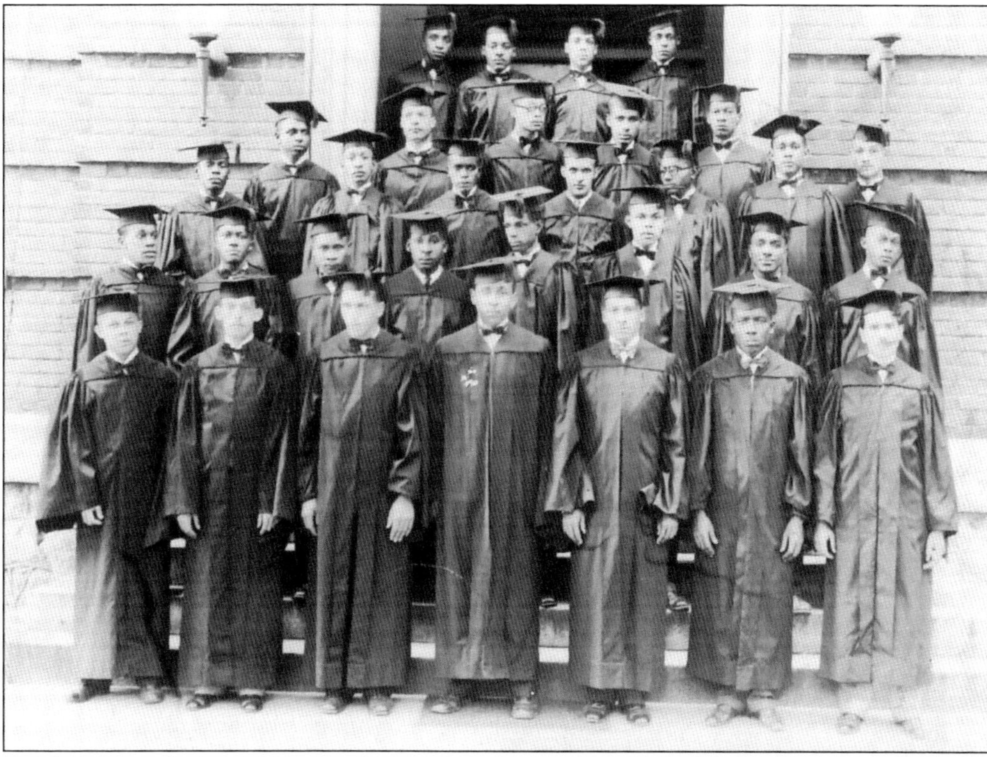

Graduating in the Morehouse College Class of 1929 was William Holmes Border (third row, second from right); Borders would become the pastor of Wheat Street Baptist Church on Auburn Avenue The commencement ceremony was held on Tuesday, June 4, in Sale Hall. It was in this class that 16 men completed the academy. Morehouse also awarded degrees to six women: Alice Umestine Bell (the second wife of John Lewis, president of Morris Brown), Hannah Elizabeth Buchanan, Mary Emma Burney, Rebecca Dickerson, Florence Mae Harvey, and Tena Beatrice Maxey.

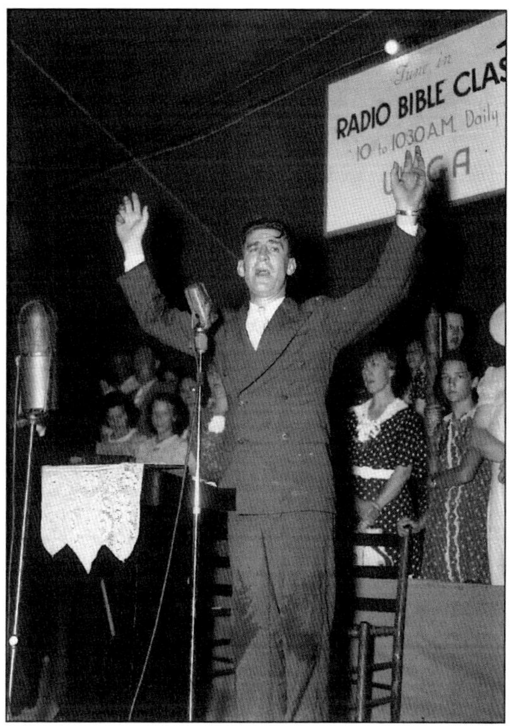

Reverend J.M. Hendley (right) and worshippers, young and old, are pictured at a tent meeting in Atlanta's Inman Park in 1939. Revivals such as this remain an important part of religious life to many in the Bible Belt. (Courtesy Atlanta History Center.)

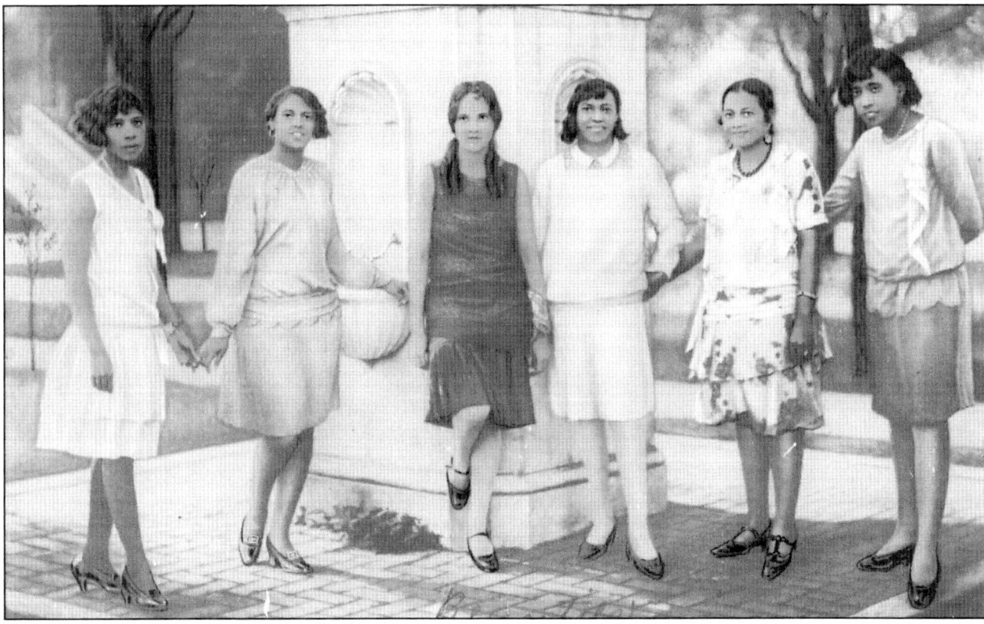

A group of Spelman coeds posed in front of the Grover Werden Memorial Fountain, which was dedicated on May 31, 1927. Spelman hosted the annual conference of the Student YWCA with representatives from nine Southern states numbering over a hundred students. (Courtesy Digging It Up Archives.)

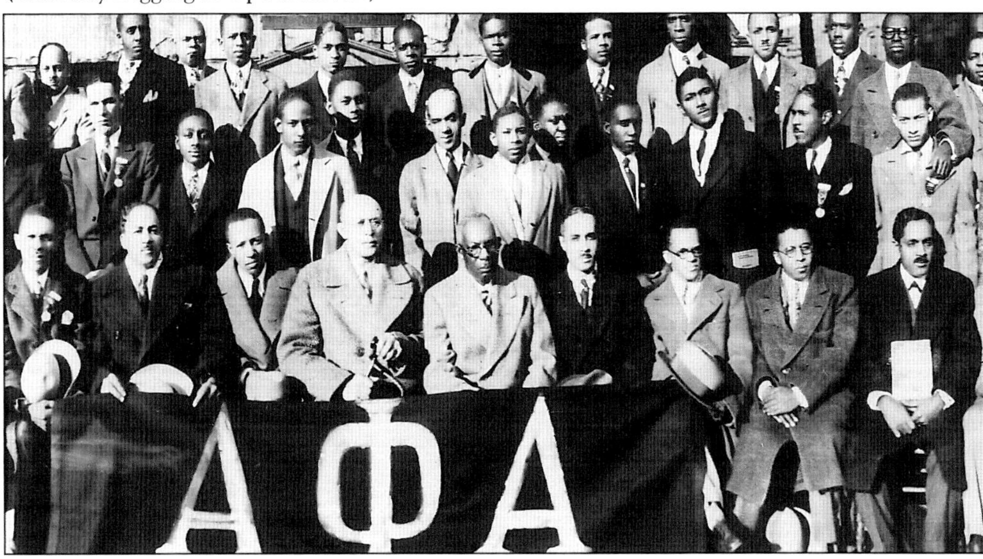

In December of 1929, the National Organization of Alpha Phi Alpha Fraternity held its 22nd General Convention in Atlanta, which featured three of the founders of the organization. The organization was founded in 1906 at Cornell University. During the convention, members of the Ku Klux Klan marched down Auburn Avenue to protest their convention. With a theme "Jim Crow Must Go," the Alphas helped Atlanta close out the decade of the twenties. (Courtesy Digging It Up Archives.)

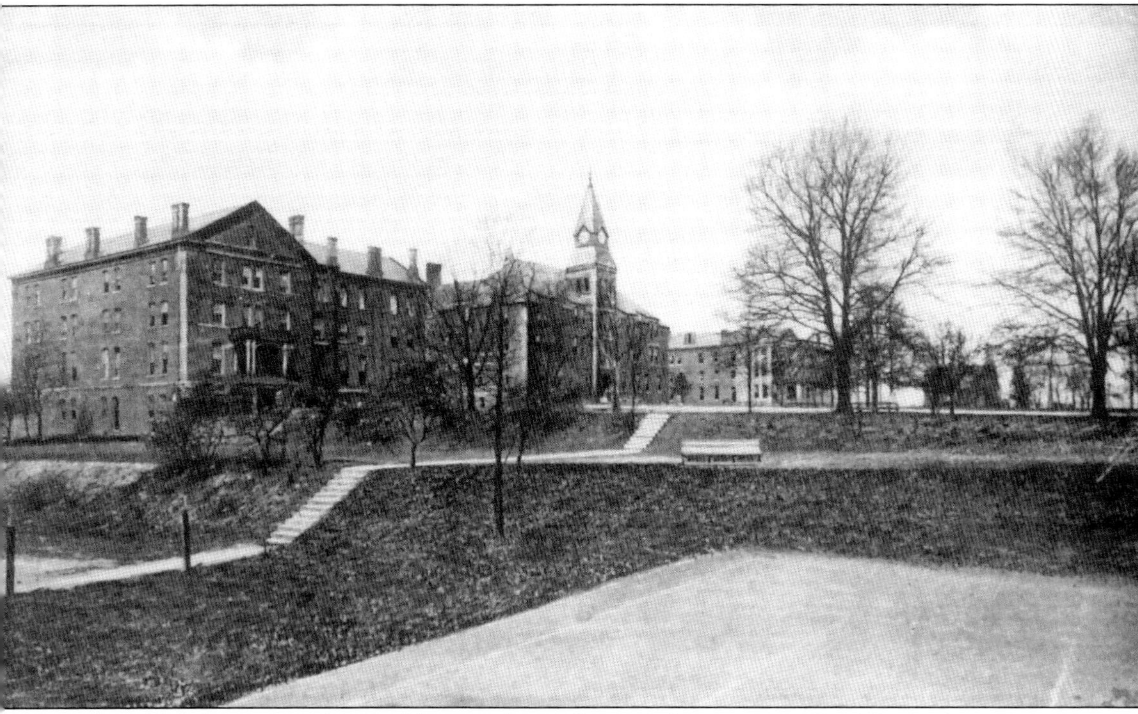

Atlanta had the unique factor of having five colleges and universities for African-American students. Though founded at different times and in different areas, these schools comprised the Atlanta University Center, the largest consortium of African-American colleges and universities in the country. During the 1920s, all of the schools were still in their infancy in developing their college curricula. Most of the schools offered private elementary and high school courses. By the end of the 1920s, the schools had redeveloped their scope and foci.

Atlanta University was founded in 1865. By the decade of the 1920s, "AU" was experiencing rapid growth and change simultaneously. In 1927, the Atlanta University choir recorded the "Negro National Anthem" on Columbia Records. Atlanta University would abandon the above campus and move closer to Morehouse and Spelman, which it merged with in 1929 to form Atlanta University Center. Morris Brown University would occupy the campus and lease it from "AU."

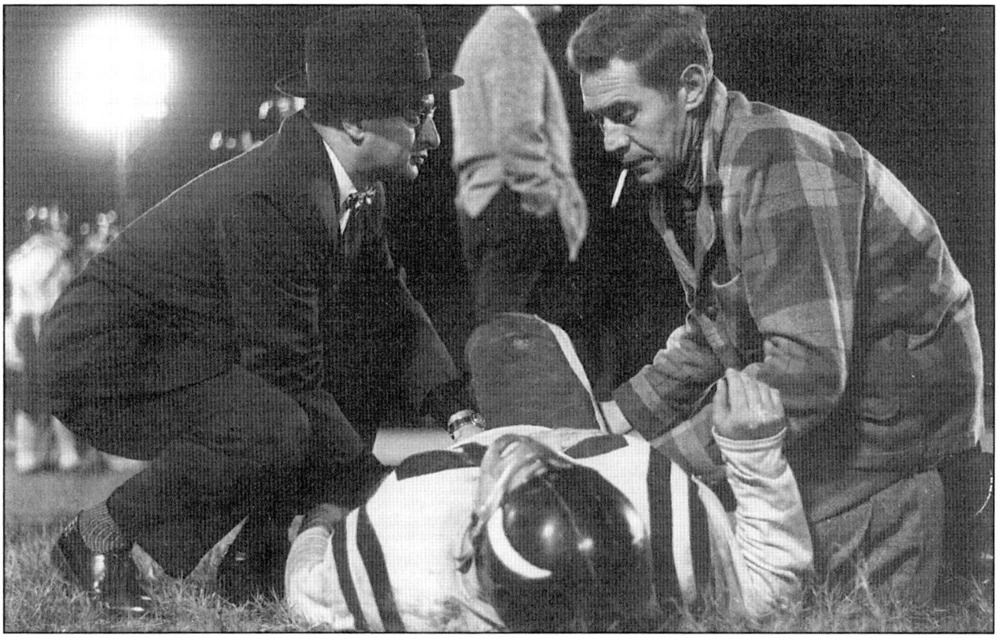

For several decades, Marietta High School's Friday night football games have been a community event, drawing citizens of all ages to cheer the home team. This 1957 scene includes Dr. Tony Musarra (left) and Romeo Hudgins taking care of an injured player. Marietta Coach French Johnson is standing in the background. (Photo by Joe McTyre.)

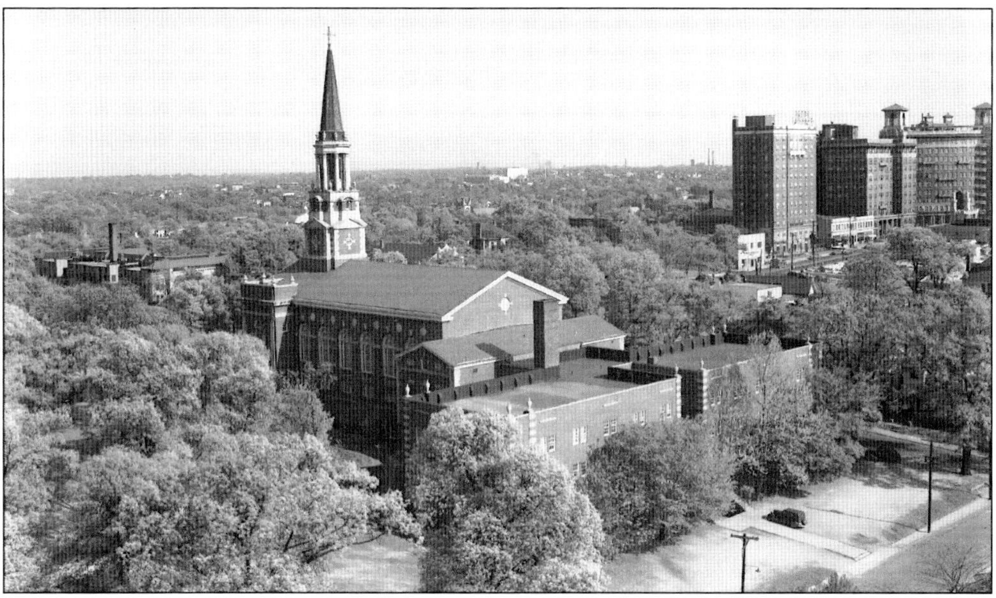

The multistoried steeple of the First Baptist Church, designed by the firm of Stevens and Wilkinson, stands sentinel over Peachtree Street in Midtown Atlanta. Built in 1929, the church is located just north of the Georgian Terrace and Ponce Apartment buildings (far right). (Courtesy Atlanta History Center.)

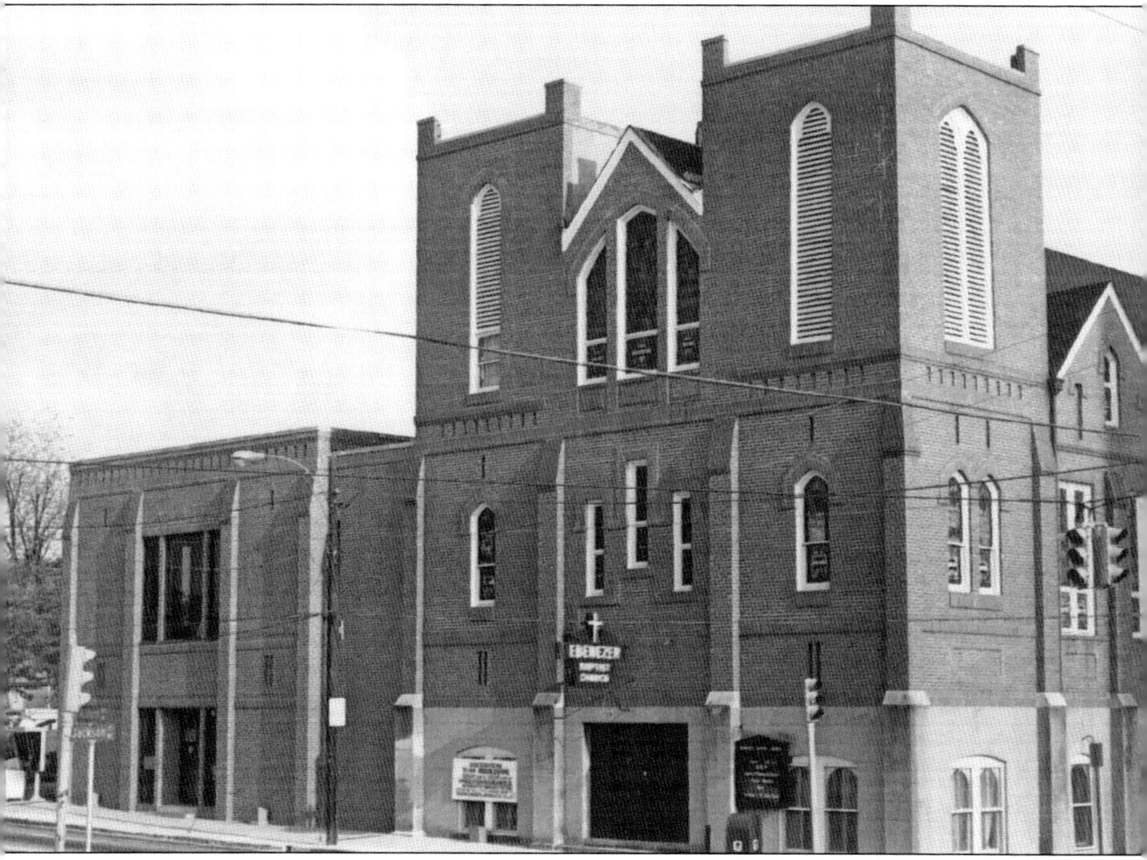

One of the historic landmarks of Atlanta, Ebenezer Baptist Church is known to all as the place where Martin Luther King, Jr. preached. At the corner of Auburn Avenue and Jackson Street, the Church saw the pastoral tenure of King's father, King's baptism, and later, his ordination as a minister. King established the Southern Christian Leadership Conference here. (Published by Thomas Warren Enterprises, Atlanta.)

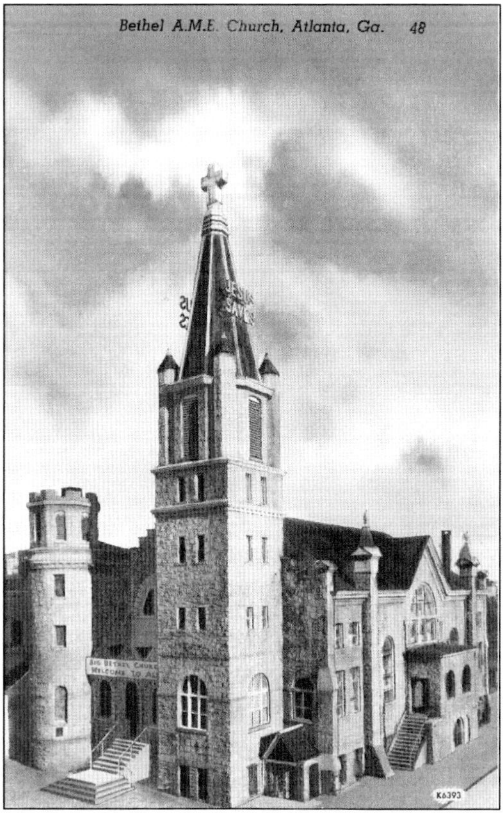

Known as "Big Bethel," the African Methodist Episcopal Bethel A.M.E. Church was organized and built in 1865–1866, at the close of the Civil War. Located at 220 Auburn Avenue, it is made of granite blocks from Stone Mountain and indeed looks as solid as a medieval fortress. The tower is complemented with the sign "Jesus Saves," and its well-known pageant, *Heaven Bound*, is presented annually. (Published by R and R News Co., Atlanta.)

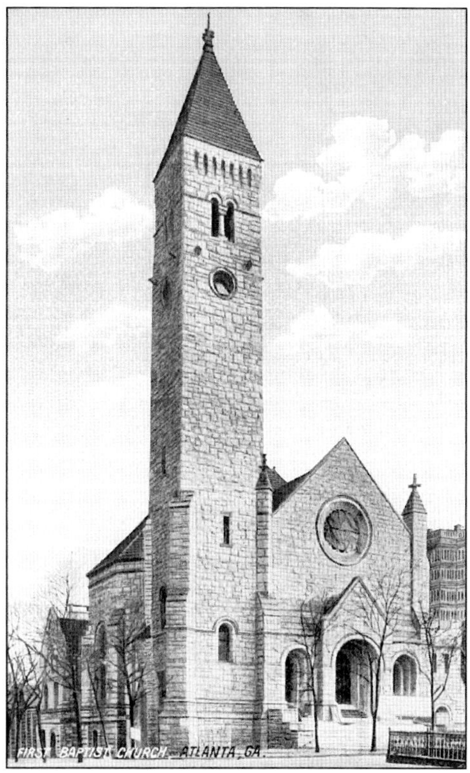

In 1906, this new building was constructed at Peachtree and Cain Streets. The First Baptist congregation moved to this location after 47 years at the building on Forsyth and Walton Streets. The granite structure of Norman Gothic design remained at this location for 22 years. The subsequent church building, opened in 1930, occupies a four-acre site on Peachtree and is bounded by Fourth, Fifth, and Cypress Streets. (Published by S.L. and Co., Germany; card sent 1908.)

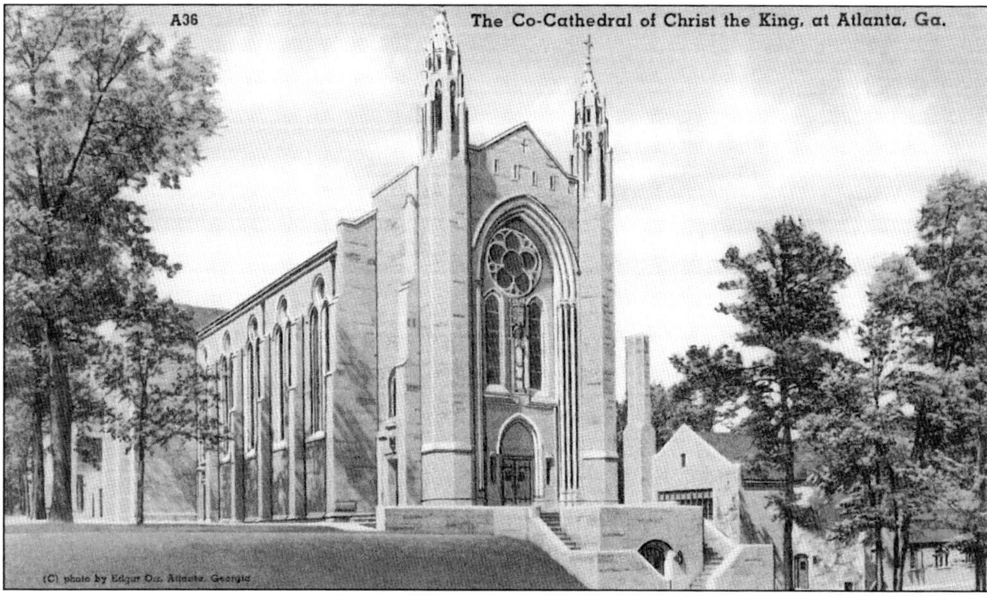

One of Atlanta's architectural showplaces, the beautiful limestone Co-Cathedral of Christ the King was built in 1938 to the designs of Henry Dagit and Sons of Philadelphia. Dedication ceremonies on January 18, 1939, drew a host of Catholic dignitaries, including Dennis Cardinal Dougherty, Archbishop of Philadelphia, who presided. Three archbishops, 12 bishops, and 150 priests took part, watched by hundreds of interested observers. One of the guests was Hiram Evans, Imperial Wizard of the Ku Klux Klan, on whose property the cathedral was built. (Published by Tichnor Bros., Boston; card sent 1943.)

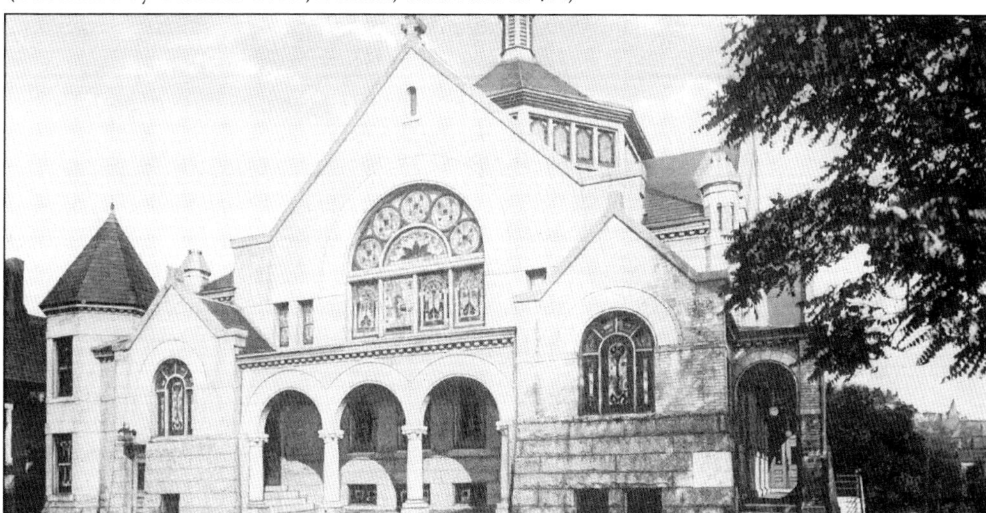

Christian churches in Atlanta have a long history. Organized in the 1850s, the first church building was destroyed in 1864. Another building, constructed in 1869 on Hunter Street between Pryor and Loyd, was exchanged for the present building on the northeast corner of Pryor and Trinity in 1907. The Peachtree Christian Church was built in 1926 at Peachtree and Spring Streets. (Published by Imperial Post Card Co., Atlanta.)

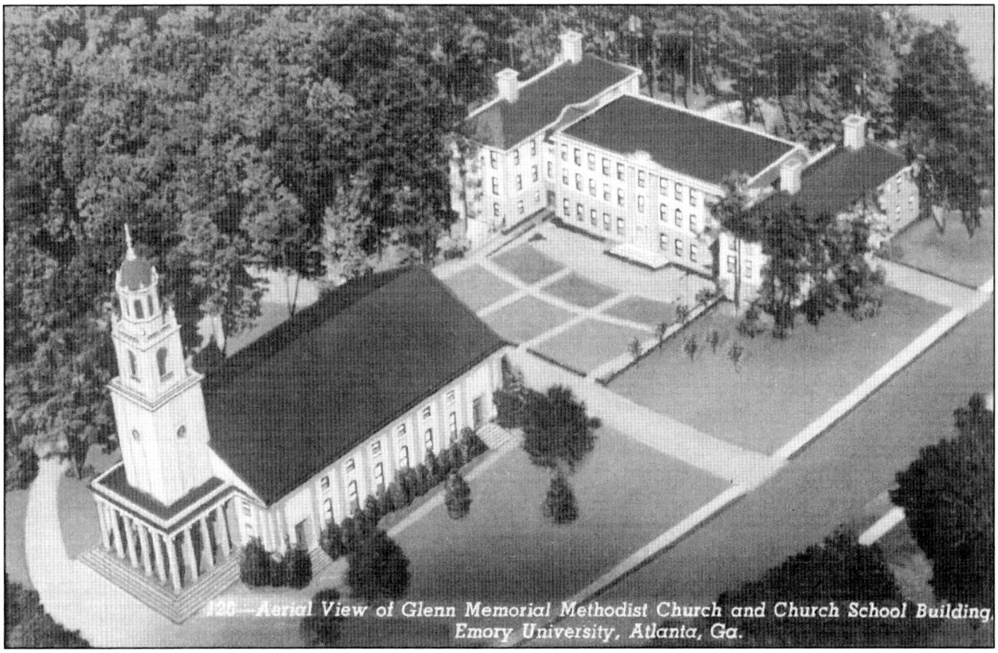

This cream-colored, stucco Methodist church stands near the entrance of the Emory campus at North Decatur and Oxford Roads. The Glenn Memorial Church, built in 1931, was given by Mrs. Charles H. Candler and Thomas K. Glenn in memory of their father Dr. Wilbur Fisk Glenn, a well-known Methodist minister. It serves both as a community church and as a university chapel. (Published by R and R News Co., Atlanta.)

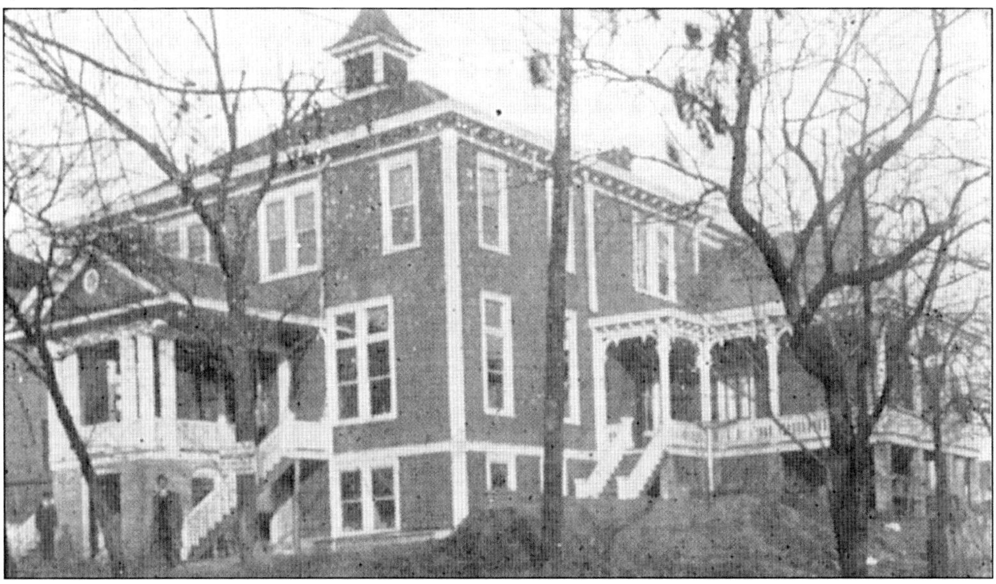

According to its description on the front of the postcard, the Atlanta Bible School opened in 1904 with its founder, Rev. Rolfe Hunt, as president. Rev. Hunt was also editor of *The Watchman*, a Baptist periodical.

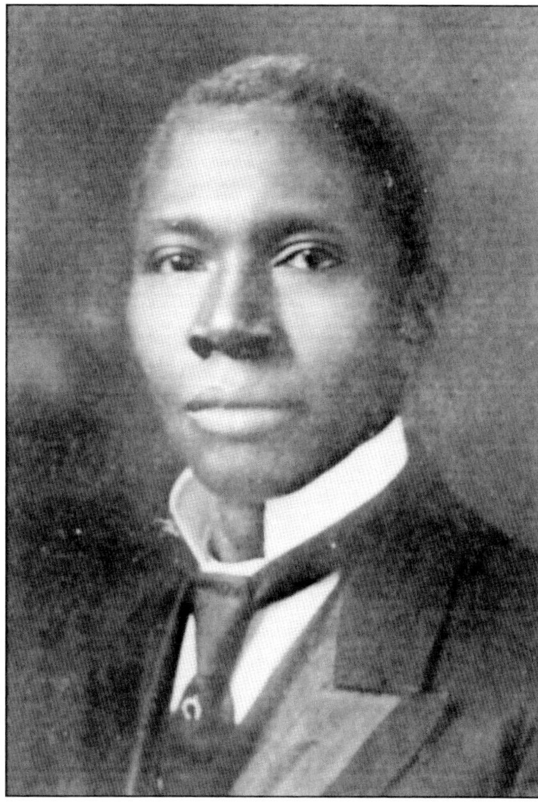

Rev. Peter James Bryant was a major leader in the African-American community. He became pastor of Wheat Street in 1898, organized the Atlanta Benevolent Protective Association in 1904, and was associate editor of the *Voice of the Negro*, a monthly magazine. He was also chairman of the board of the Carrie Steele orphanage. His wife, Sylvia Bryant, operated the Bryant Baptist Institute on Auburn Avenue and was the first president of the Phyllis Wheatley YWCA. Rev. Bryant and his wife were pillars of the civic and religious life of Atlanta at the time. In 1920, Rev. Bryant and his congregation moved into a new sanctuary on the corner of Auburn and Hilliard Street. The Gothic Revival structure was built by African-American contractor Robert E. Pharrow, who also built the Odd Fellows Building. (Courtesy Digging It Up Archives.)

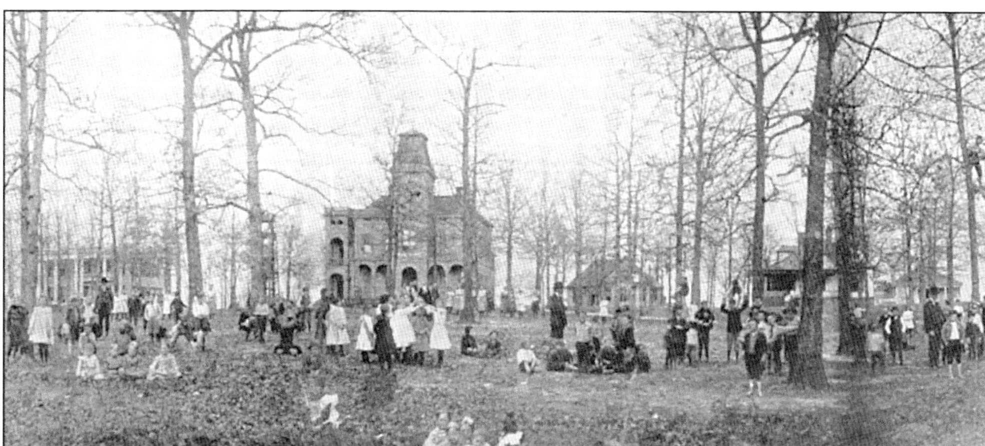

Located on the former property of William H. Clarke on Flat Shoals Road (Columbia Drive), the Decatur Orphan's Home opened in the 1870s and has been developed and enlarged through the years. In 1934 its name was changed to the Methodist Children's Home at Decatur. (Card sent 1908.)

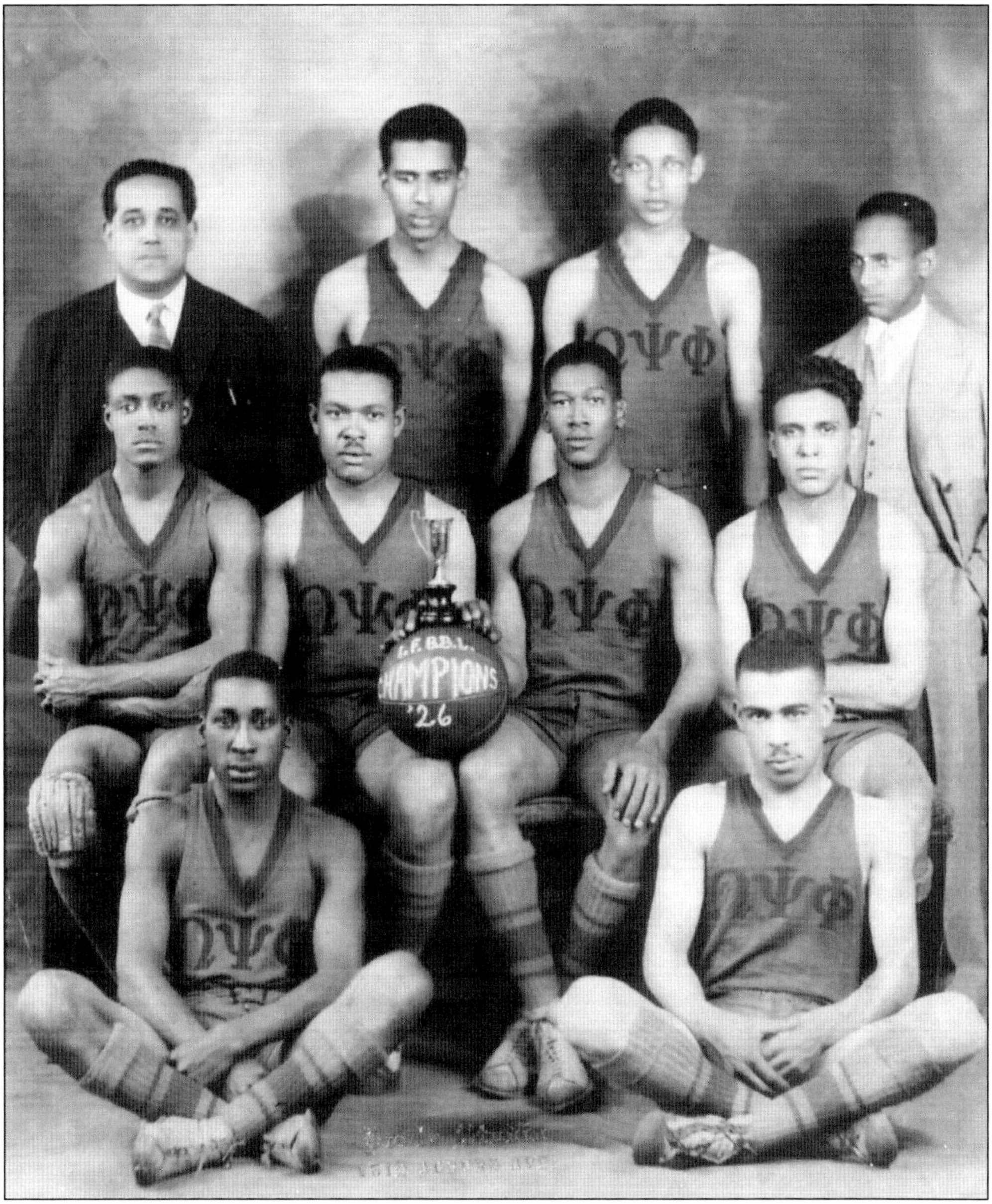

The Omega Psi Phi basketball team, coached by "Chief" Walter Aiken, were the 1926 inter-fraternity basketball champions. The team consisted of members from Tau Chapter at Atlanta University, Psi Chapter at Morehouse, and Beta Psi Chapter at Clark College. The fraternity was established in Atlanta on December 27, 1919, as the Eta Omega Chapter, and was composed of college men from Morehouse, Clark, and Atlanta University during the 1920s. Harold H. Thomas, Harvey Smith, L.R. Harper, Horace A. Hodges, and C.E. Warner organized the chapter. In 1924, they opened a fraternity house on Ashby Street. Some prominent Omega men during the 1920s were W.J. Faulkner, Jesse O. Thomas, C.L. Harper, and John Wesley Dobbs. This team portrait was taken by Paul Poole. (Courtesy Digging It Up Archives.)

Five

The Civil War

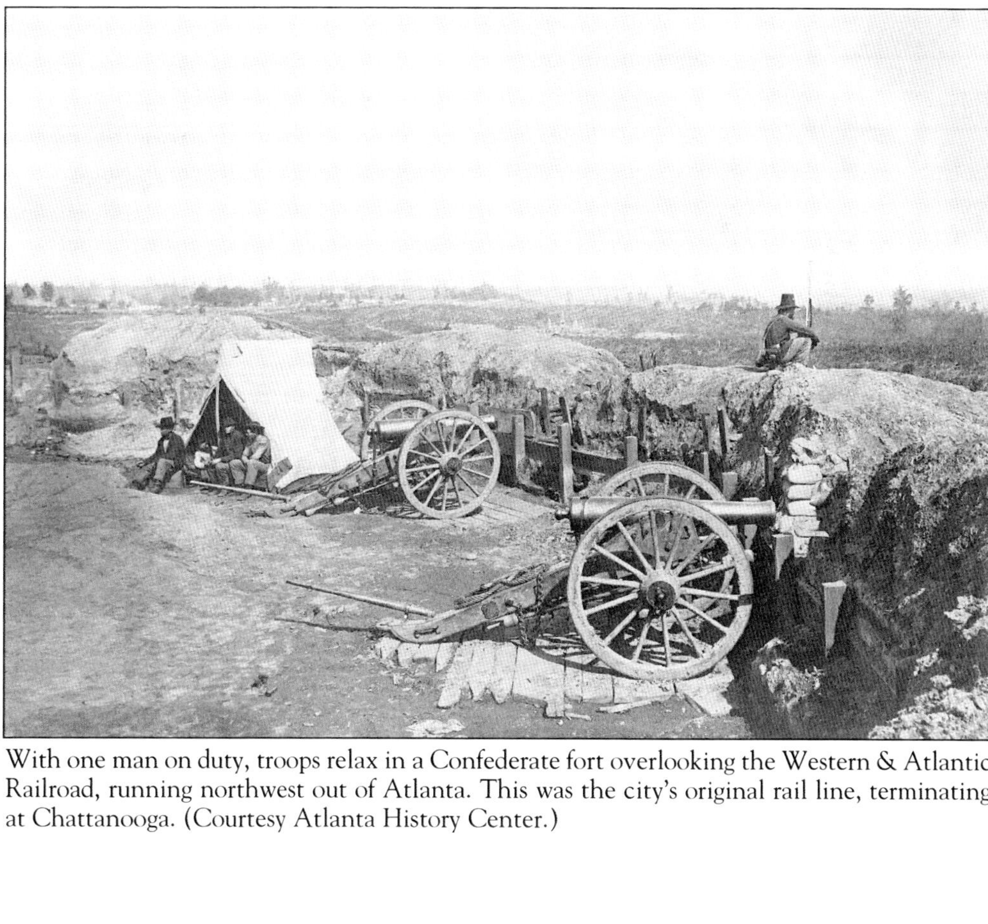

With one man on duty, troops relax in a Confederate fort overlooking the Western & Atlantic Railroad, running northwest out of Atlanta. This was the city's original rail line, terminating at Chattanooga. (Courtesy Atlanta History Center.)

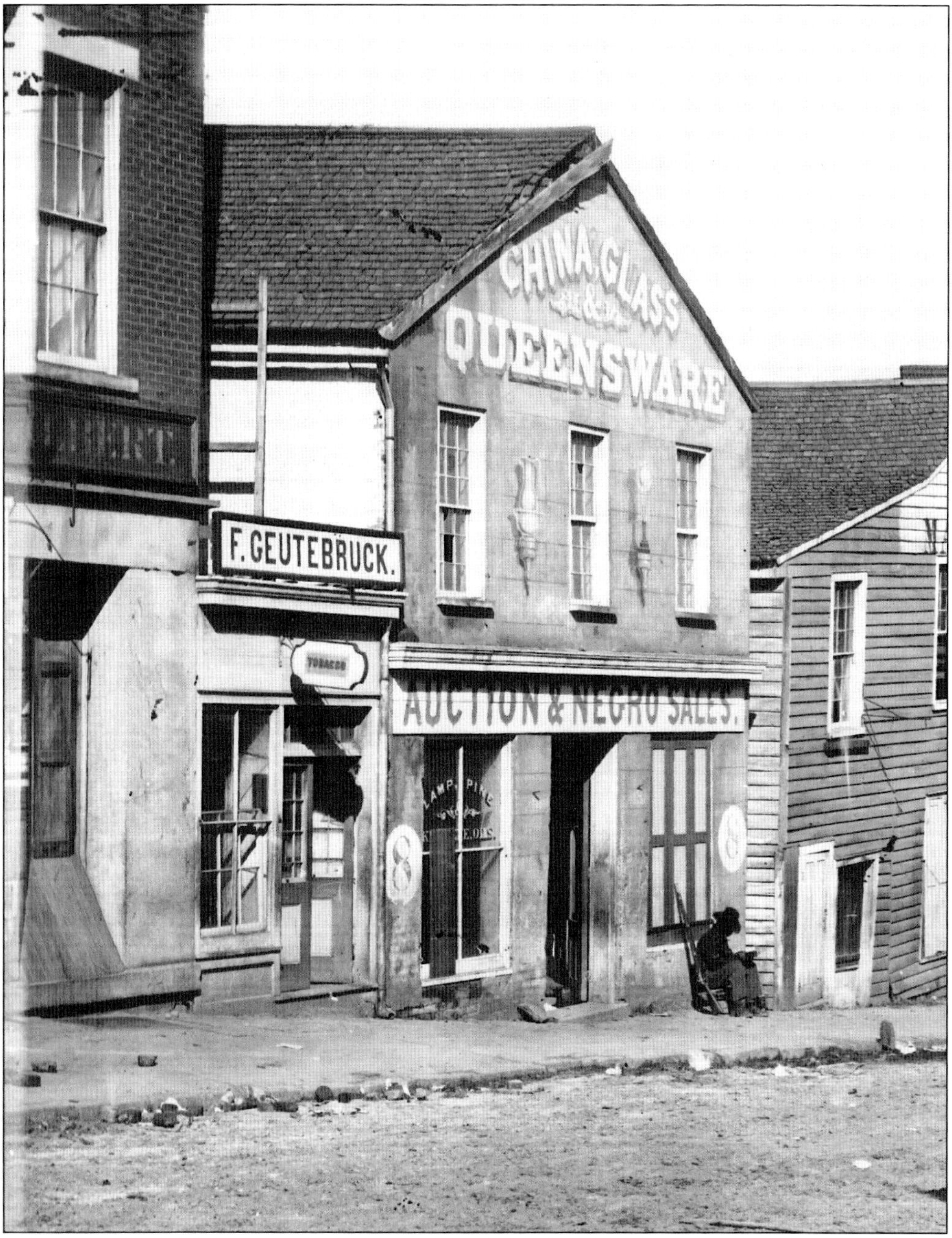

A visual icon of the Atlanta campaign, this is one of Barnard's most famous images of the city. The Crawford, Frazer & Co. slave market was located at No. 8 Whitehall Street between Alabama and Hunter [Martin Luther King Jr. Drive] Streets. L.C. Butler remembered the benches surrounding the room on which slaves were seated. "Here," he said, "the prospective buyers made their selections just as they would have a horse or mule at a stockyard." (Courtesy Atlanta History Center.)

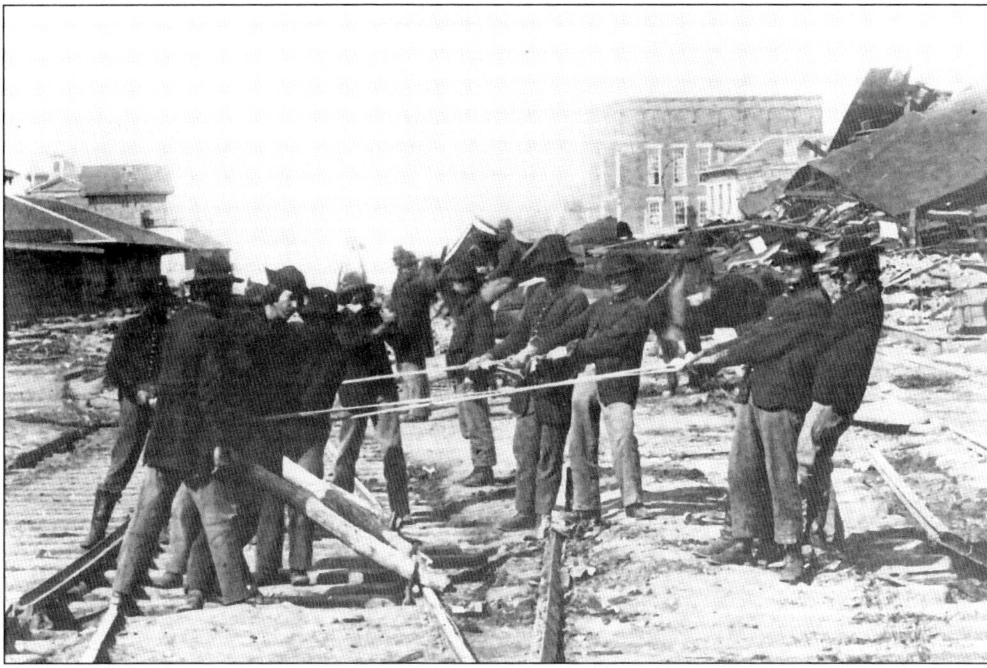

With the ruins of the Car Shed at right, soldiers demonstrate methods used to pull entire sections of track to loosen spikes attaching rails and ties. Ties were then used as bonfire fuel over which rails were laid, softening them to bend and twist into "Sherman's neckties." The men became skilled at the practice, with teams performing each step in the process. (Courtesy Atlanta History Center.)

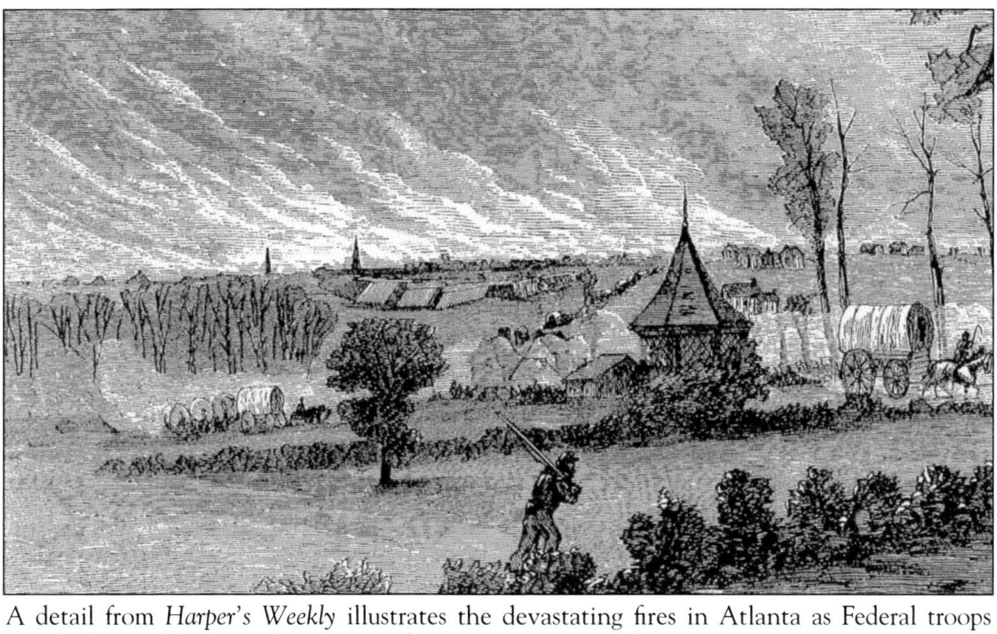

A detail from *Harper's Weekly* illustrates the devastating fires in Atlanta as Federal troops marched out of the city. (Courtesy Atlanta History Center.)

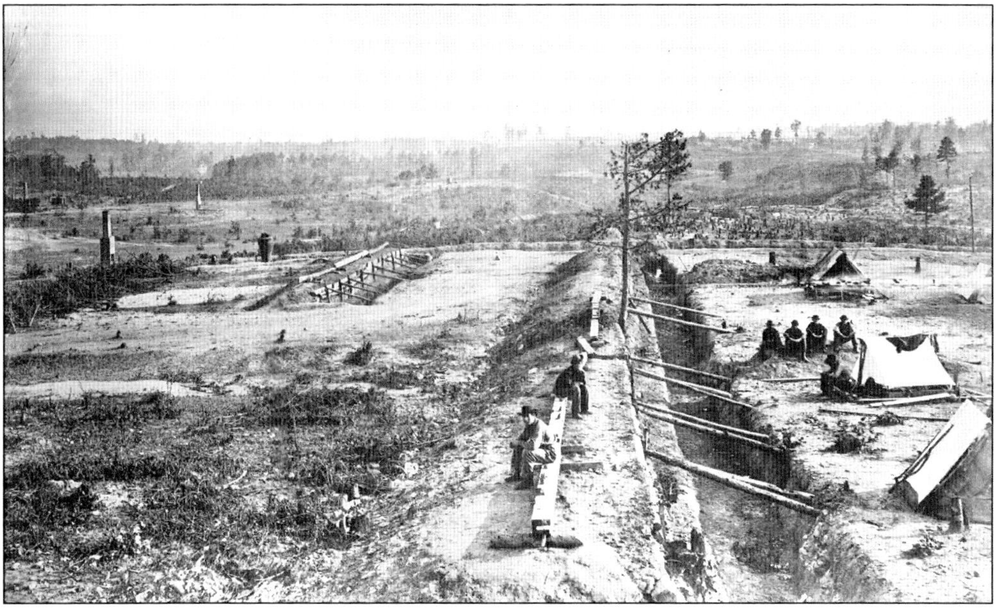

Here, two men sit on head logs near Confederate rifle trenches protecting the Georgia Railroad. The railway sits in a deep, steep-sided cut just beyond the trench at left; at left center can be seen just the smokestack of a locomotive. Head logs allowed troops to fire under them while protecting their heads from enemy fire. The skid poles lying across the pit offered safety in case the logs were dislodged. (Courtesy Atlanta History Center.)

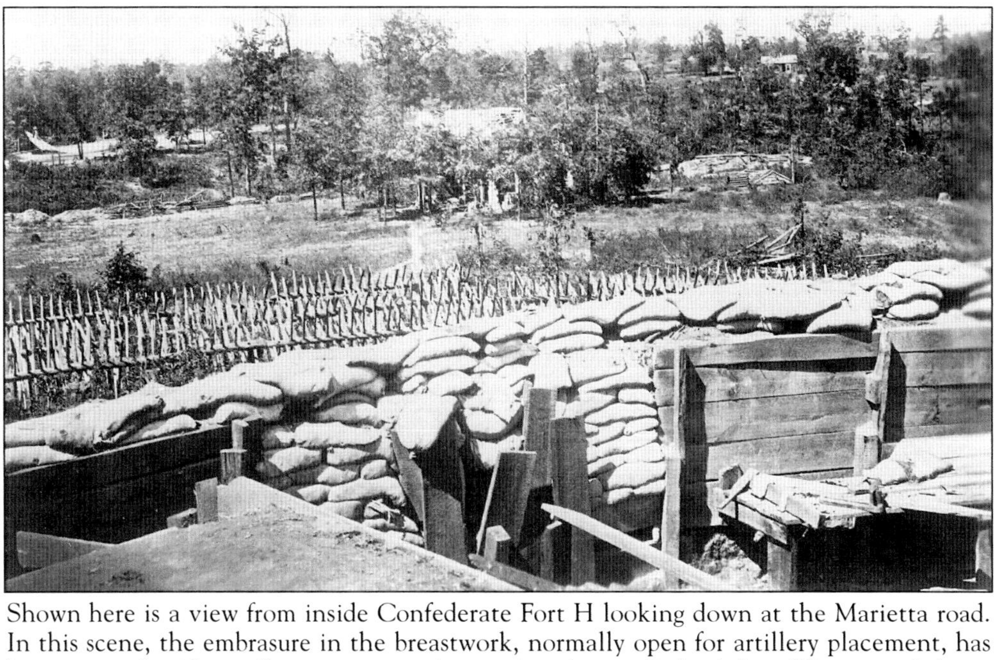

Shown here is a view from inside Confederate Fort H looking down at the Marietta road. In this scene, the embrasure in the breastwork, normally open for artillery placement, has been secured with sandbags as protection against heavy Federal fire. (Courtesy Atlanta History Center.)

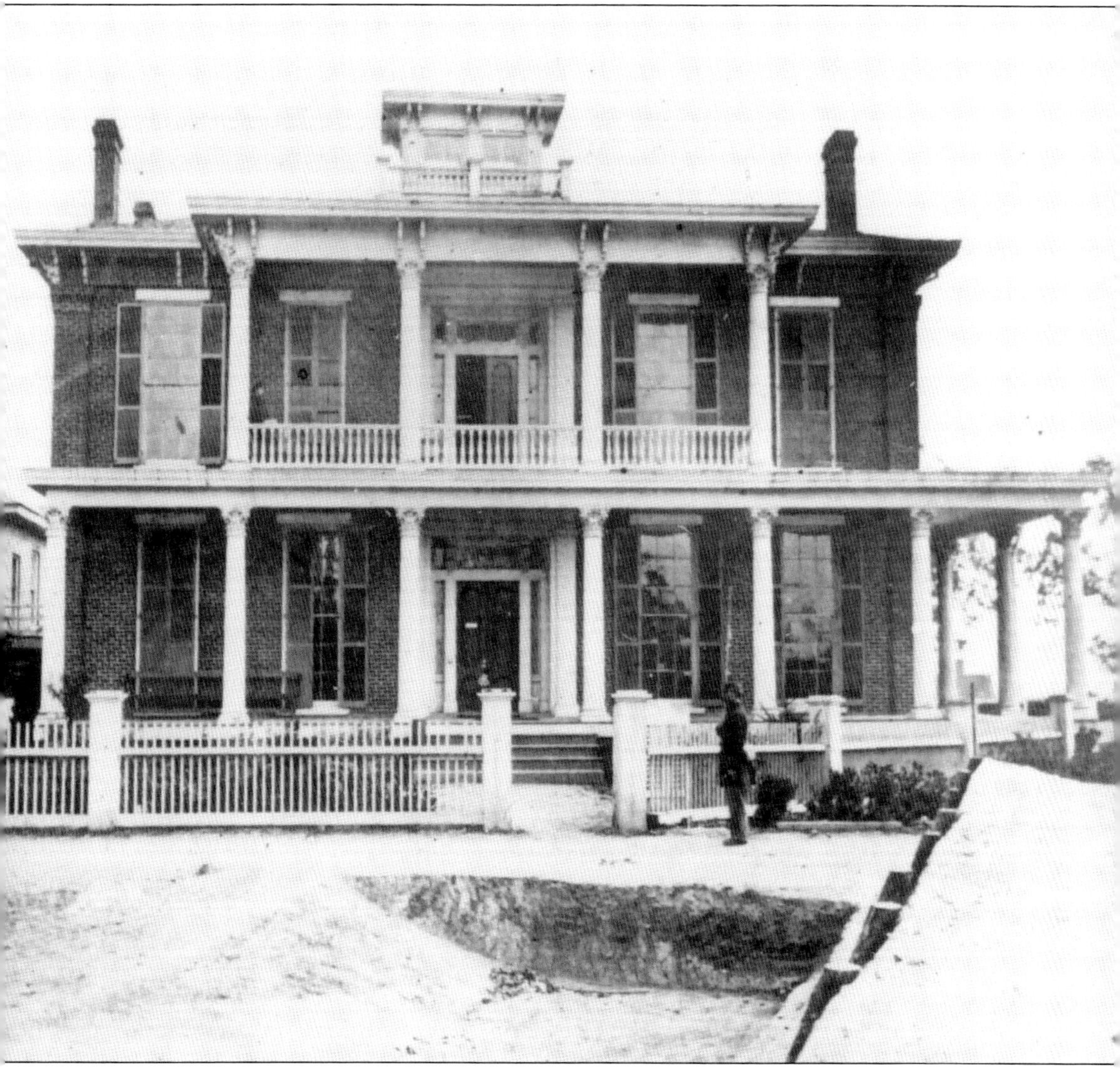

Guarded by a sentry and showing evidence of defense works surrounding city hall in the right foreground, the William Solomon residence on Mitchell Street served as the Federal army's post headquarters during the occupation of Atlanta, September–November 1864. (Courtesy Atlanta History Center.)

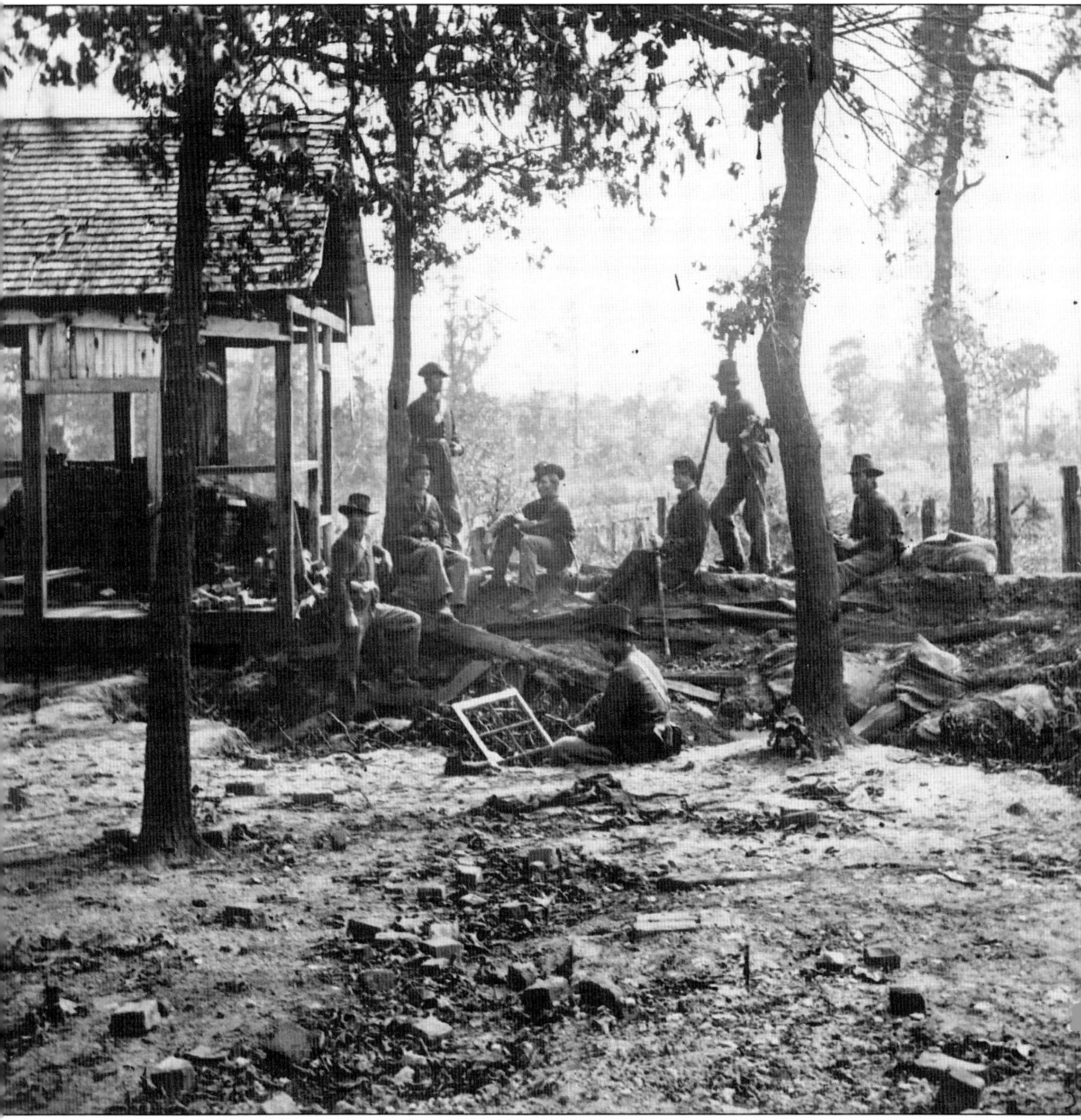

Following the Battle of Bald Hill (Atlanta), Federal troops such as these pictured here occupied their own trench lines around the city while the Confederate army settled in for a long siege: "We are still standing quite [quiet] since our big fight on last Friday," wrote Evan Park Howell of Howell's Battery, Georgia Light Artillery. "We occupy the ditches around town, and the enemy just in front of us; sharp shooting and cannonading now and then. The enemy shell the city once in a while, doing no other damage than kill a few women and children." (Courtesy Atlanta History Center.)

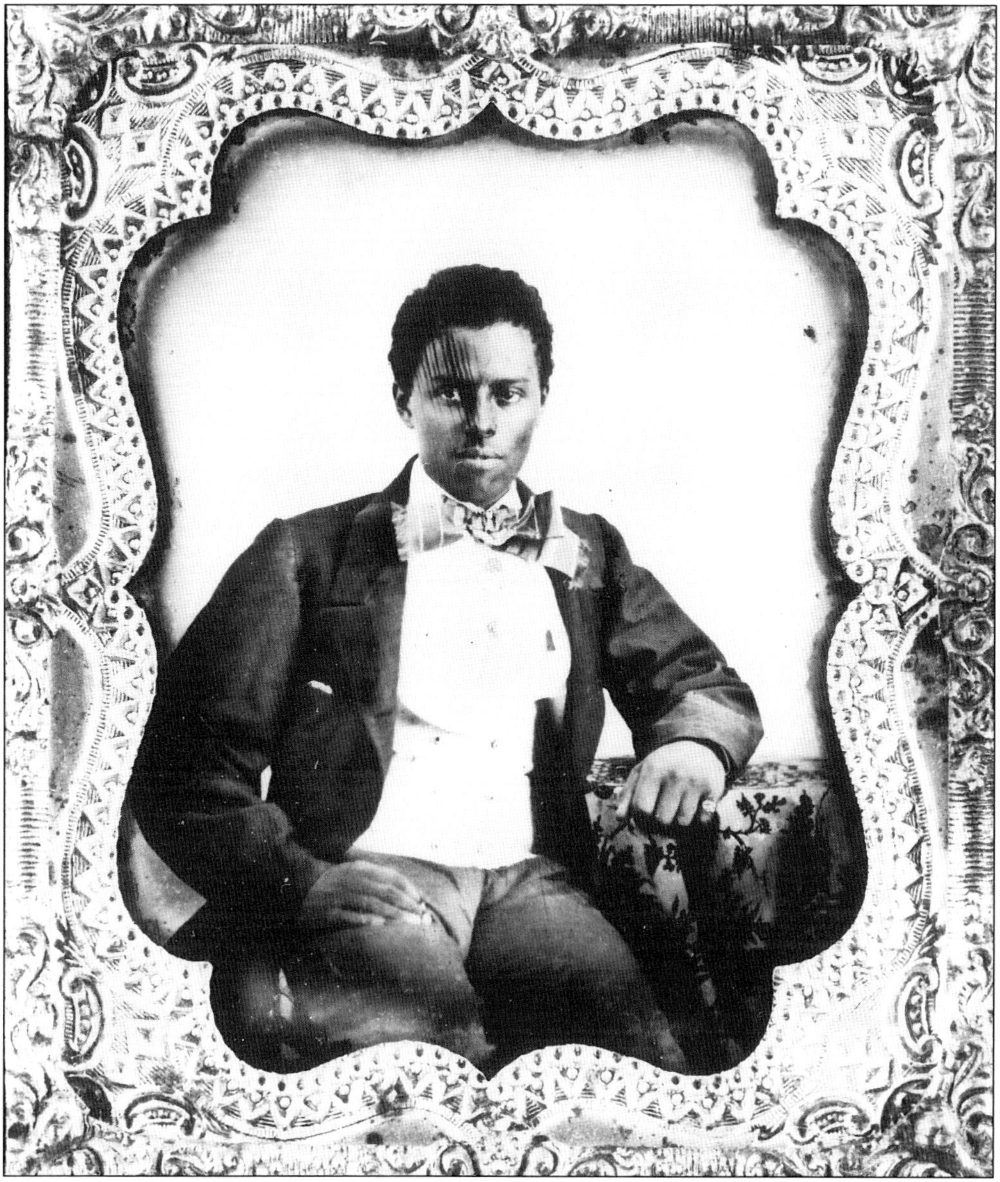

"That red day in August . . ." August 9, 1864, was the worst day of the siege. Solomon Luckie, a free African American, ran a barber shop and bathing salon in the Atlanta Hotel. While at the corner of Whitehall and Alabama Streets that day, Luckie was struck by shell fragments from the bombardment. Taken by Thomas Cruselle and others to the Atlanta Medical College, Dr. Pierre-Paul Noel D'Alvigny amputated his leg. Suffering from shock, Luckie failed to recover and died a few hours later. (Courtesy Atlanta History Center.)

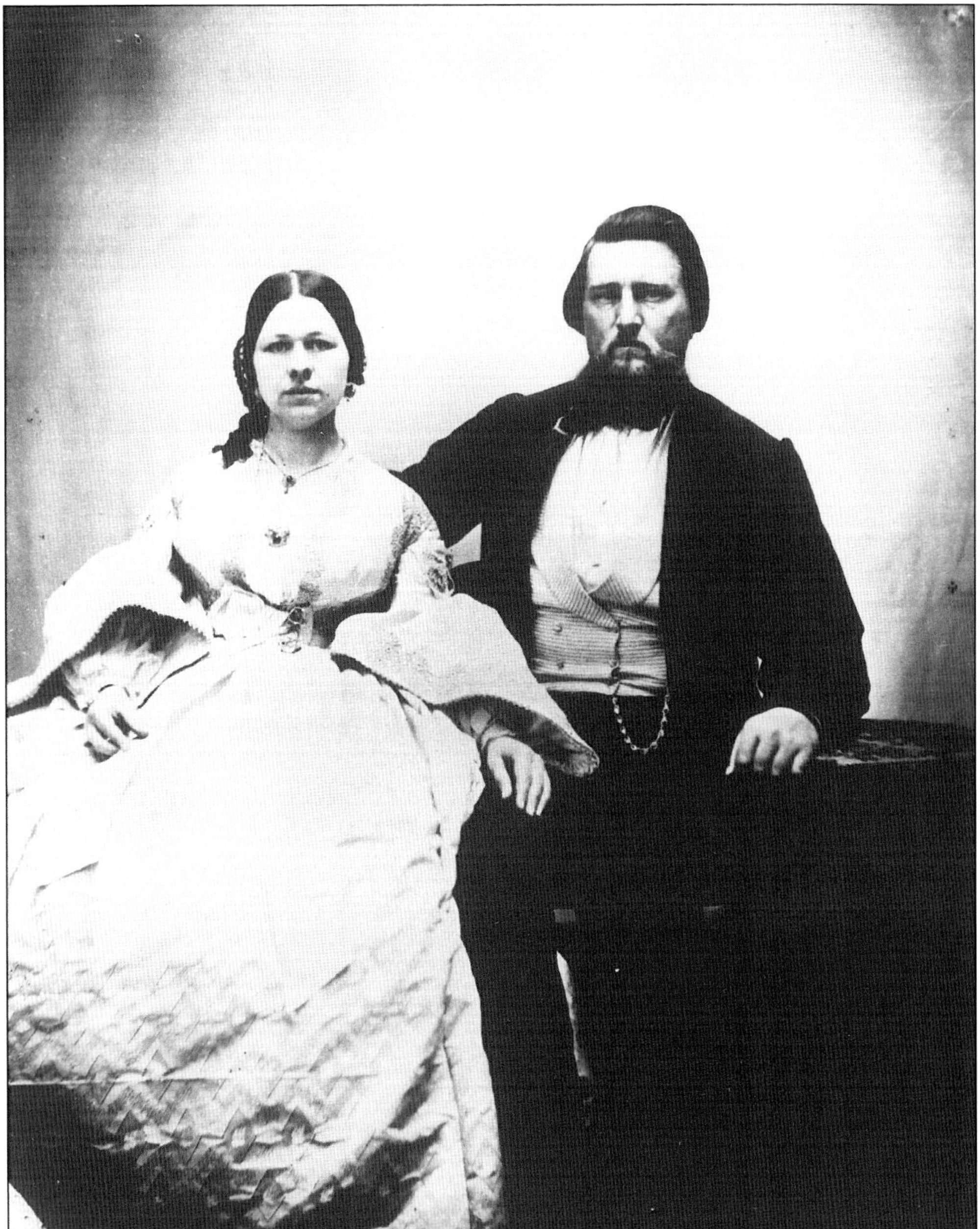

Cotton factor and merchant Robert Flournoy Maddox and his wife, Nancy J. Reynolds, pose for a whole-plate ambrotype in the Whitehall Street studio of William H. DeShong in 1861. Moving to Atlanta in 1858, Maddox organized and served with the Calhoun Guards No. 2, 42nd Georgia Regiment, fighting at Vicksburg and Missionary Ridge. After the war, Maddox was president of the Maddox-Rucker banking firm and the Old Dominion Guano Company. (Courtesy Atlanta History Center.)

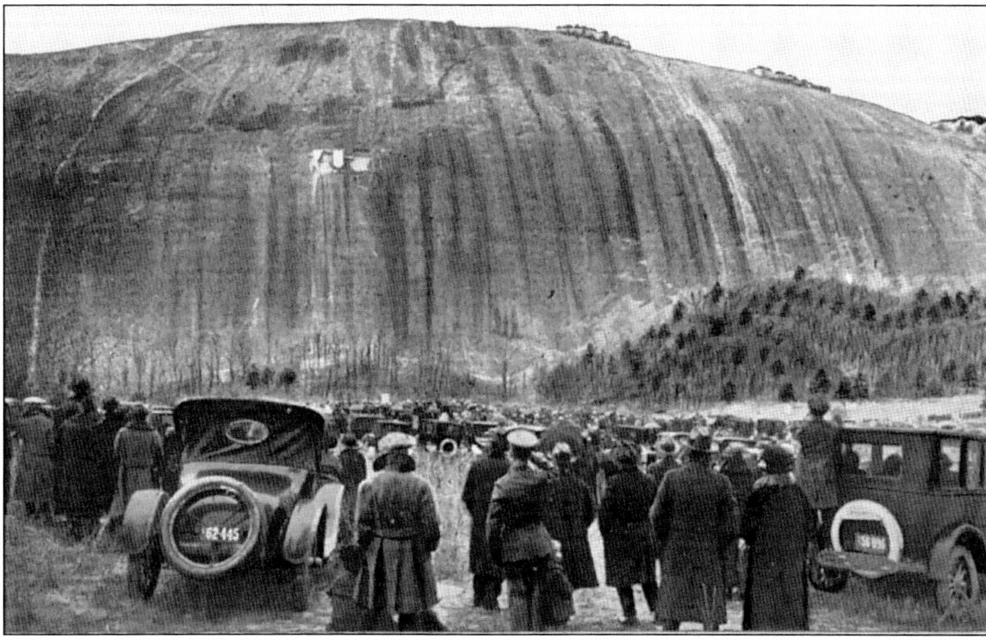

On January 19, 1924, the partially completed head of General Lee was unveiled to the public with great ceremony. Over 10,000 people came to witness the event, including five governors. (Published by R. and R. News Co., Atlanta.)

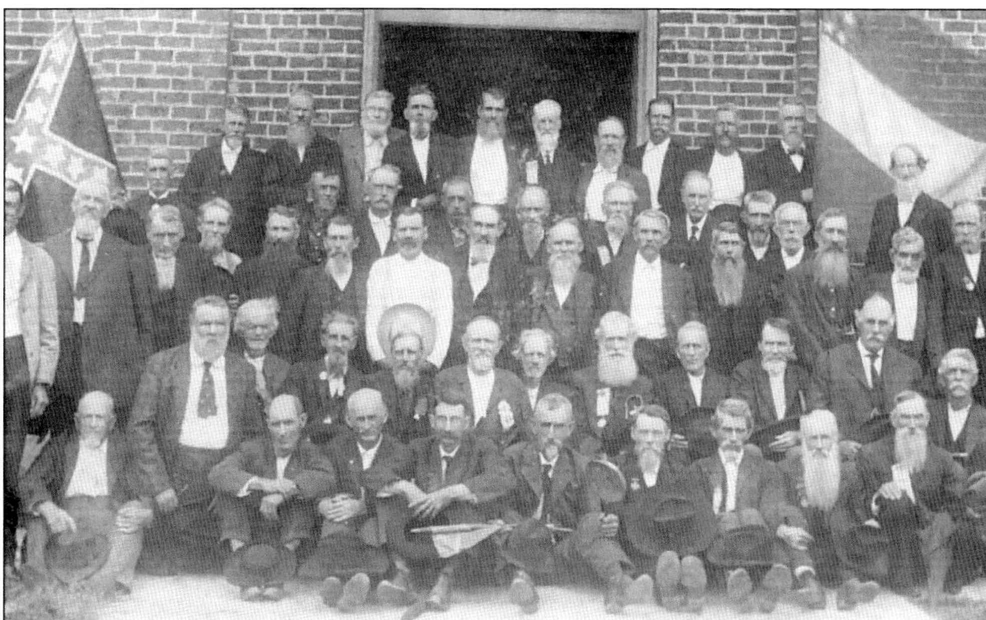

This remarkable picture of Confederate veterans was taken in September 1909 at Alpharetta by an amateur photographer who made it into a postcard. The war ended 44 years earlier; these 65 or 70 year olds look dignified and eager in their expressions of survival and patriotism.

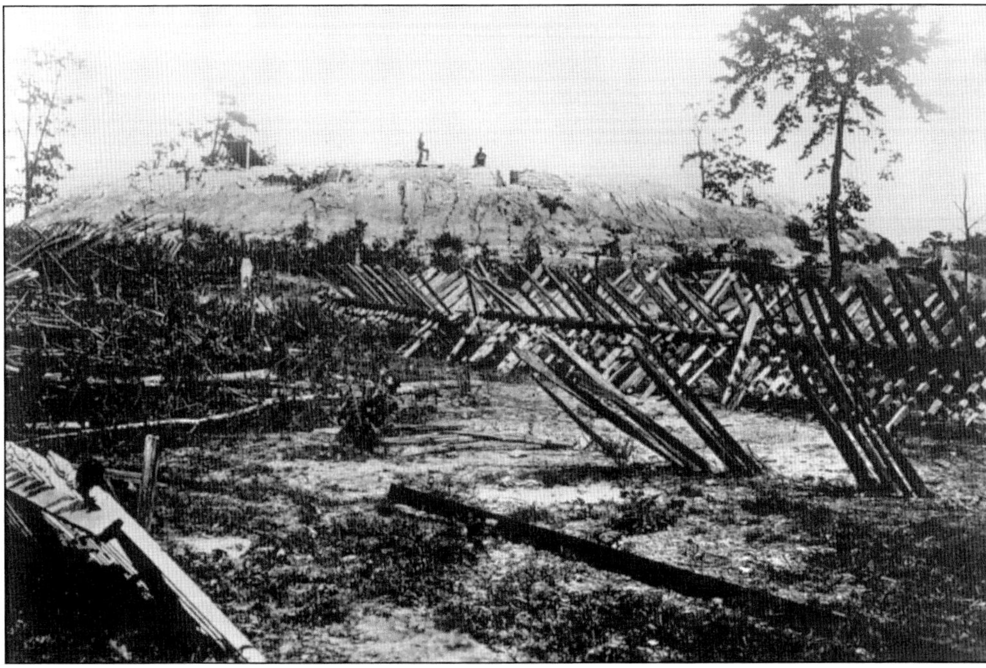

Here, two soldiers stand atop Confederate Fort H guarding Marietta Street and the Western & Atlantic rail line running northwest of the city. The approach to the fort is protected by a series of *fraises*, *chevaux-de-frise*, *abatis*, and at left foreground, a white picket fence. (Courtesy Atlanta History Center.)

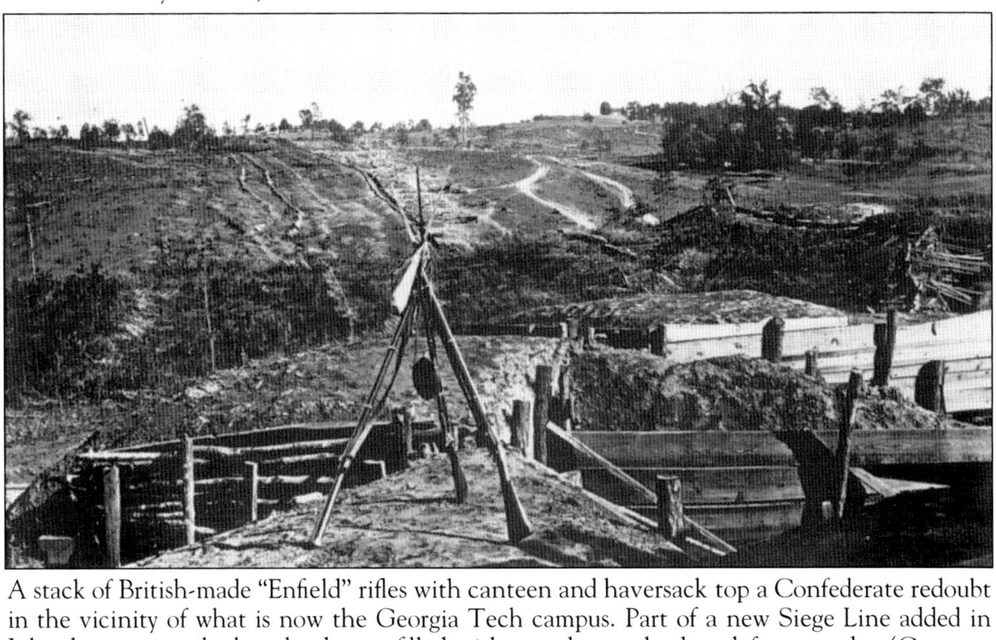

A stack of British-made "Enfield" rifles with canteen and haversack top a Confederate redoubt in the vicinity of what is now the Georgia Tech campus. Part of a new Siege Line added in July, the post overlooks a landscape filled with trenches and other defense works. (Courtesy Atlanta History Center.)

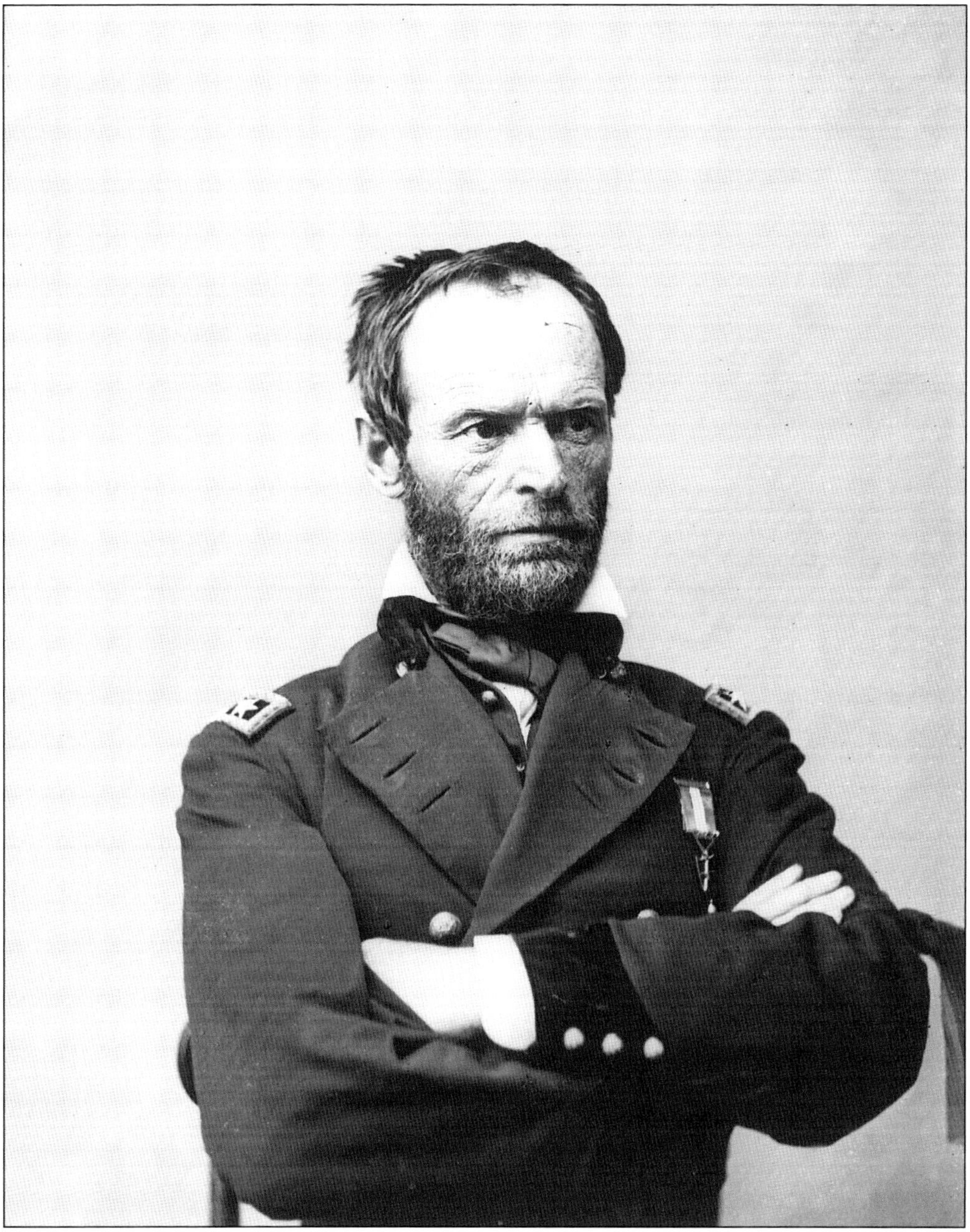

In addition to seizing Atlanta, Major General William T. Sherman sought to prevent the transfer of Confederate troops to relieve Robert E. Lee in the struggle against Grant in Virginia. Nevertheless, destruction of the Southern war capability remained a critical element in Grant's war strategy, asserting Sherman's mission was to inflict "all the damage you can against their War resources." Thus this single object within these two goals was Atlanta. Separating Sherman and the city were the north Georgia mountains and the Confederate army. (Courtesy Atlanta History Center.)

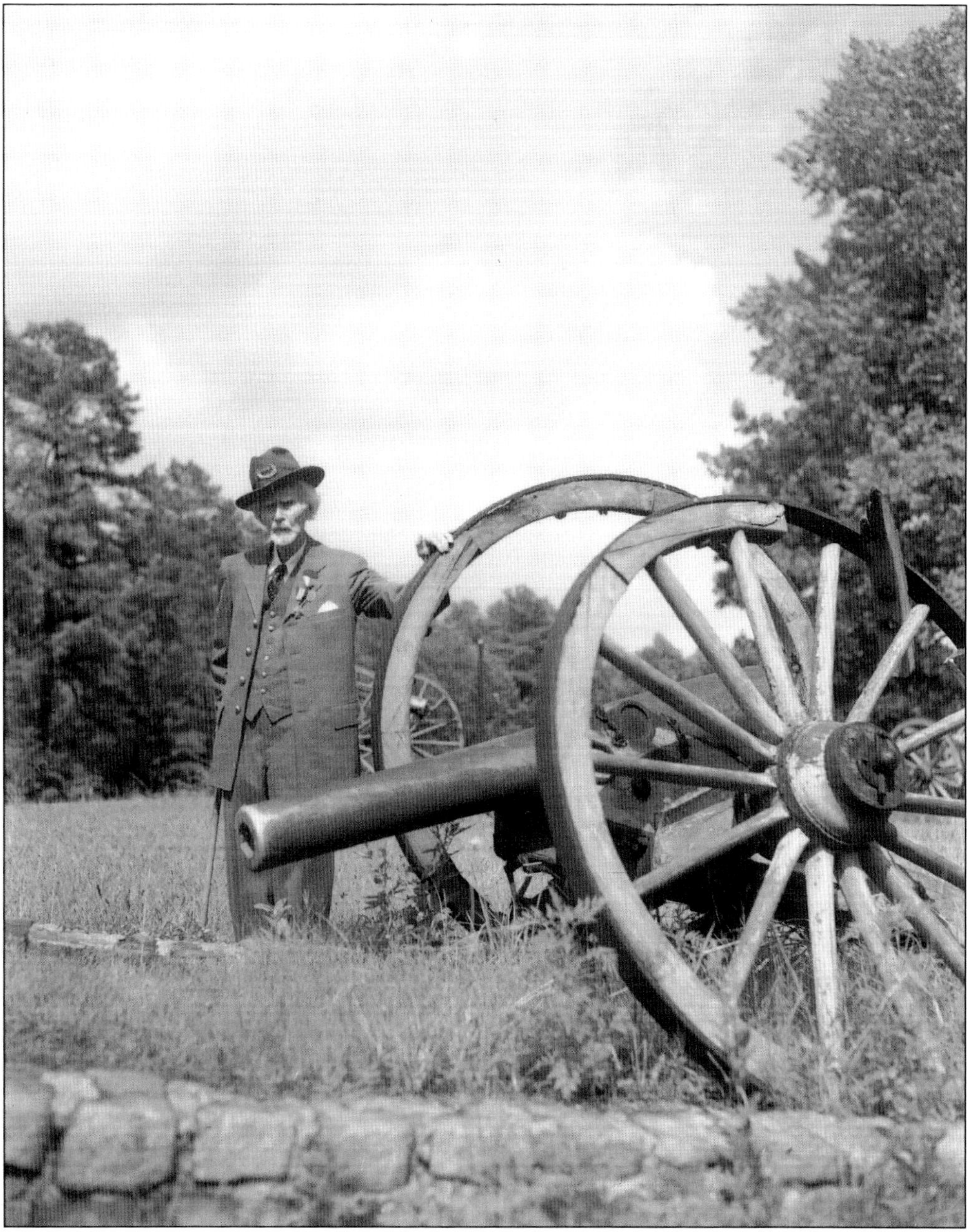

Henry T. Dowling, shown here when he was 98 years old, was the last Confederate general to reside in Atlanta's Confederate Soldier's Home. (Courtesy Atlanta History Center.)

Six

Recreation

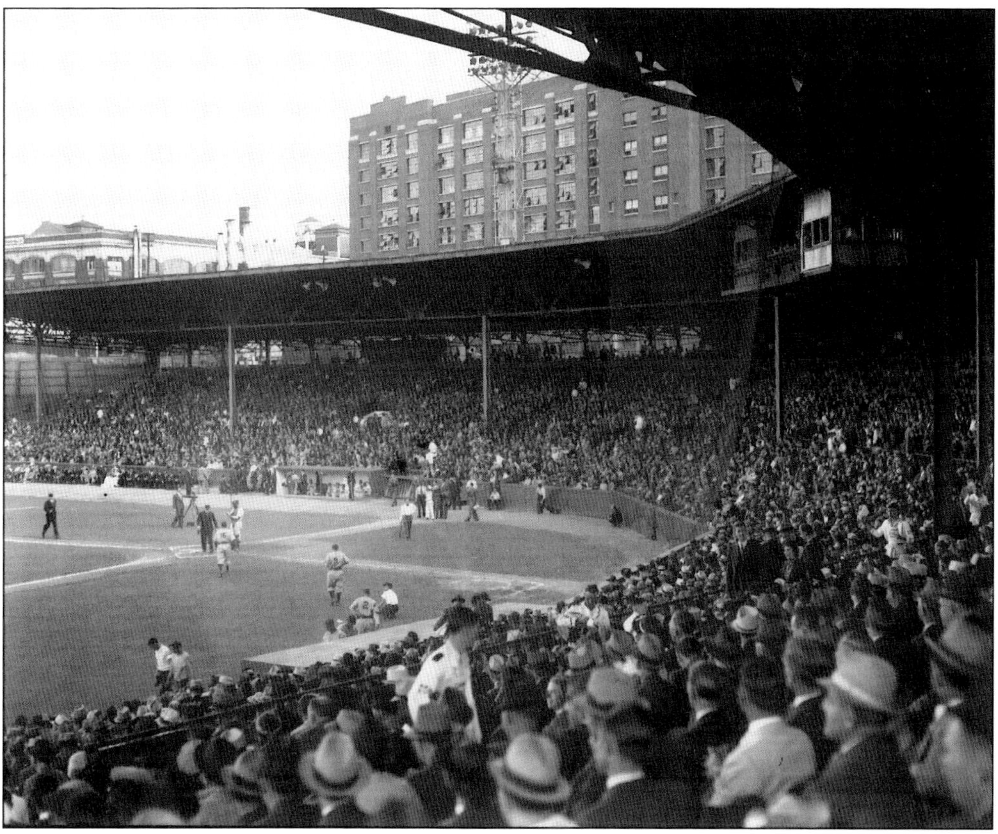

A crowd watches a game at R.J. Spiller Field, more commonly known as Ponce de Leon Ballpark, 1940. The park was home to the minor league Atlanta Crackers, and on occasion to the Atlanta Black Crackers, until the mid-1960s.(Courtesy Atlanta History Center.)

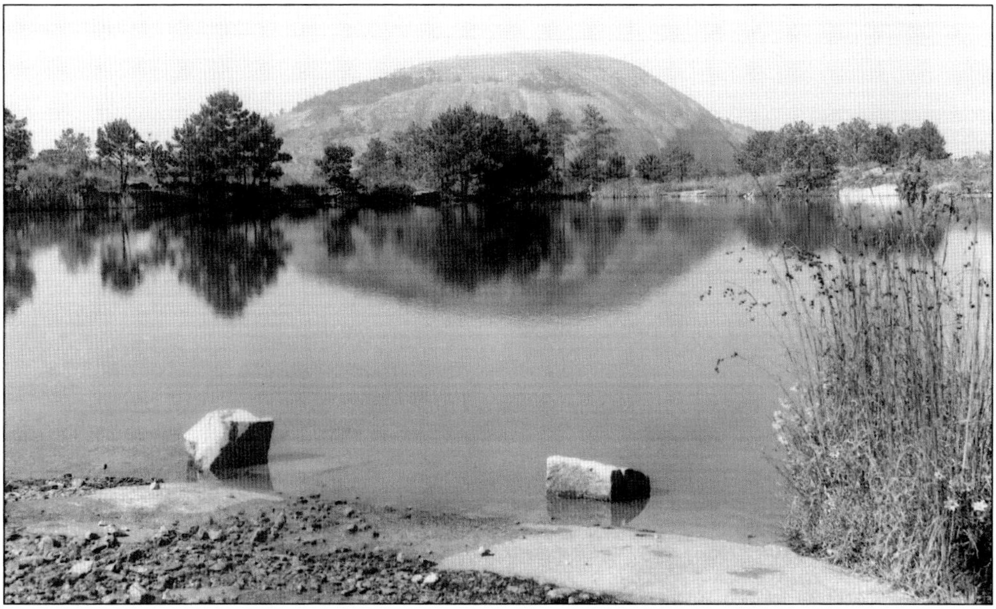

Stone Mountain, located just east of Atlanta, is the largest exposed mound of granite in the world. Stone Mountain Park has long served as a favorite recreation, sport, and historic site for leisure-seeking Atlantans. (Courtesy Atlanta History Center.)

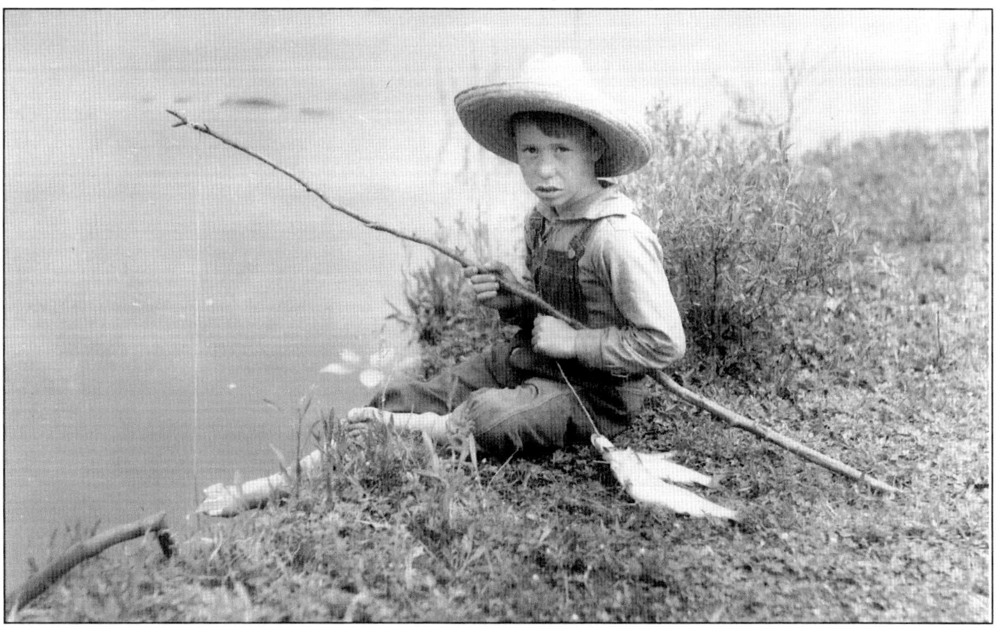

Just as many of his rural landscapes sought to idealize the South, Rogers' images of children include shots of the "ideal" Southern youth, such as a boy at Grant Park with his bike and schoolchildren at play. Others include a boy with the straw hat and fishing pole, and two smiling youngsters, which was actually taken at a 1936 political debate. (Courtesy Atlanta History Center.)

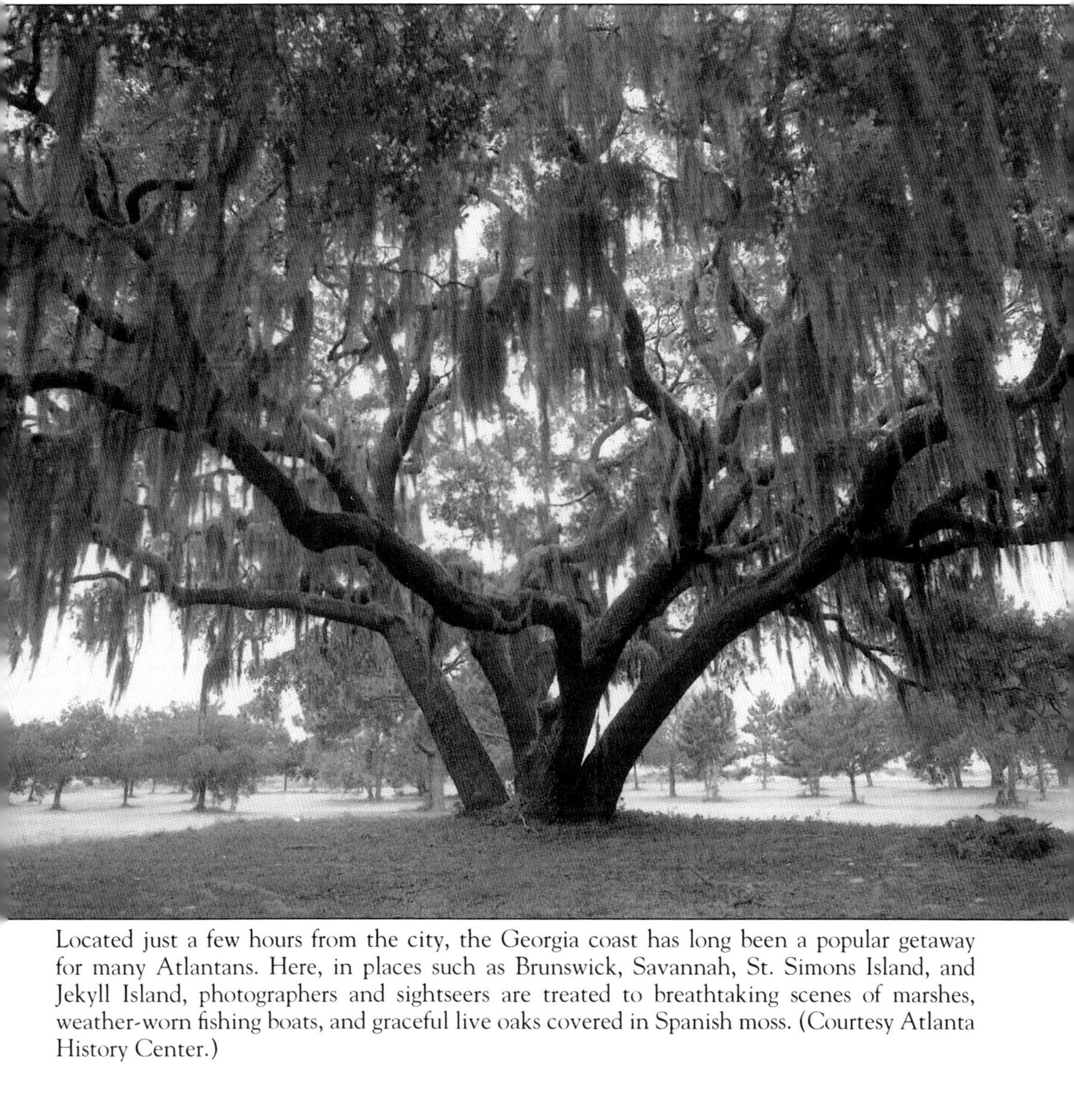

Located just a few hours from the city, the Georgia coast has long been a popular getaway for many Atlantans. Here, in places such as Brunswick, Savannah, St. Simons Island, and Jekyll Island, photographers and sightseers are treated to breathtaking scenes of marshes, weather-worn fishing boats, and graceful live oaks covered in Spanish moss. (Courtesy Atlanta History Center.)

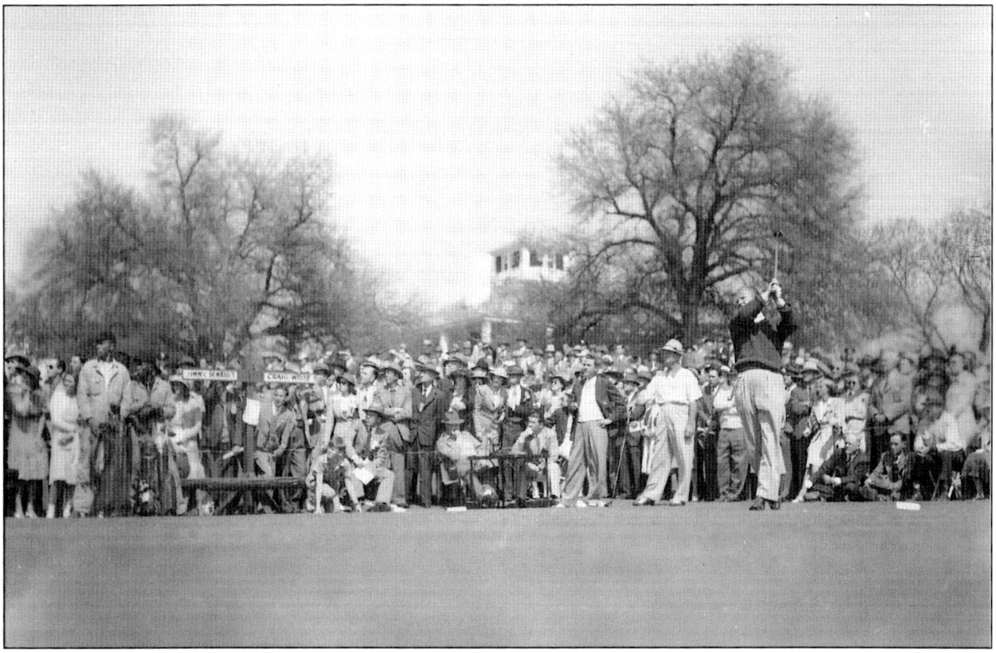

Shown here are scenes from the Masters tournament of April 1940; Jimmy Demaret won the tournament that year with a score of 280. Started by Atlanta golfer Bobby Jones in 1934 and hosted by the Augusta National Golf Club, this annual golf tournament and Georgia tradition has, since 1940, been held the first full week of April, when many of the state's prized azaleas and dogwoods are in bloom. (Courtesy Atlanta History Center.)

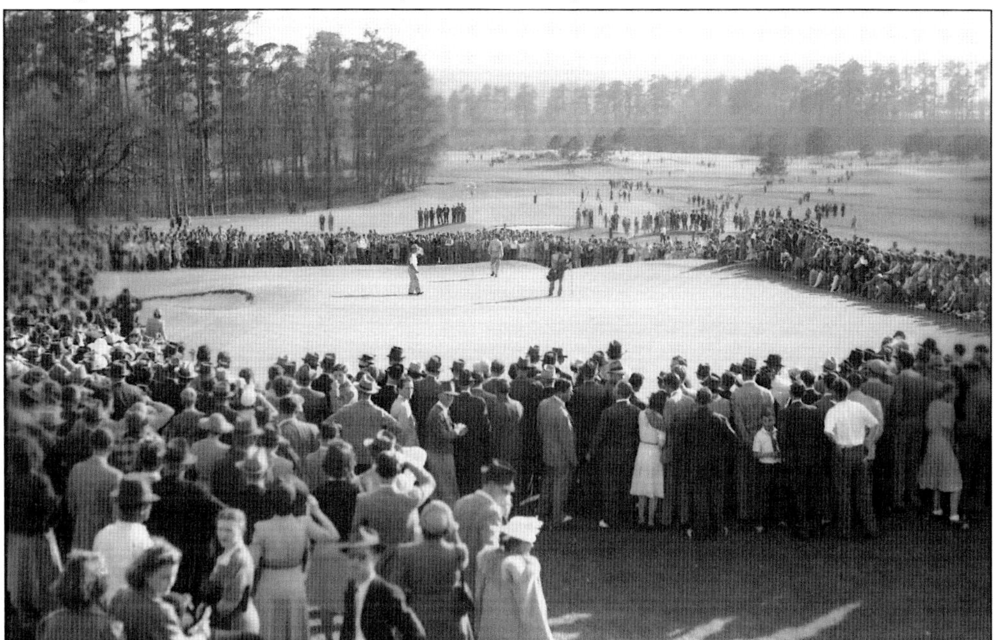

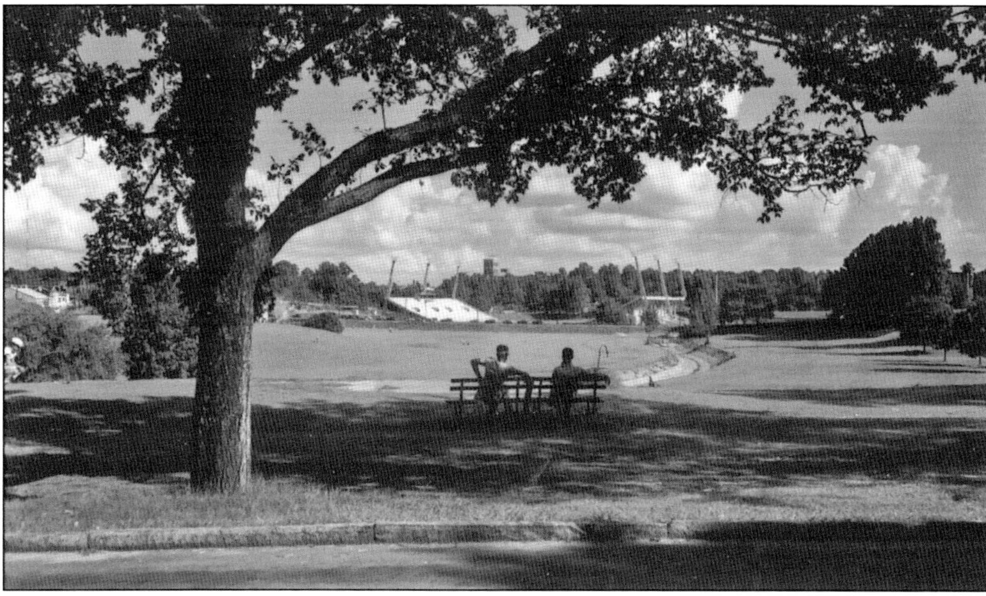

Piedmont Park was the site of the Piedmont Exposition of 1887 when its location, beyond the city limits, was still considered country. The park later hosted the Cotton States and International Exposition (1895); some of the park's landscaping and support structures date from that event. (Courtesy Atlanta History Center.)

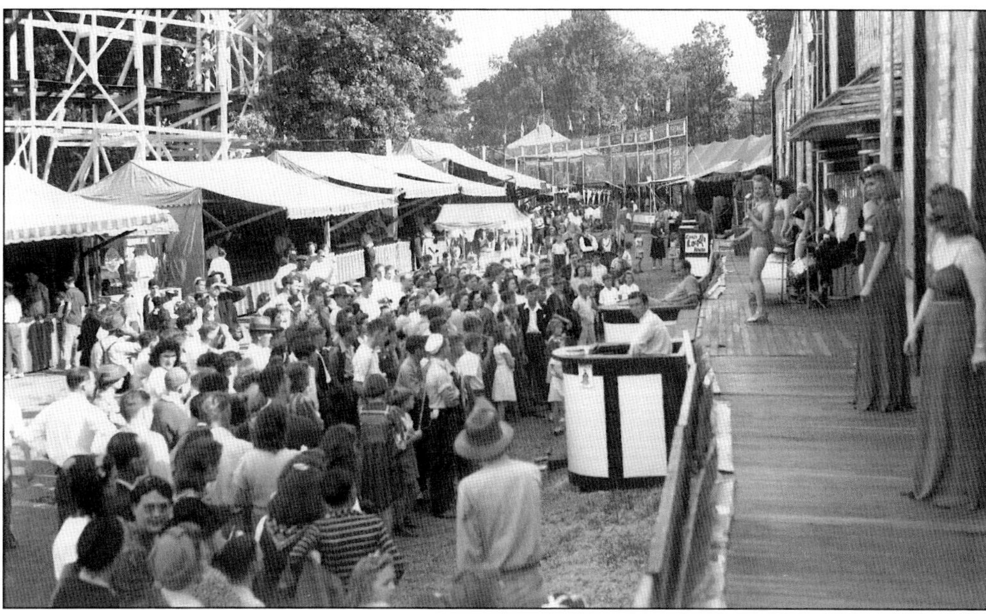

As early as 1909, Lakewood Park hosted racing events at "the fastest track in the world," but the park is perhaps best known for its annual Southeastern Fair, which started in 1916. Events as diverse as midway rides, agricultural exhibitions of poultry and livestock, art shows, and the Star and Garter hoochie-coochie show, entertained Atlantans until the fair's demise in 1975. (Courtesy Atlanta History Center.)

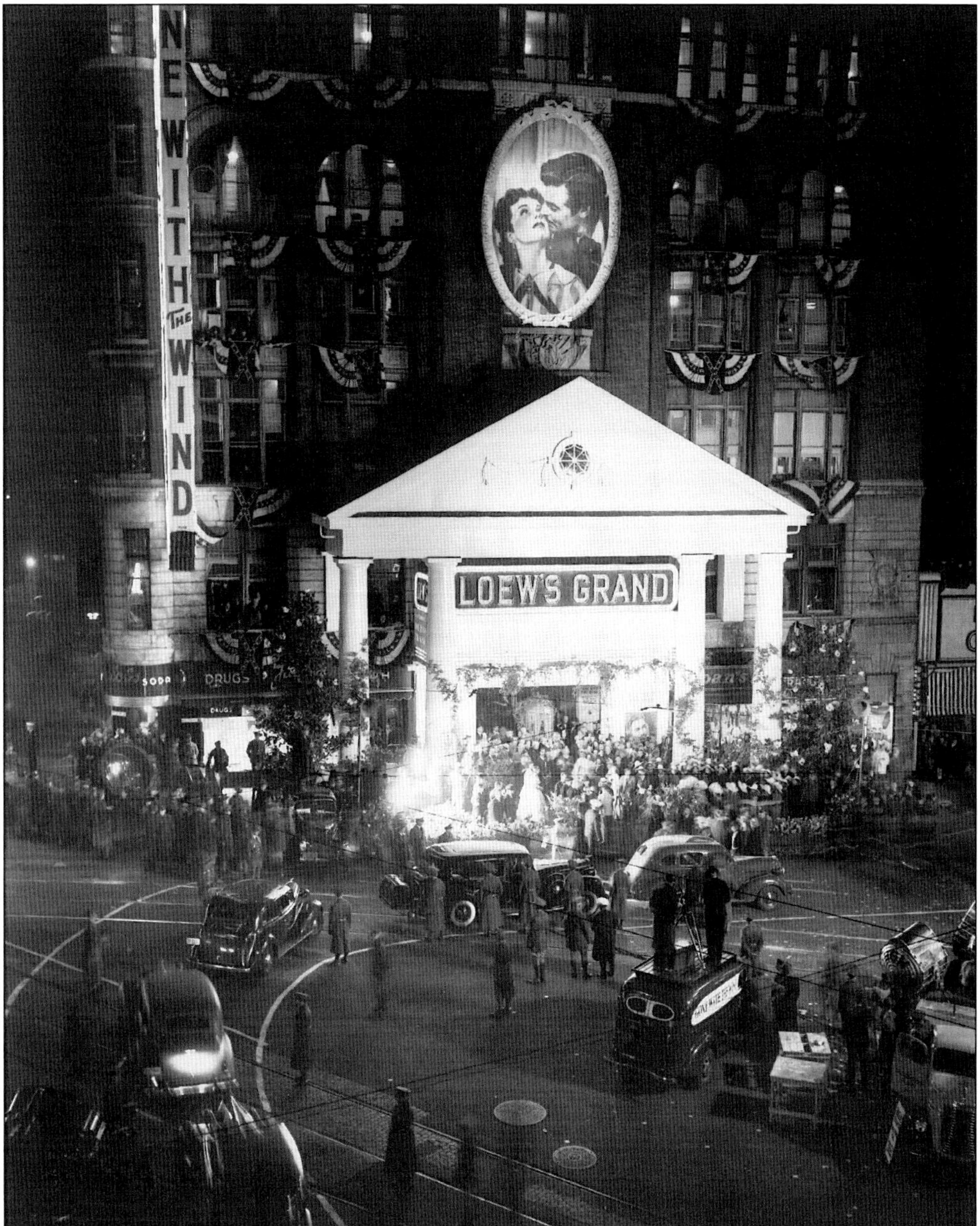

A state holiday was declared on December 15, 1939—the day of the star-studded *Gone With the Wind* movie premiere. For this momentous occasion, Loew's Grand Theater was outfitted with a facade of the fictitious Twelve Oaks plantation house and bathed in the greatest wattage of lights ever used for a film premiere. (Courtesy Atlanta History Center.)

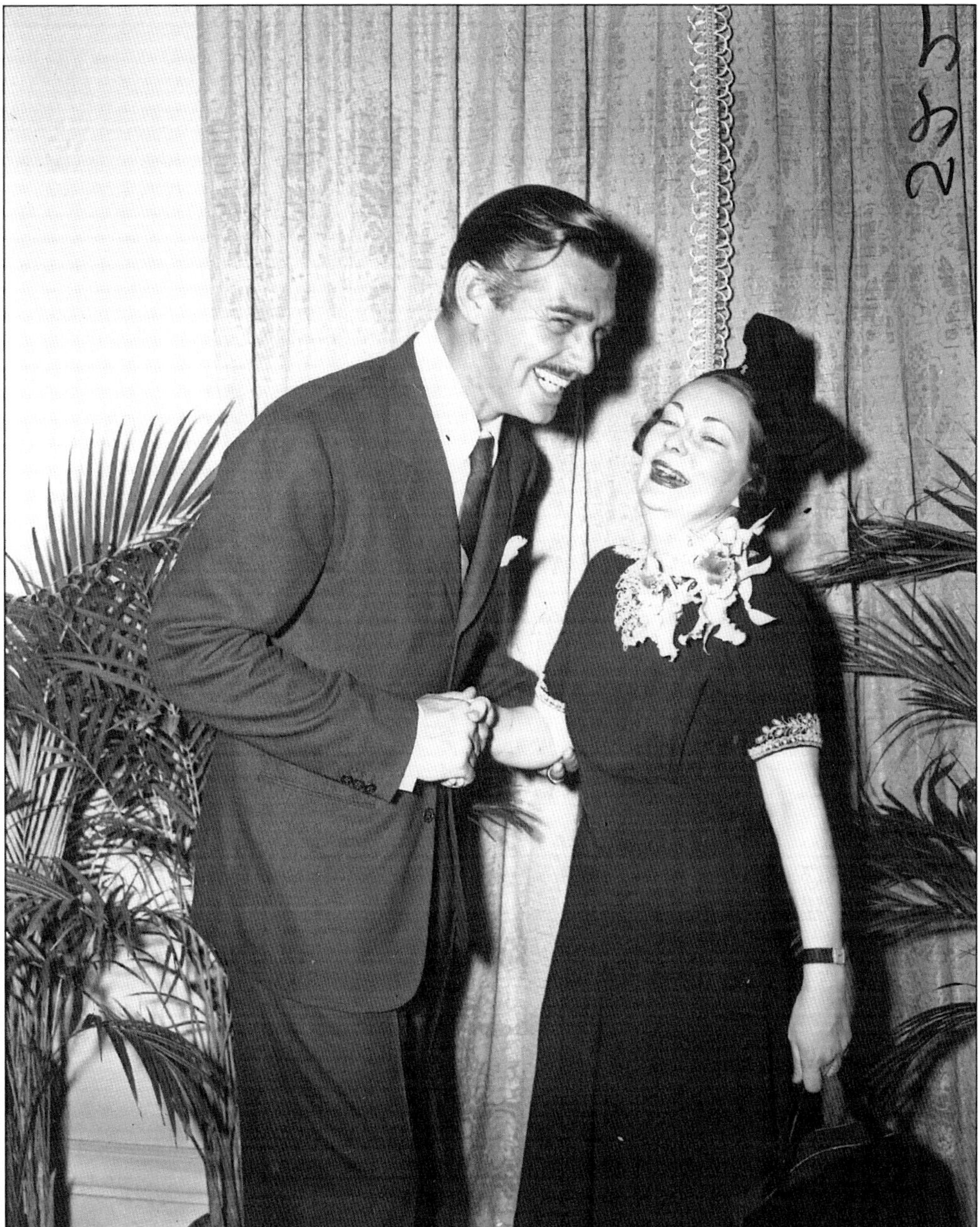

In a spontaneous burst of laughter, Clark Gable and Margaret Mitchell share an unguarded moment at the Piedmont Driving Club following the successful premiere of *Gone With the Wind*. (Courtesy Atlanta History Center.)

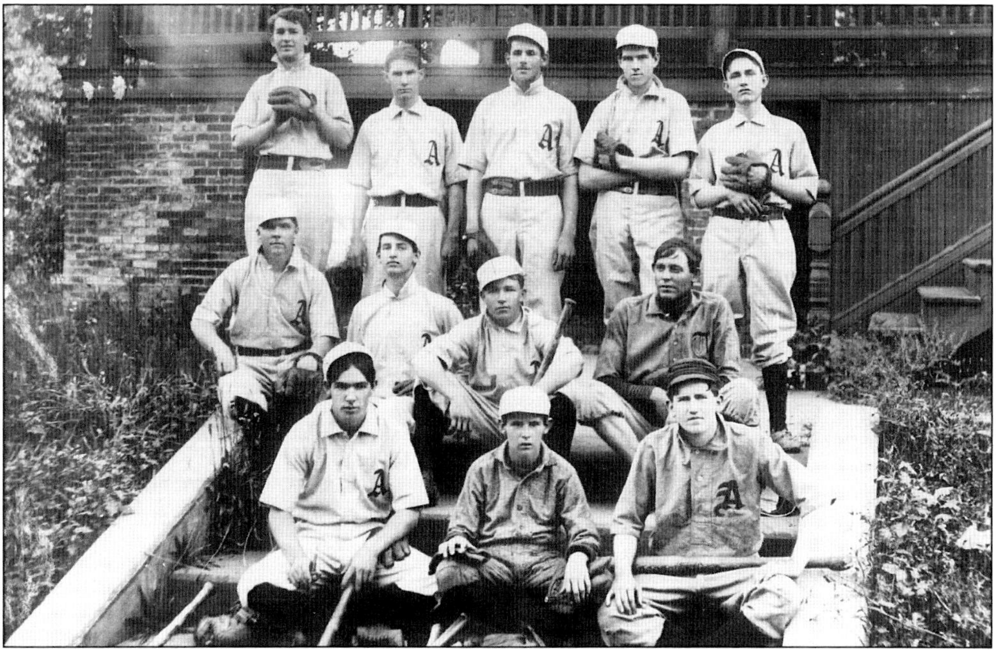

The Atlanta Athletic Club baseball team poses here in 1906. Founded in 1898, the club later assumed responsibility for the East Lake Country Club, which produced famous golfer Bobby Jones. (Courtesy Atlanta History Center.)

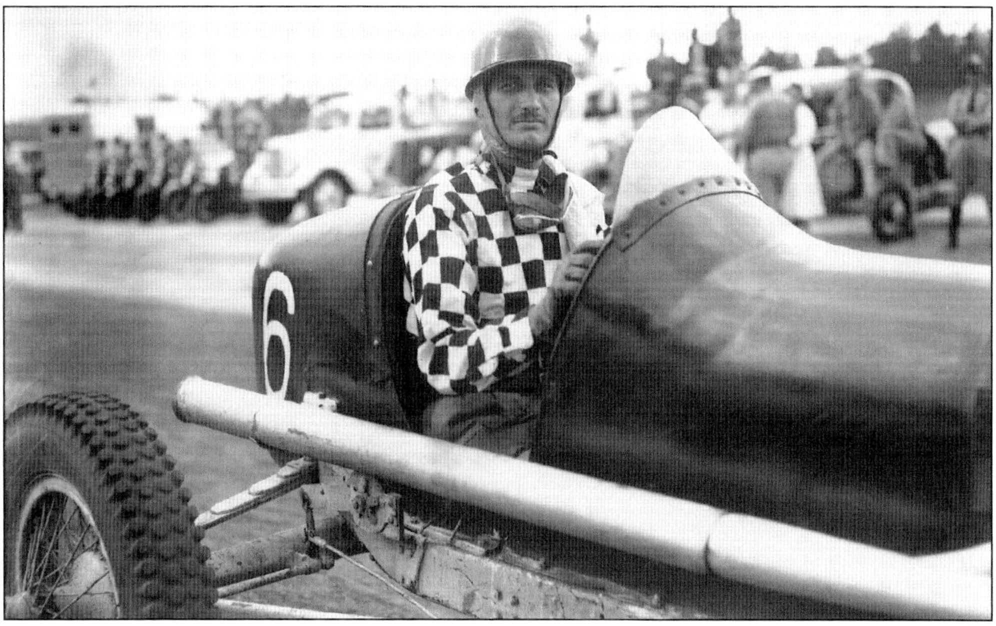

Automobile racing has been popular with Atlantans since 1909, the year the Atlanta Speedway opened (on the site that would later become the Atlanta Municipal Airport). Pictured here is a race car driver, c. 1940, at the Lakewood Park racetrack. (Courtesy Atlanta History Center.)

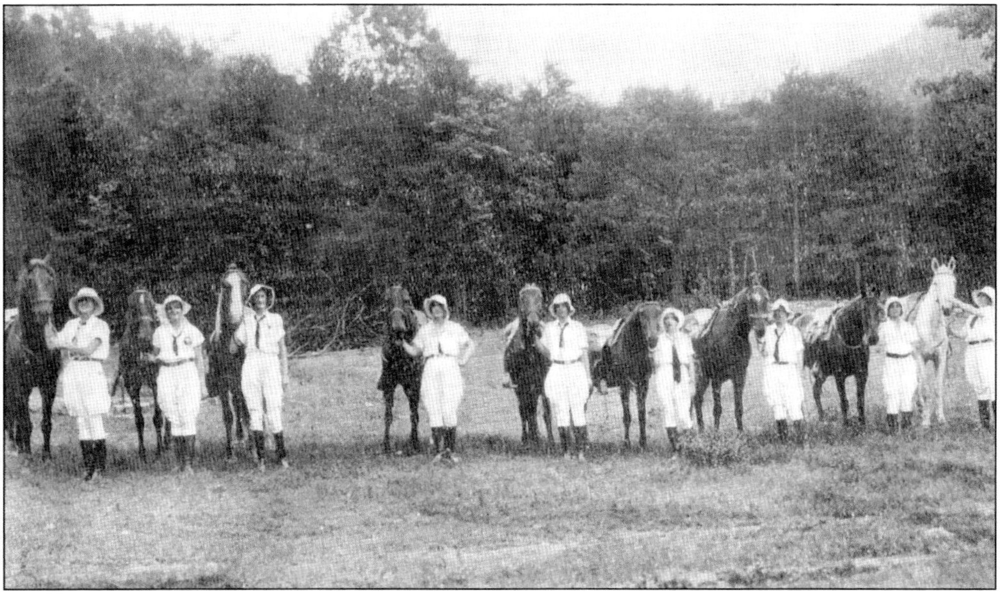

On the reverse side of this card is the following text: "After school closes . . . what? In city, languidness—lassitude; in camp, happiness—health. Spend your vacation at Camp Dixie for Girls, Blue Ridge Mountains. Winter address: 414 Rhodes Building, Atlanta, Ga." (Published by Artvue Post Card Co., New York; card sent 1930.)

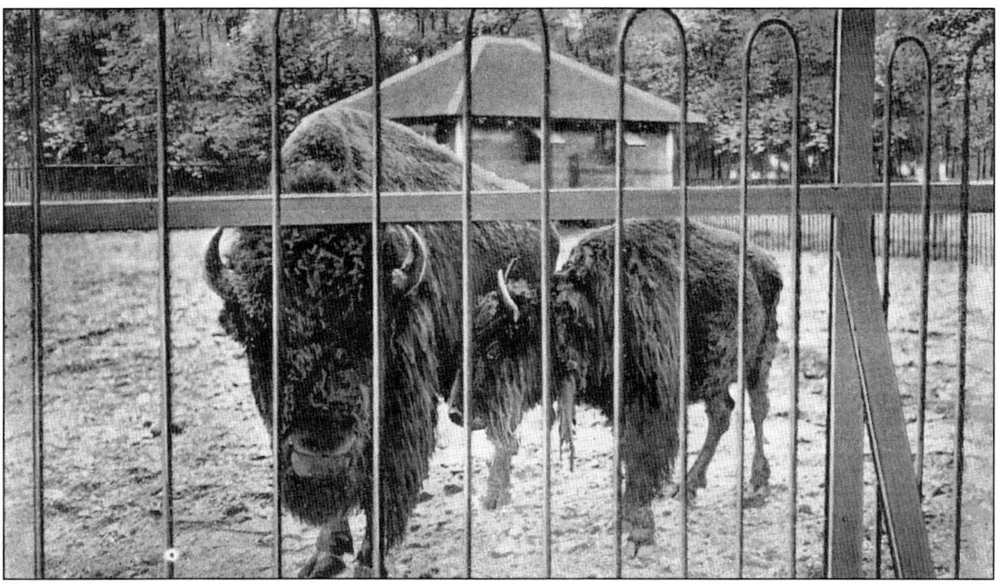

A notable addition to the Grant Park Zoo came in 1935, when Asa G. Candler, Jr. gave his private collection of animals to the city. Candler had assembled 84 fine species of animals and birds on his estate on Briarcliff Road; however, neighbors objected to them and taxes were heavy. He offered his menagerie to the zoo, provided that appropriate shelters were built for them; volunteer contributions of dimes from school children and other donations accomplished the task. (Published by I.F. Co., Atlanta.)

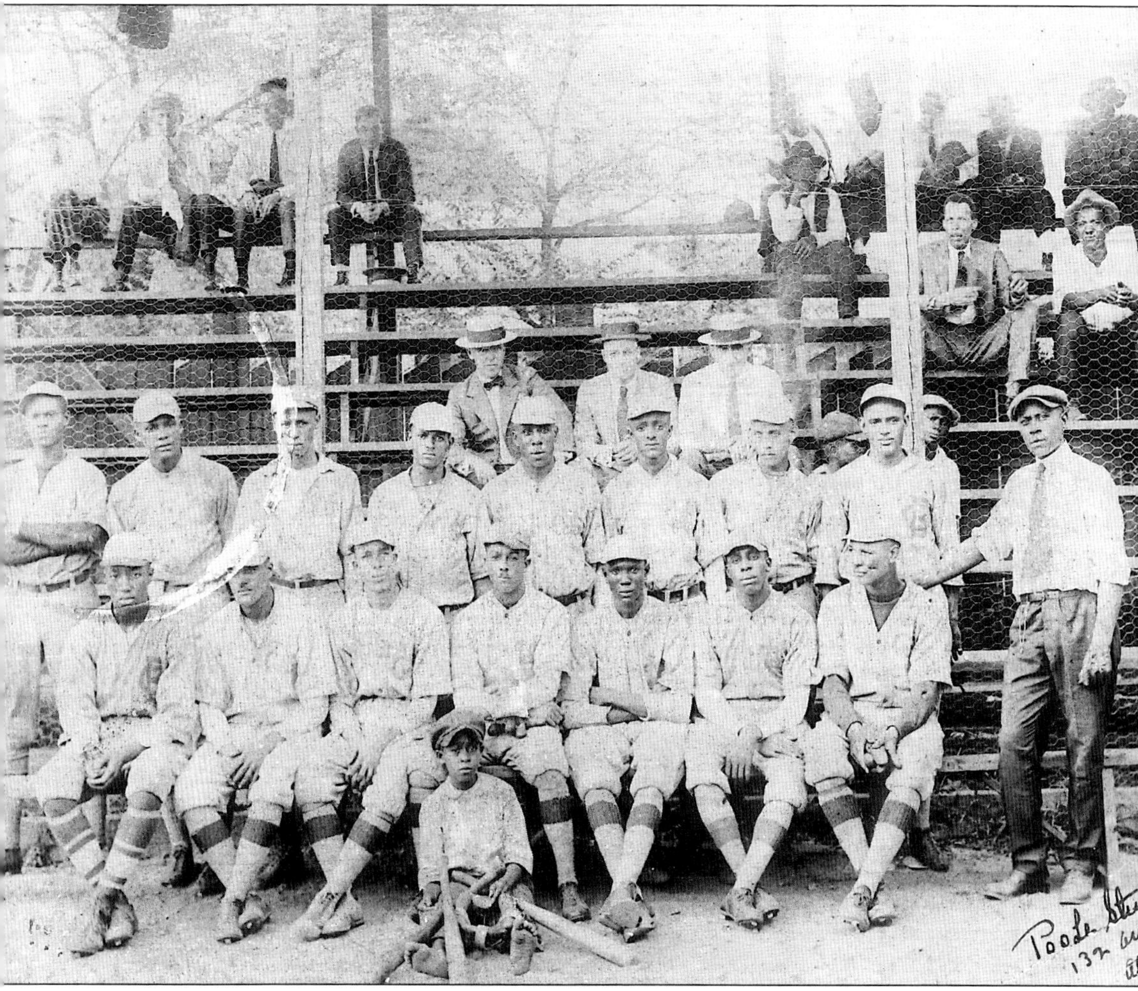

The Atlanta Black Crackers Baseball team was organized in 1919. By 1920, it was under the ownership of Bill Shaw and consisted of very talented players. Shaw was a most industrious businessman, operating a restaurant, running the Roof Garden, and ultimately purchasing the Odd Fellows Building in 1935. He later sold the building to the Georgia Baptist Convention. The Black Crackers were members of the Southern Colored League teams, and the games were played at the Morris Brown University field and the old Spiller's Field across from what would become the Ponce De Leon Ballpark. (Edward Bowen.)

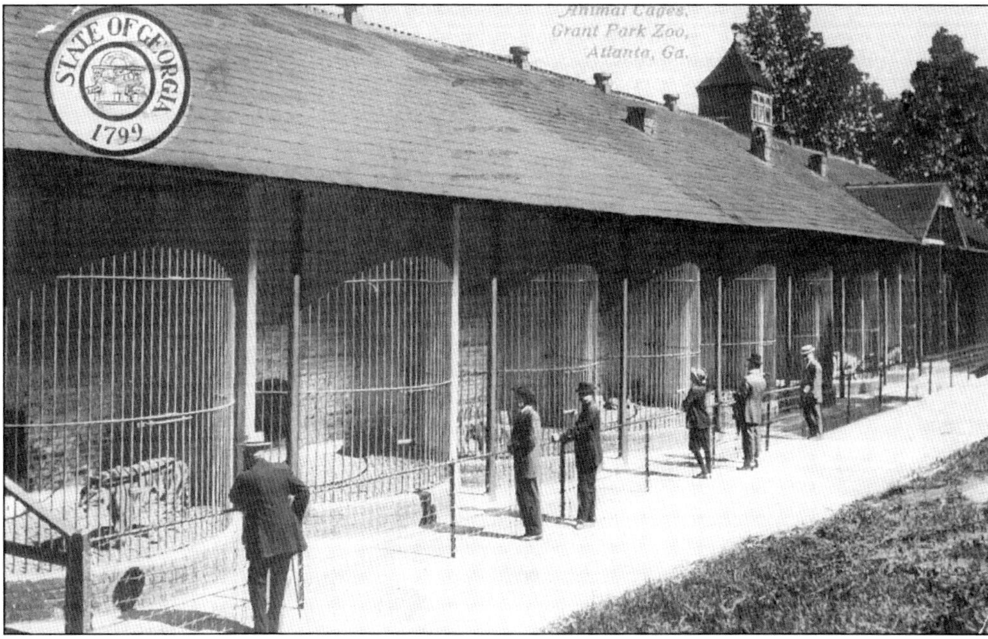

The zoo began in 1889 with a gift from G.V. Gress, a wealthy merchant of Atlanta. He presented the city with the menagerie of a bankrupt circus he had bought in order to secure its heavy wagons for his lumber business. He also erected the first shelters for the animals. In early years, the collection was known as the Gress Zoo. (Published by Witt Bros., Atlanta; card sent 1913.)

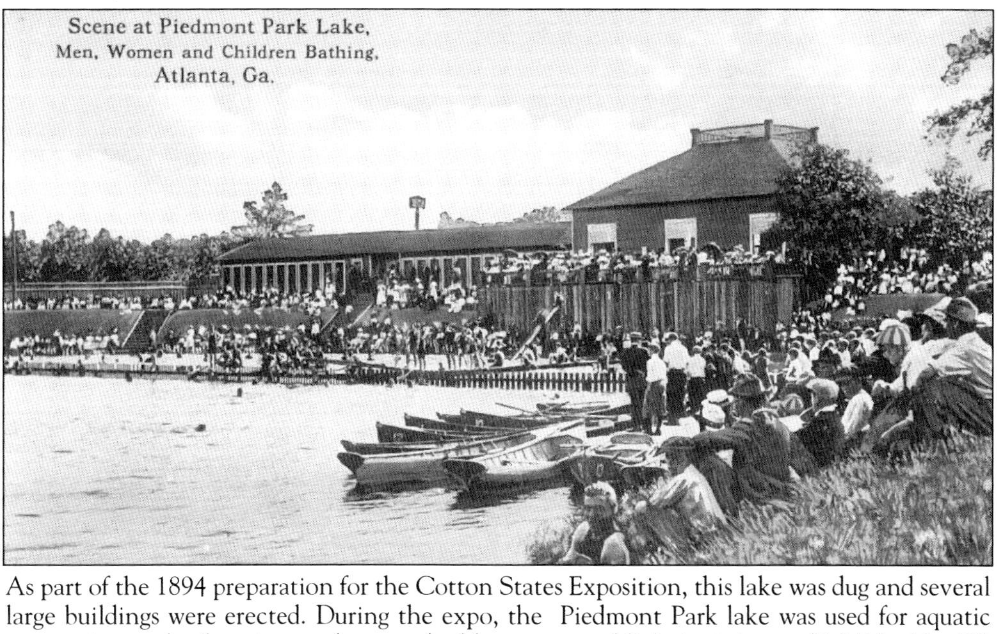

As part of the 1894 preparation for the Cotton States Exposition, this lake was dug and several large buildings were erected. During the expo, the Piedmont Park lake was used for aquatic events; it was the first time such sports had been seen publicly in Atlanta. (Published by I.F. Co., Atlanta.)

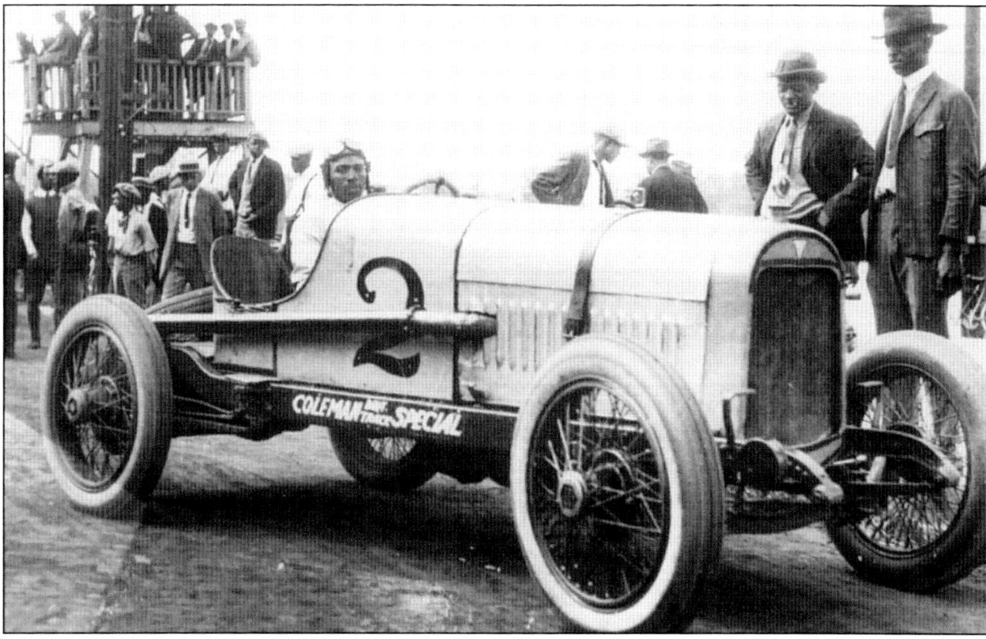

During the 1940s and 1950s, the Lithonia Speedway and Country Club was nestled in a secluded area off Highway 12, on Rodgers Lake Road. It was a perfect venue for African-American stock car drivers, of which there were many, including George Muckles. An African-American dentist, Dr. Anderson initially operated the Anderson Lake Country Club until Otis Easley took over the club and renamed it. (Courtesy Herman "Skip" Mason Jr.)

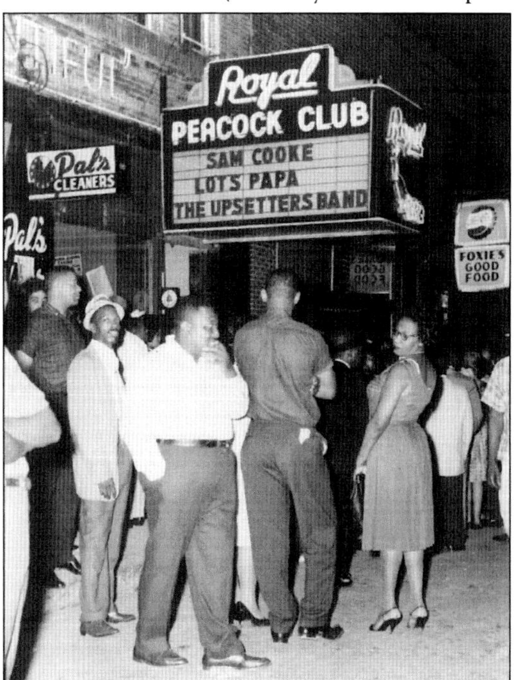

In the fall of 1949, the Top Hat closed, only to reopen a few months later as the Royal Peacock. After a successful 12-year run with the Top Hat Club, owners Blayton, Yates, and Milton decided to sell the club. Carrie Cunningham was interested in acquiring the club for her son Red McAllister so that he could stay off the dangerous, segregated roads with his band (there was often trouble and arrests on the roads for McAllister and his boys). Mrs. Cunningham paid $31,000 for the second floor of the building on Auburn Avenue, and redecorated so that it would accommodate 350 patrons. (Courtesy of Digging It Up Archives.)

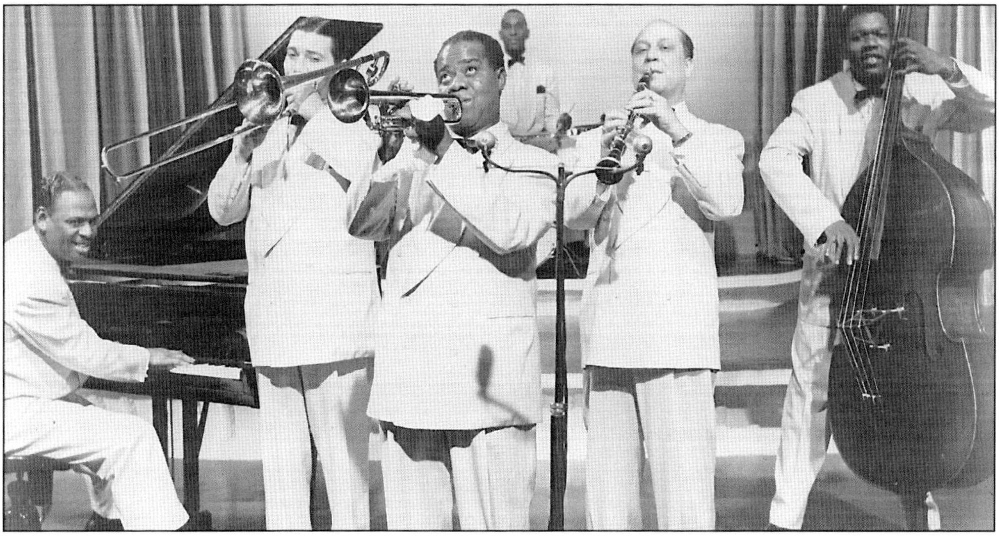

Local promoters brought such popular acts as Cab Calloway and Louis Armstrong (seen here) to the City Auditorium. In 1934, Louis Armstrong and Duke Ellington and his 15-piece orchestra "rocked" the City Auditorium with his vocalist Ivie Anderson (Armstrong would later return under the Southeastern Artist promotion). The show also offered a 30-minute amateur contest featuring the Mills Brothers, impersonators, and demonstrations of the dance "Snake Hips." (Courtesy of Digging It Up Archives.)

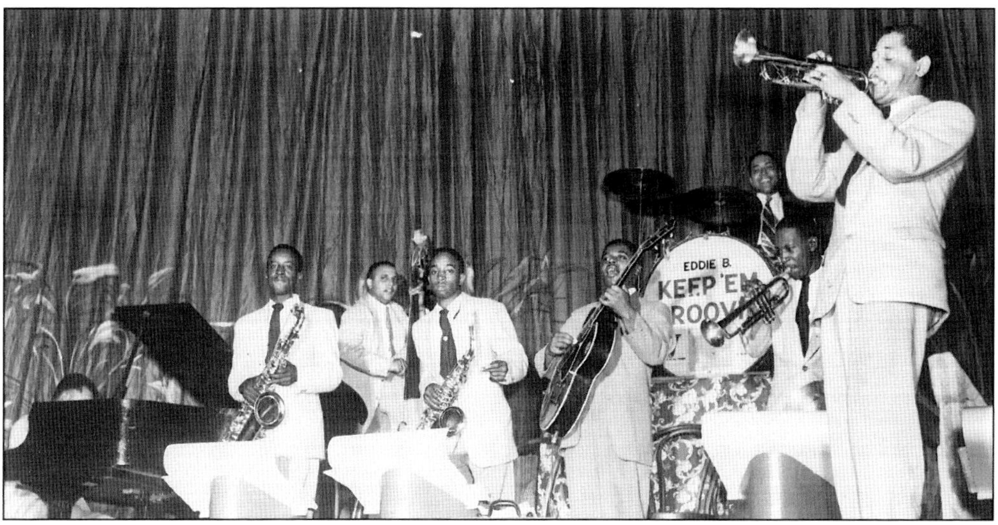

Noted writer Lawrence D. Reddick recalls one of Dizzy Gillespie's visits to Atlanta. Uncertain of local race relations etiquette in Atlanta, Reddick had vowed that he would not patronize any Jim Crow theaters or gatherings. However, a new music form, "be-bop," interested him, and the "Bop King" was in town. At this concert at the City Auditorium, blacks and whites were sitting on the auditorium main floor. The auditorium was only half-filled. Reddick attributed it to the inclement weather but observed that when the "Silas Green from New Orleans" show appeared the week before, it was packed and the weather was not that much better. Reddick saw that the blacks present were younger than the whites. (Courtesy of Digging It Up Archives.)

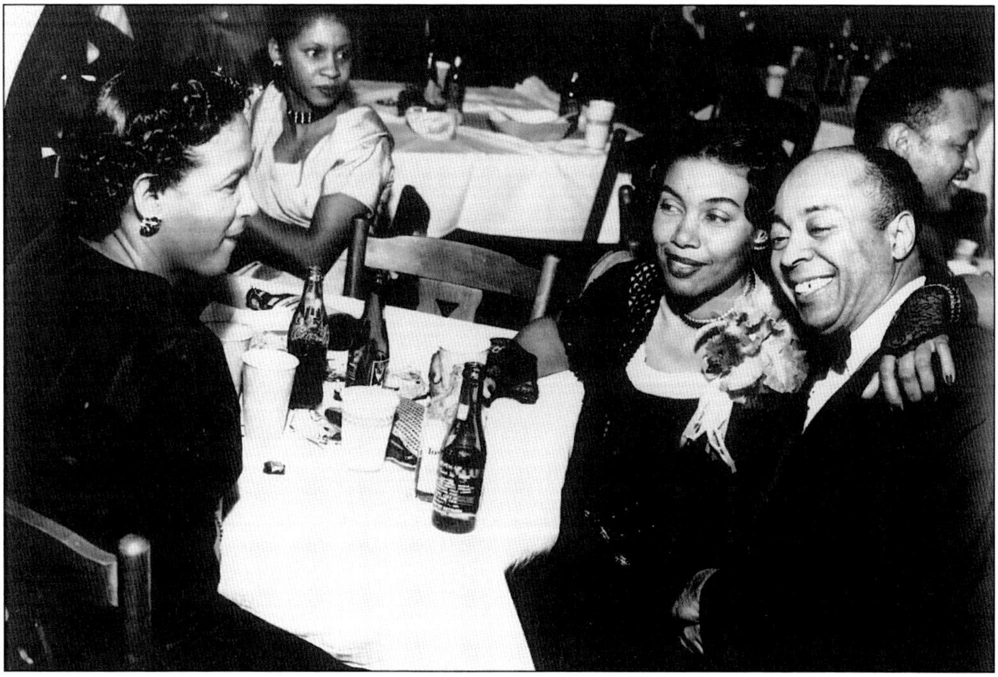

The legendary "Lady Day," or Billie Holiday (seen here at left), performed at the Magnolia in March 1959, three months before her death. Miss Holiday is pictured with B.B. Beamon and an unidentified guest. Jazz was a popular medium at the Magnolia. Jazz artists such as Art Blakely and the Jazz Messengers, Stan Keaton, and Lionel Hampton performed there. (Courtesy of B.B. Beamon.)

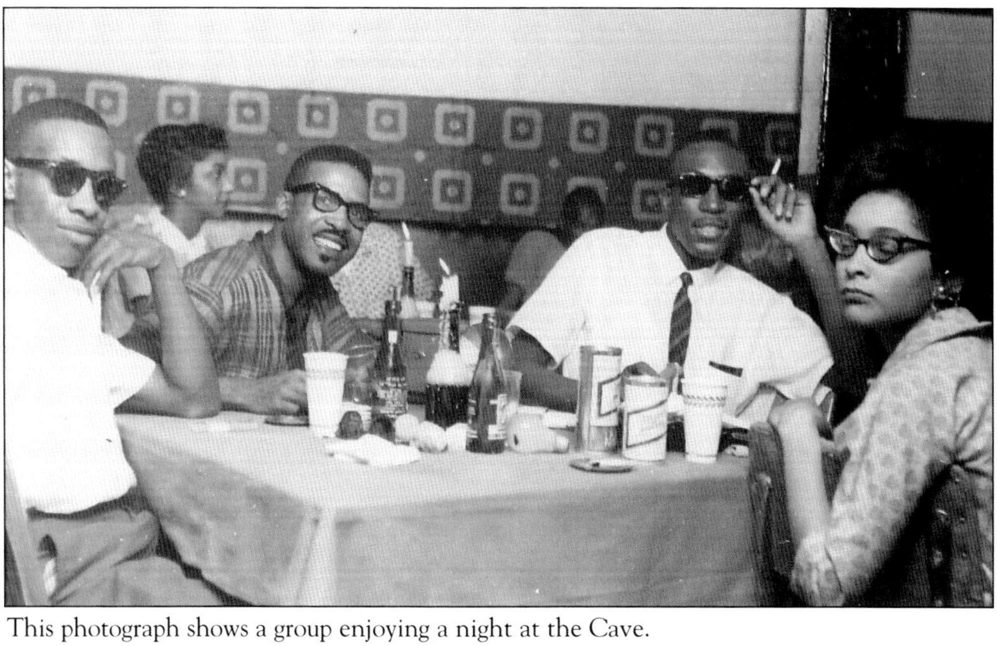

This photograph shows a group enjoying a night at the Cave.

Seven

PERSONALITIES

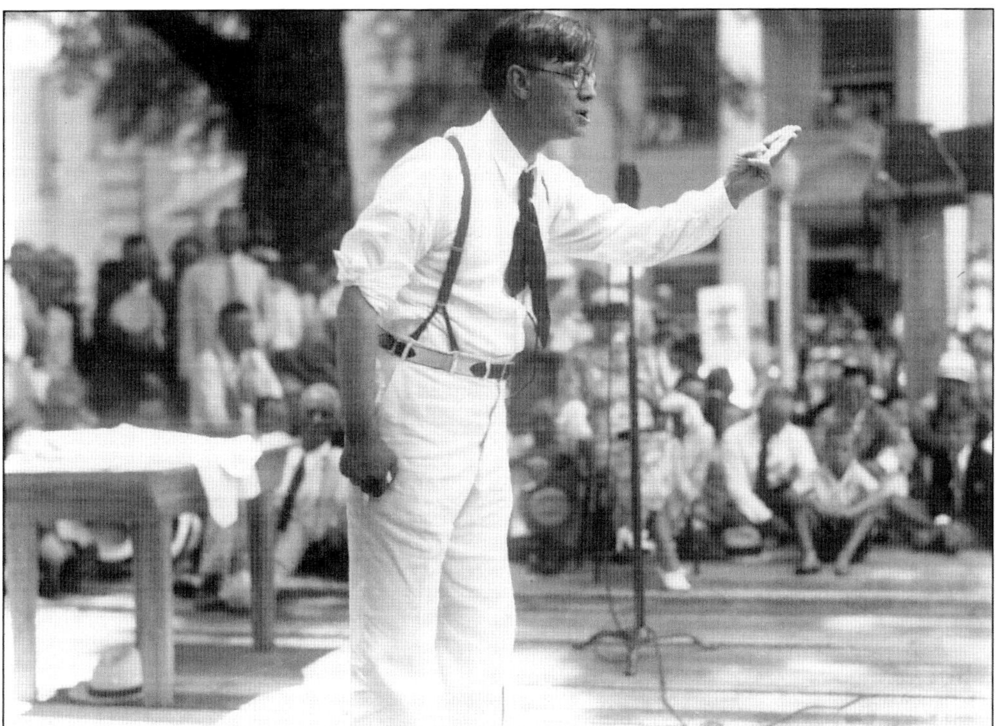

Georgia Governor Eugene Talmadge is pictured during his 1946 campaign. Talmadge was a colorful orator and his campaign rallies were often a combination of politics, barbecue, and country music. Talmadge's three terms as governor were characterized by his passionate defense of the state's rural population and its agrarian culture. (Courtesy Atlanta History Center.)

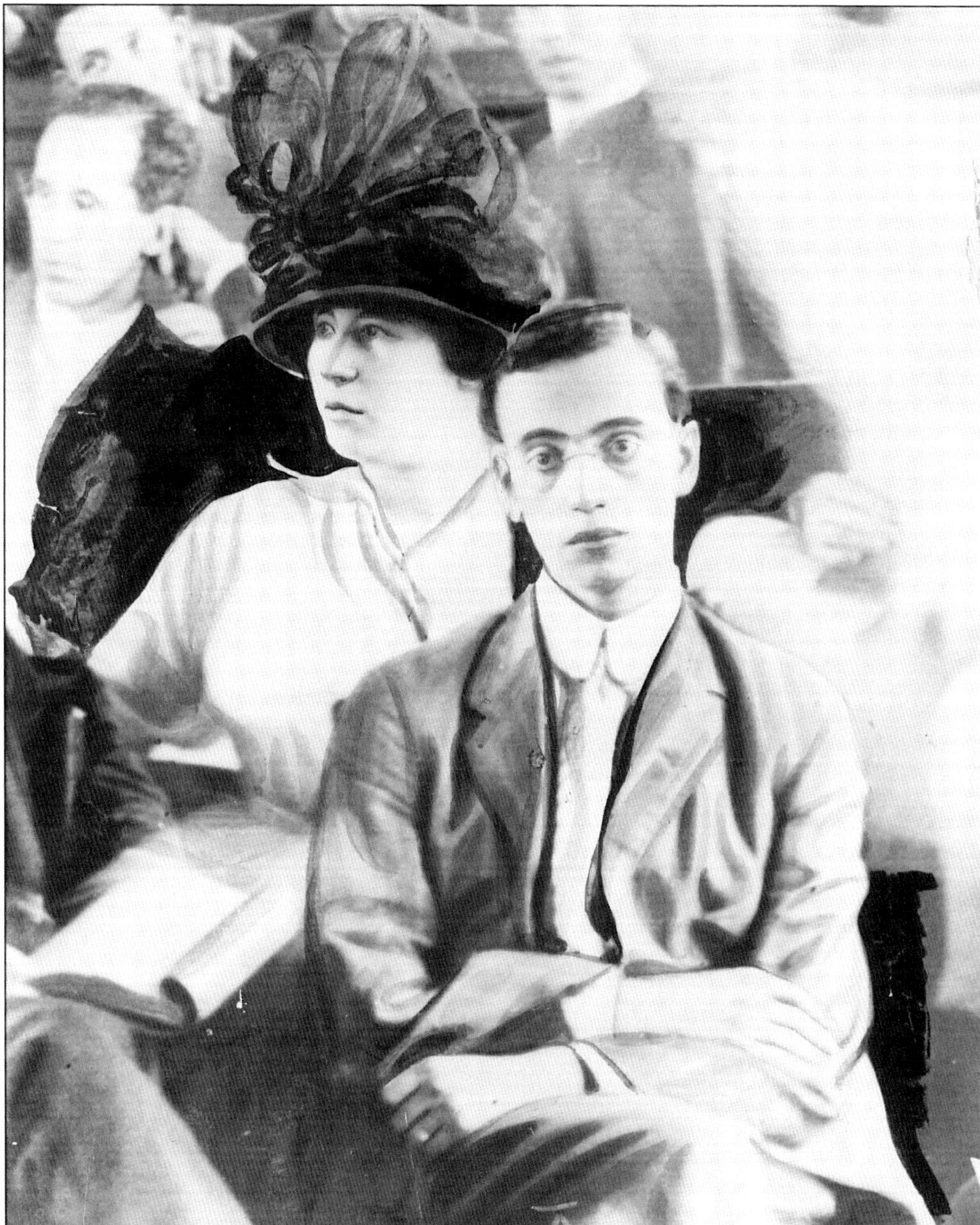

In 1913, Leo Frank, a prominent member of Atlanta's Jewish community and manager of the National Pencil Company, was charged with the murder of 13-year-old Mary Phagan, one of his employees. Amidst sensationalist press coverage tinged with anti-Semitism, Frank was found guilty and sentenced to death. After numerous appeals, Frank's sentence was commuted to life in prison, but vigilantes angry with the decision abducted Frank and lynched him in Phagan's hometown of Marietta, Georgia. This image shows Leo Frank sitting in the courtroom during his trial. (Courtesy Atlanta History Center.)

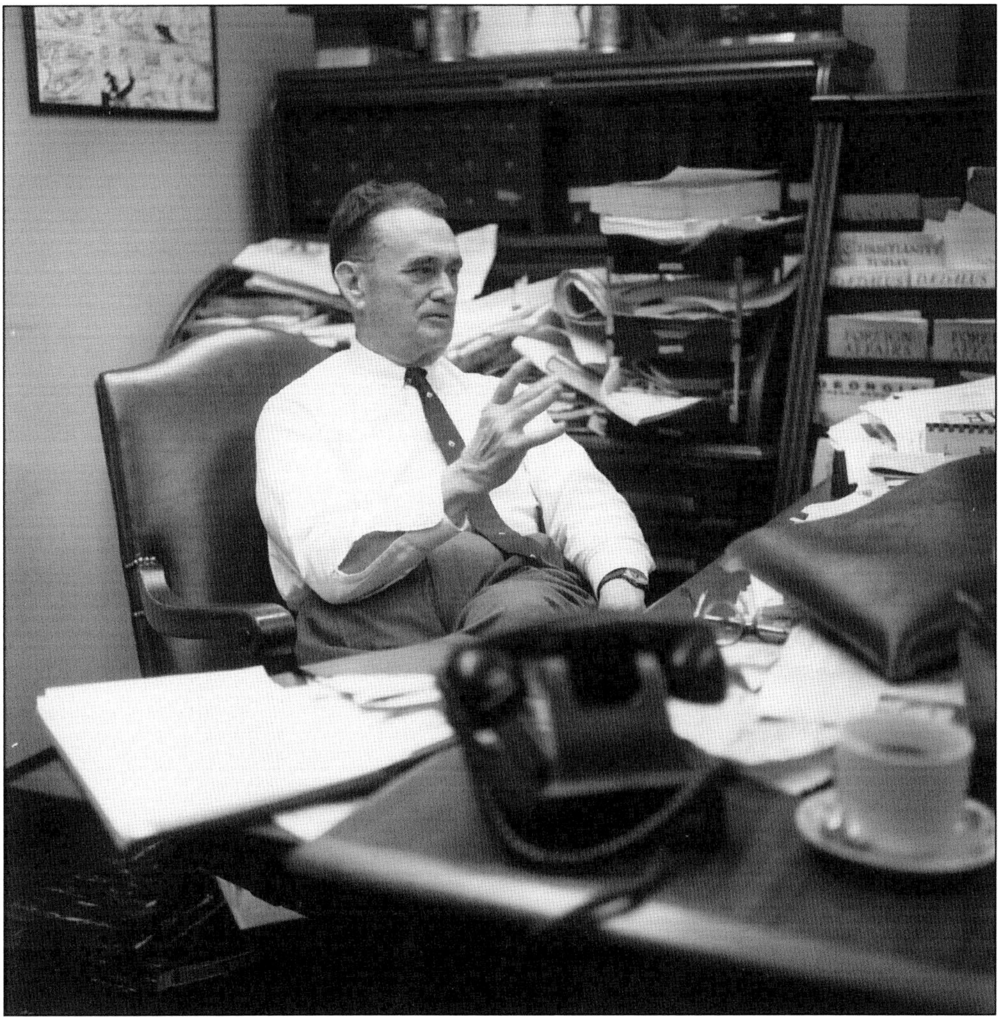

Atlanta Constitution Editor Ralph McGill, pictured in the 1960s, was arguably the most influential Georgia journalist in the twentieth century. McGill's columns favoring social justice and opposing segregation earned him designation as "the conscience of the South"—as well as many enemies. (Courtesy Atlanta History Center.)

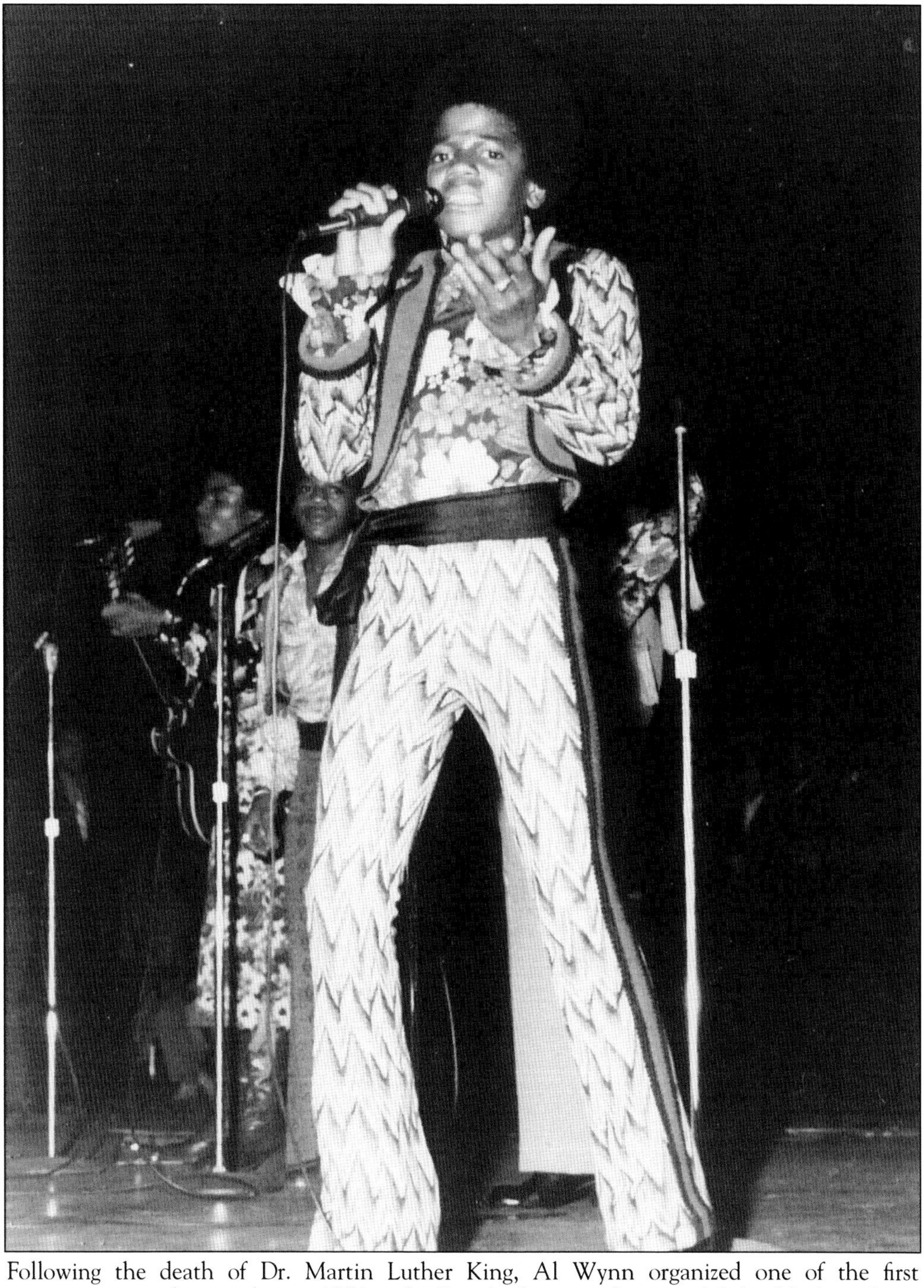

Following the death of Dr. Martin Luther King, Al Wynn organized one of the first entertainment tributes to him in 1971 at the City Auditorium, featuring Michael Jackson (seen here) and the Jackson Five and "Moms" Mabley. Wynn promoted shows until 1973, with one of his last shows featuring Marvin Gaye. (Courtesy Atlanta History Center.)

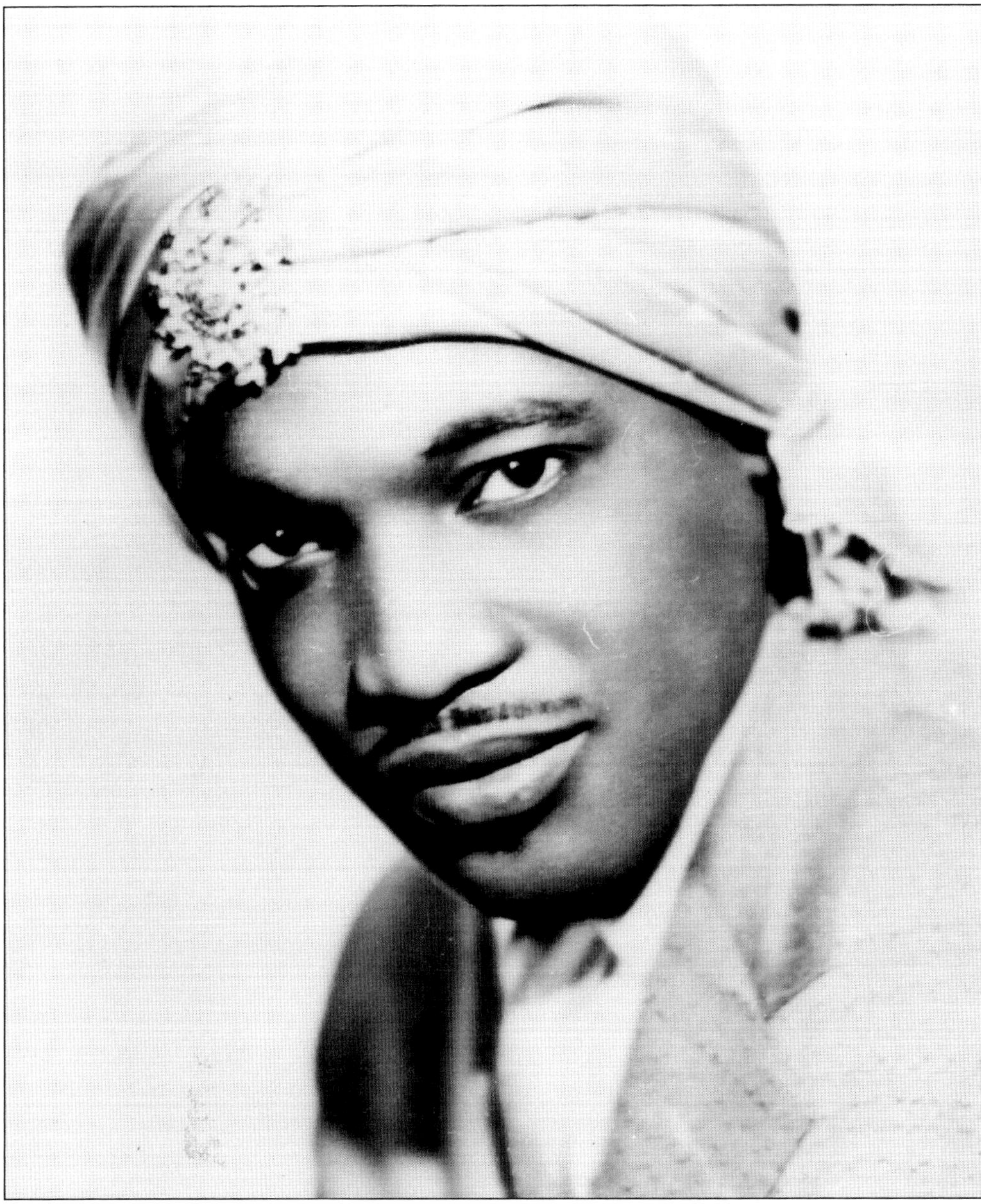

Born Harold "Chuck" Willis on January 31, 1928, in Atlanta, Willis grew up near the Bell Street area. By the late 1940s, Willis was performing the floorshows of the Club Zanzibar and singing vocals with the Red McAllister and Roy Mays band. He was very popular at the teenage canteens sponsored by the YMCA. Willis was a local celebrity until Zenas "Daddy" Sears began to showcase him at talent shows. Sears eventually became manager for Willis and helped him to get a weekly television show and introduced him to an executive at Columbia Records, recording several tunes including "Can't You See." In 1952, he wrote "My Story," which shot all the way to number two on the Billboard "Juke Box" Rhythm and Blues list for two weeks. Willis died tragically at the age of 30 in April 1958. (Courtesy of Clarence Hubbard.)

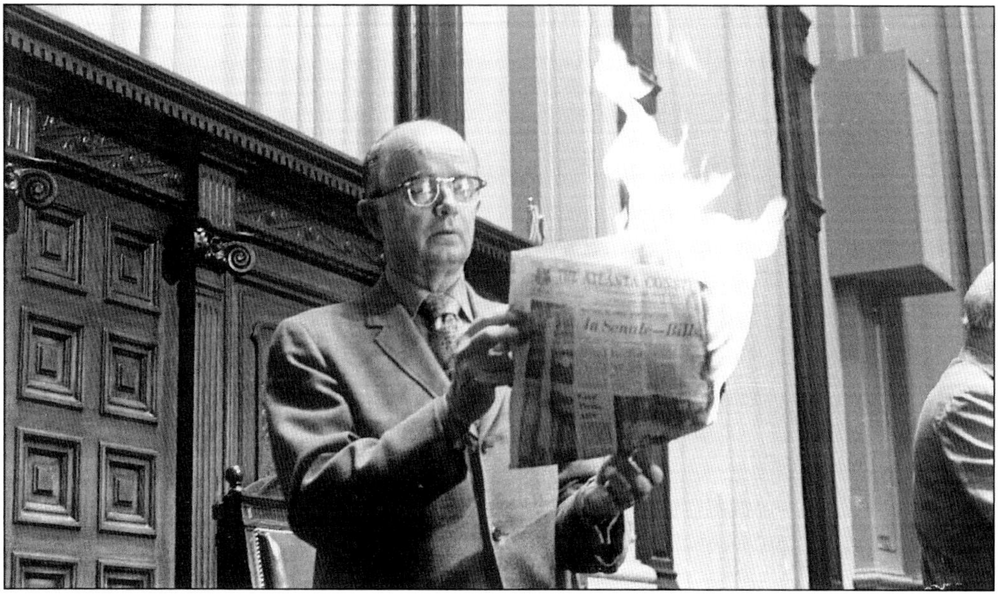

After delivering a 30-minute denunciation of the Atlanta newspapers, Lieutenant Governor Lester Maddox burned a copy of the *Atlanta Constitution* to protest an article critical of the state senate. After hearing about Maddox's action, photographer Bill Wilson asked him to repeat the stunt and Maddox happily obliged. (Courtesy Atlanta History Center.)

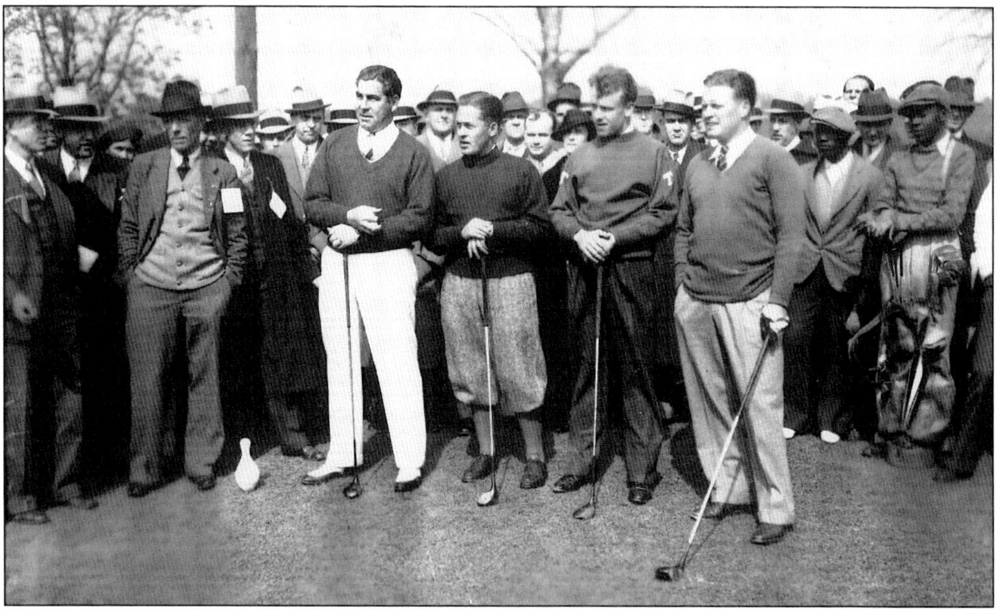

In 1930, Atlanta native Robert "Bobby" Tyre Jones became the only man to win the Grand Slam of golf: the United States Amateur, United States Open, British Amateur, and British Open. Upon his return to Atlanta, he was met with a victory parade, followed by speeches at City Hall. Above, Jones (second from left) is seen with fellow golfers Olin Dutra, Charlie Yates, and Jimmy Thompson (from left to right). (Courtesy Atlanta History Center.)

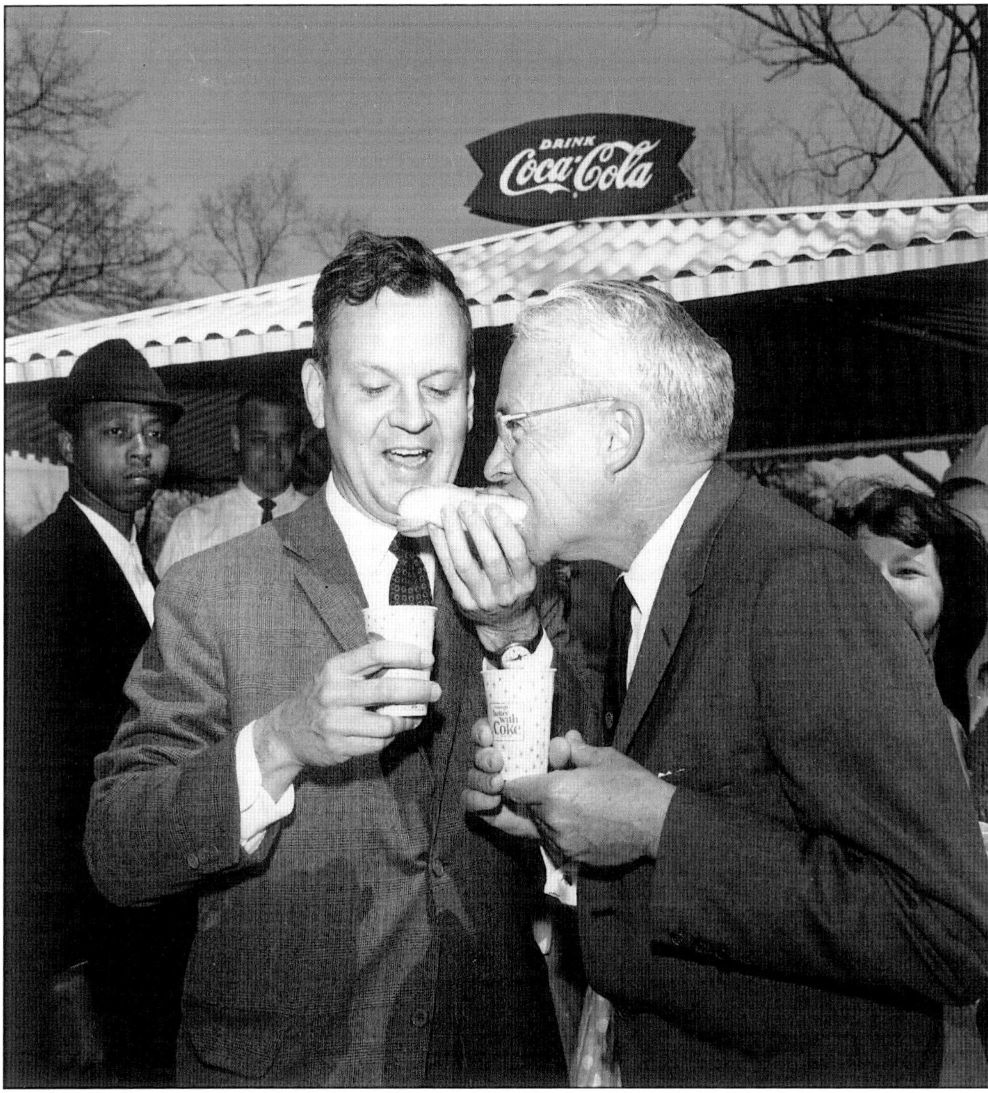

With a Coke, a smile, and a hot dog, Arthur Montgomery, president of the Atlanta Coca-Cola Bottling Company, and Ivan Allen Jr., mayor of Atlanta, celebrate groundbreaking at Atlanta-Fulton County Stadium, 1964. The two were driving forces in bringing professional baseball to Atlanta. (Courtesy Atlanta History Center.)

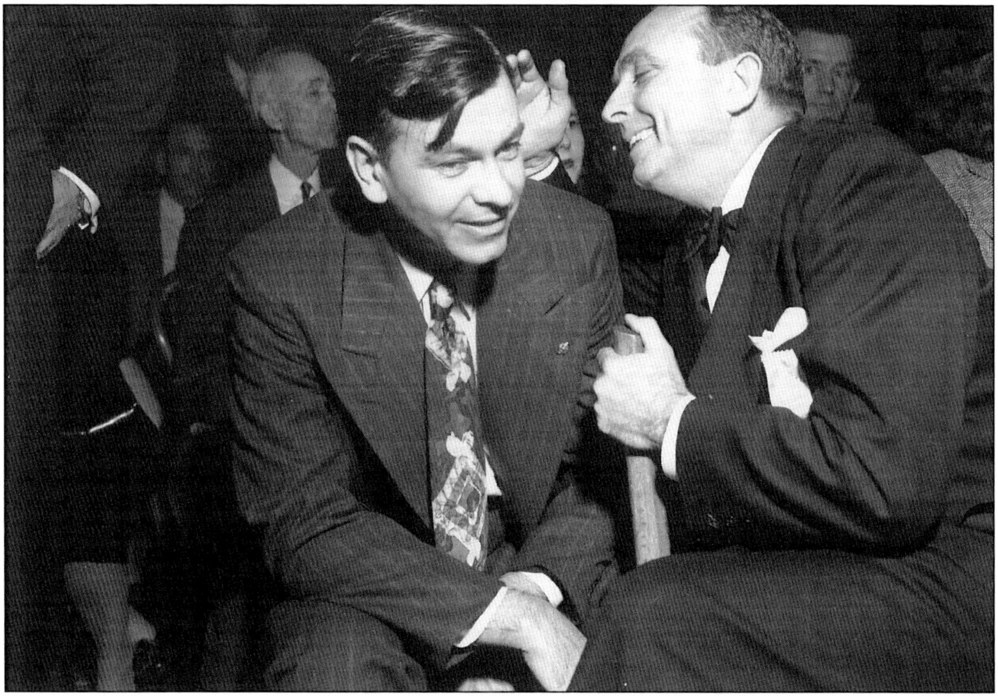

Two Georgia powerbrokers, Herman E. Talmadge and E.D. Rivers, speak confidentially during a Democratic convention. Both men served as Georgia's governor, and Talmadge went on to spend a quarter-century in the U.S. Senate. (Courtesy Atlanta History Center.)

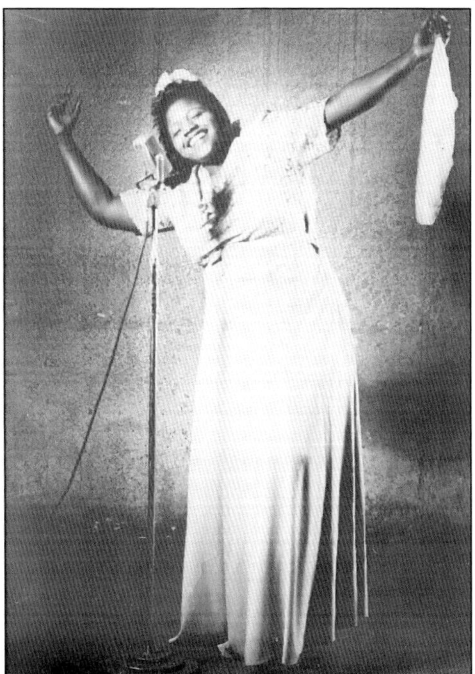

Another legend born in the annals of the Royal Peacock who benefited from Ms. Cunningham and Red McAllister was gutsy rhythm and blues singer Big Maybelle. Born Mary Belle (Mabel) Smith in Jackson, Tennessee, she began her career in 1945 with Red McAllister's band, in which she sang for several years before going to Indiana to go solo. A Royal Peacock regular, she and Willie Mae Thornton were two of the legendary "blues shouters." According to legend, Thornton introduced the song "Hound Dog," later made popular by Elvis Presley. During one of Big Maybelle's appearances in Atlanta, she forgot to bring her outfits, and, according to lore, Carrie Cunningham pulled some draperies from a window and stitched her an outfit. (Courtesy of Digging It Up Archives.)

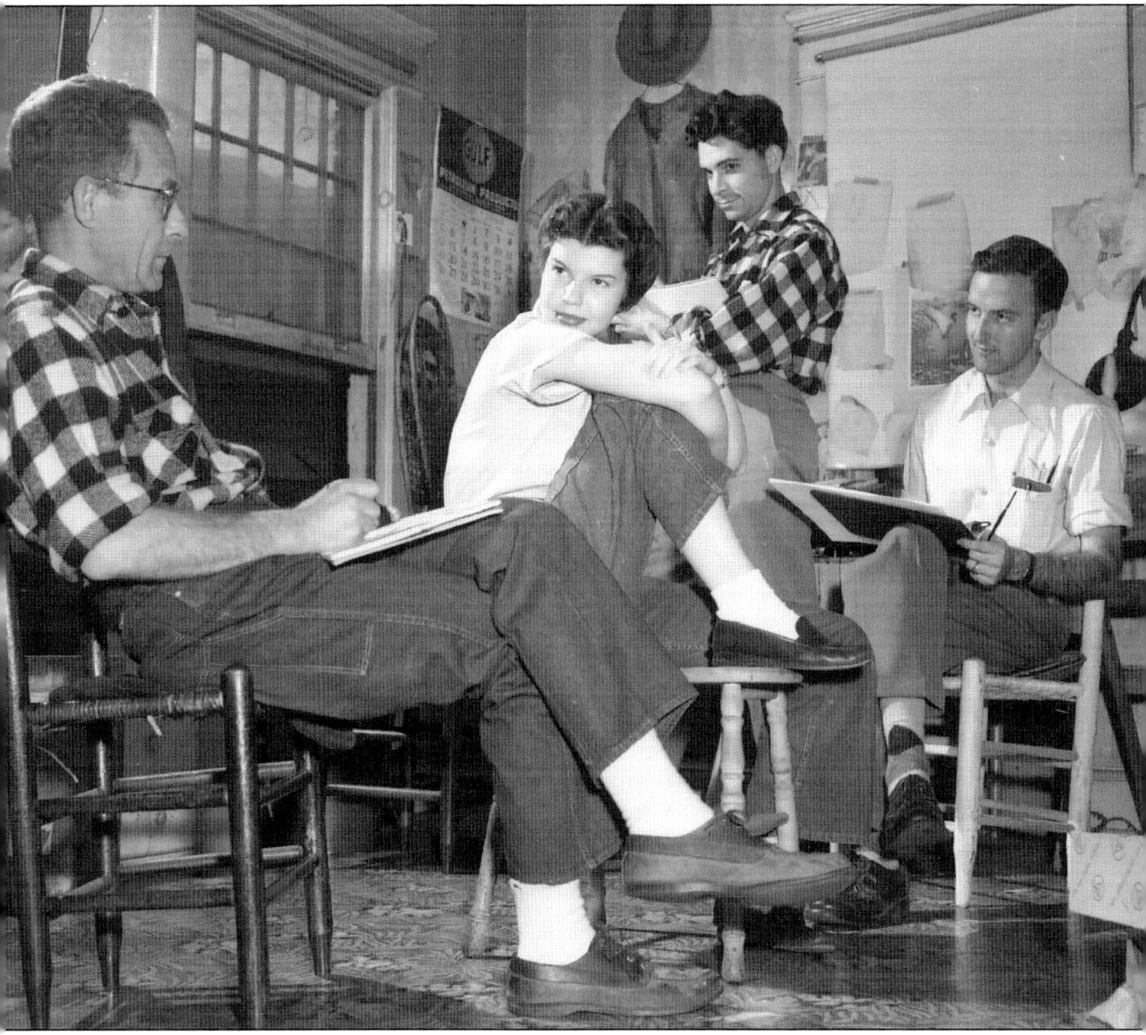

Cartoonist Ed Dodd (left), 1950, created the long-running *Mark Trail*, the first outdoor-themed comic strip. Dodd's philosophy as an artist was to arouse in people an interest in conservation.

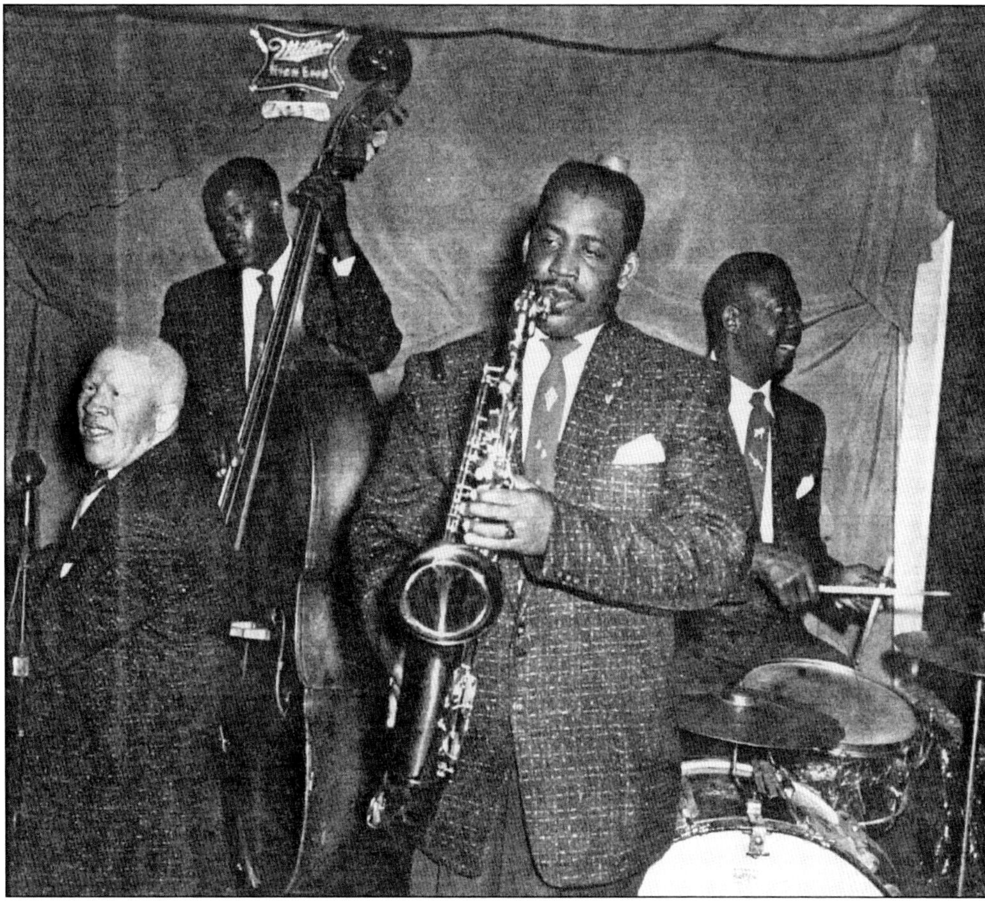

One of the greatest blues musicians to come out of Atlanta was Willie "Piano Red" Perryman. He was born in 1913 in Hamilton, Georgia, one of nine children born to sharecropping parents. In 1919, his family moved to Atlanta, and he began playing rent and house parties and fish fries in Atlanta's Summerhill community with his brother Rufus, also a musician, who was known as "Speckled Red." Perryman began to play at the local clubs. He recorded "Rocking With Red" and "You Got the Right String Baby, but the Wrong Yo-Yo" with his six-piece band called the Interns. Perryman had a large white following that was further enhanced by his gigs at Underground Atlanta. He died in July 1985.

James "Put" Jackson (seen here playing drums) was born in Madison, Georgia, and grew up in Atlanta and joined the Rambling Preps at Washington High School. He later attended Morris Brown College and had a distinguished career in entertainment, playing with Graham Jackson and Neal Montgomery. Of interest, when he was young, Jackson had to lie to his mother to get out at night to play at the nightclubs. (Courtesy of Linda Jackson.)

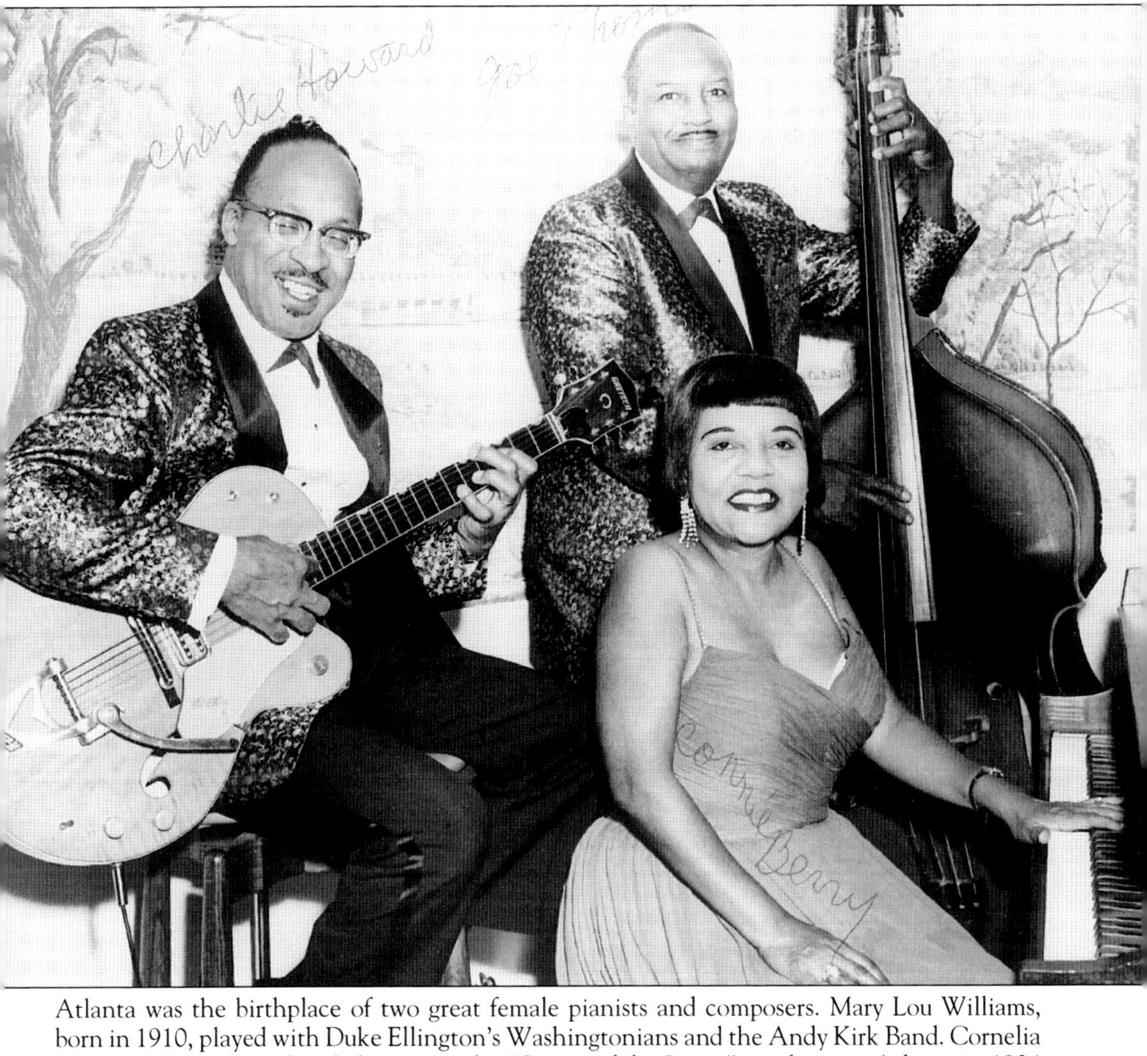

Atlanta was the birthplace of two great female pianists and composers. Mary Lou Williams, born in 1910, played with Duke Ellington's Washingtonians and the Andy Kirk Band. Cornelia "Connie" Berry (seen here), known as the "Queen of the Ivory," was born in Atlanta in 1904 and graduated from Clark College. By the 1920s and 1930s, she traveled extensively across the country playing for cafe society in New York and Hollywood, California. She performed at Harlem's Club Ubangi and Club Onyx and briefly had a New York radio show called *The Sophisticated Lady of Song*. She recorded for Brunswick Records. Miss Berry played with Tommy Dorsey and Duke Ellington and performed for President Franklin Delano Roosevelt often at his home in Warm Springs, Georgia. Connie Berry died in 1995. (Courtesy of Ralph Mays.)

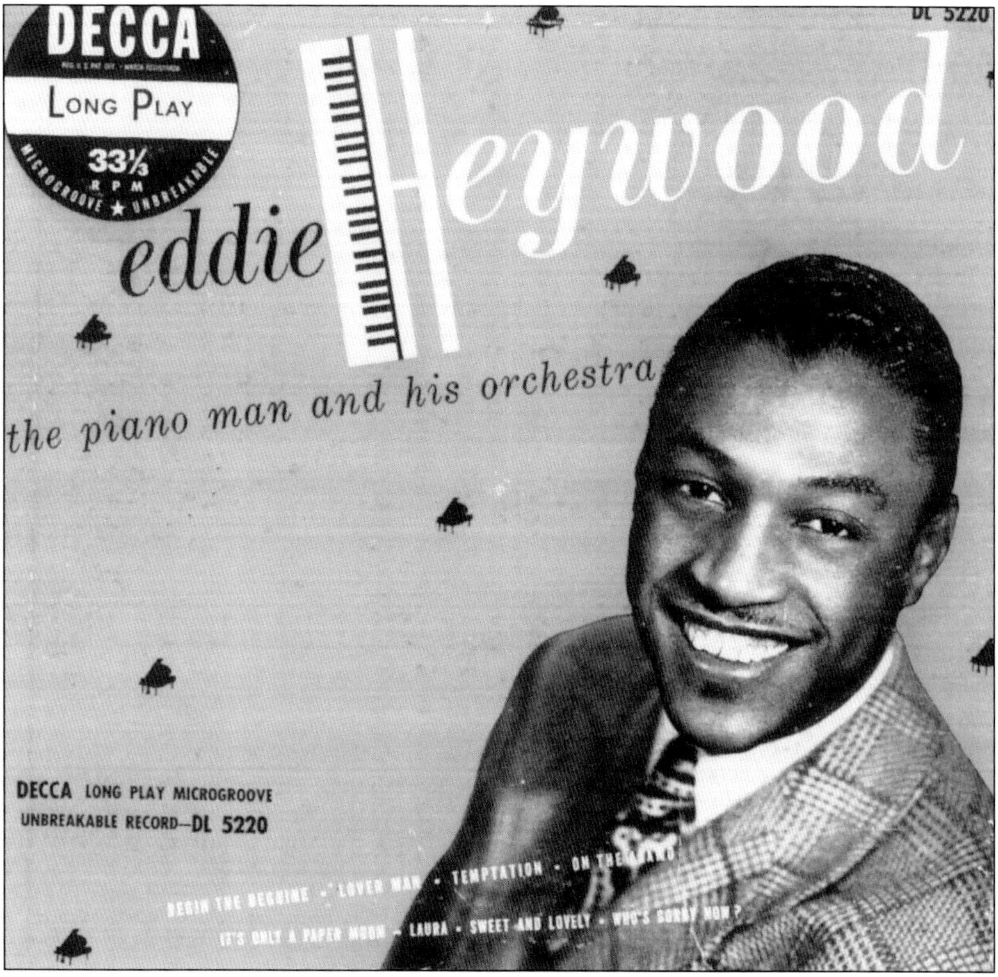

Eddie Heywood performed throughout the country until 1931, when he found himself the pianist for the Benny Carter band. It was with Carter that Heywood met Billie Holiday. She was so impressed with his work that she insisted on having him arrange for her as well as accompany her on several recording dates.

Later, he became the house pianist at the Village Vanguard. This stint would introduce him to some of the most recognized talent of the period. John Hammond, who had already helped to nurture the careers of Count Basie, Billie Holiday, and Benny Goodman, urged Eddie to organize a sextet that included trumpeter Doc Cheatham and trombonist Vic Dickenson.

From 1943 to 1947, the sextet rode a wave of popularity and was heard on radio records. He arranged music for Bing Crosby, which escalated his popularity once the records were released. He began to make a cross-country tour from New York to Hollywood, and stopped in his old hometown of Atlanta and performed at the Top Hat Club and the City Auditorium.

His arrangement of Cole Porter's "Begin with Beguine" brought him even greater fame. Cole Porter once remarked that "he wished he had written it the way Heywood arranged it." Following a temporary paralysis of his hands and subsequent therapy, Heywood came back and wrote three hit tunes: "Land of Dreams," "Soft Summer Breeze," and his biggest hit, "Canadian Sunset." Eddie Heywood Jr. died at age 73 in December 1988.

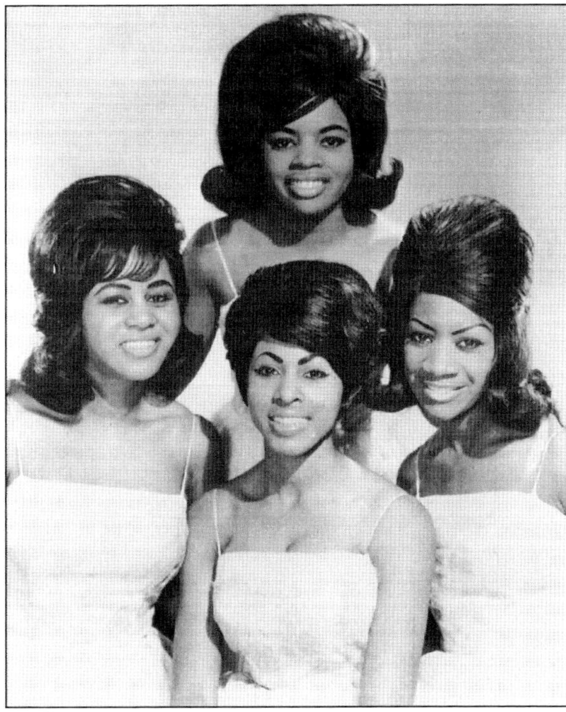

Today, Patti Labelle electrifies Atlanta audiences at the Fox Theater and Chastain Park. But during the 1960s, Patti Labelle and the Bluebells brought their harmonious melodies and their "hair" to the Royal Peacock's stage.

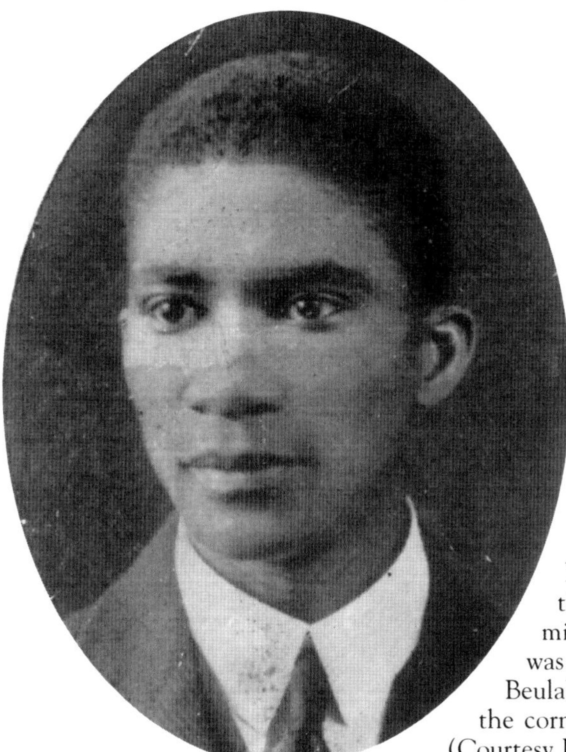

Rev. Leander A. Pinkston was one of the talented and gifted young Baptist ministers in Atlanta during the 1920s. He was pastor at one of two churches called Beulah Baptist. This church was located on the corner of Hunnicutt and Williams Streets. (Courtesy Digging It Up Archives.)

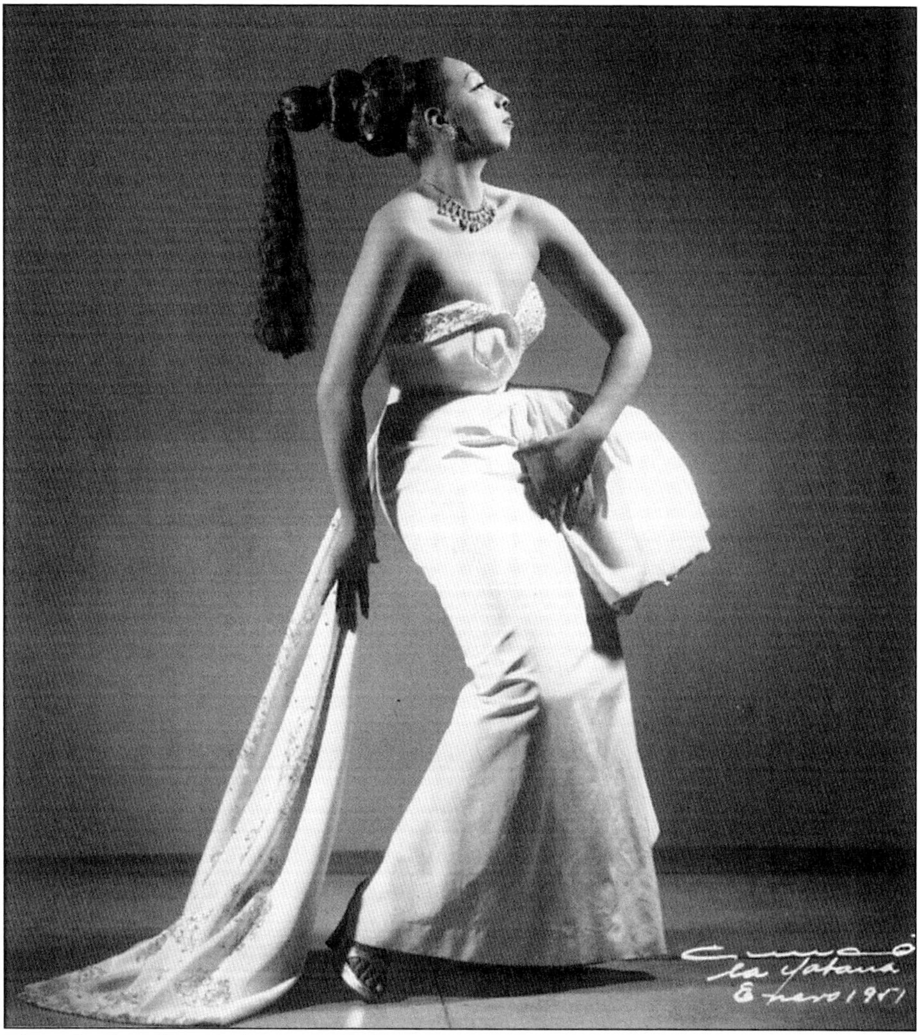

In July 1951, Josephine Baker cancelled her planned performance because she could not obtain first-class accommodations at one of the city's major hotels. Miss Baker had accepted the invitation extended by Walter White and the NAACP on June 30 with the condition that she and her party be housed in a first-class hotel, that there be no segregation in the audience, and that a mixed orchestra provide music. On Monday, May 5, 1951, Walter White unsuccessfully wired three of Atlanta's leading hotels asking for reservations for three days for Miss Baker and her party. Walter White urged Miss Baker to go on with the performance since two of her conditions had been met. Miss Baker wired a response stating the following: "It makes my heart beat with happiness to know that you not only appreciate but agree to my keeping my principles in not going to Atlanta because the hotels have refused my accommodations to me and my party. The fact of being in a white hotel does not flatter me in the least, but it is a matter of being a Negro and not being able to go wherever you desire. This situation grieves me deeply and I am all heart with you and the NAACP, Dr. Bunch and all of our people who are fighting to conquer injustice, discrimination and prejudice against people who only want to be considered as human beings. I profoundly believe in God and am absolutely certain we will win."

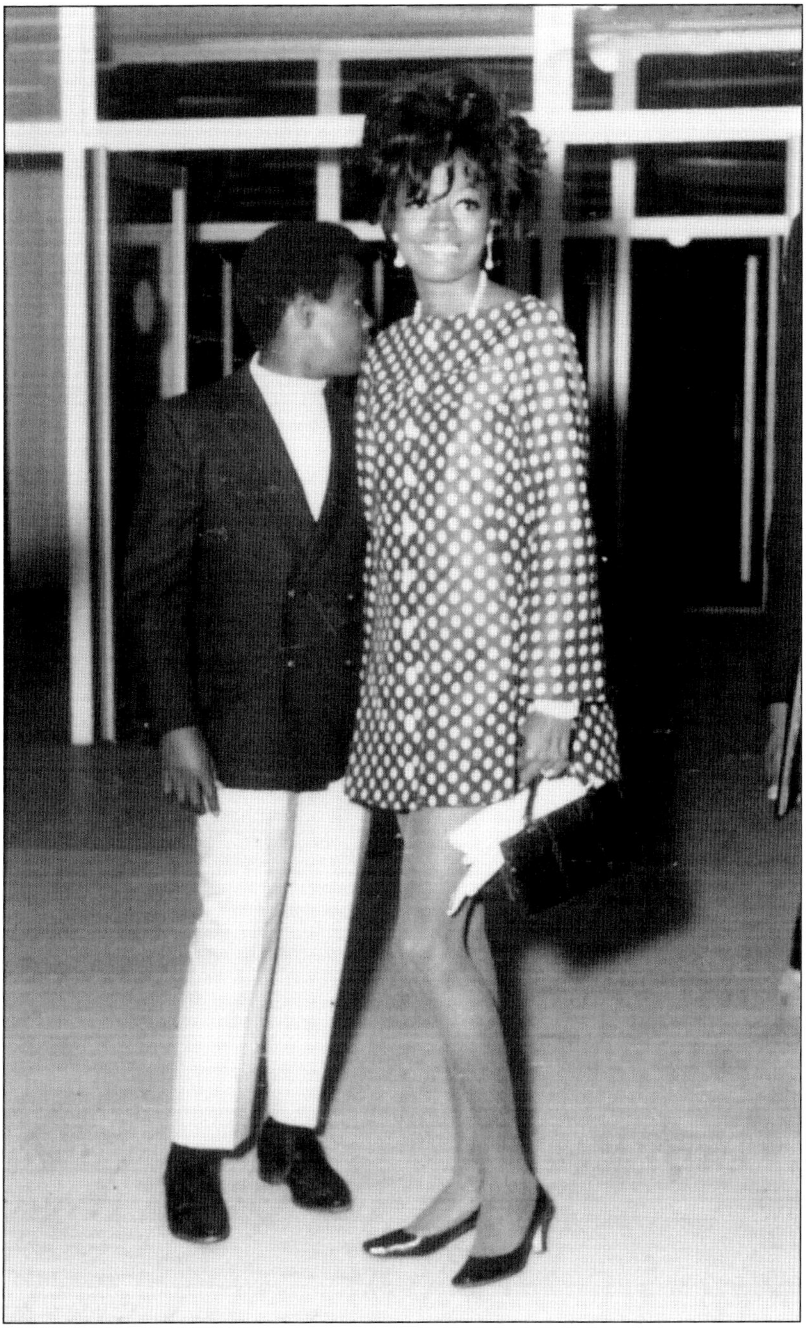

Pictured here is Diana Ross in the lobby of the Atlanta Civic Center, *c.* 1970s. Shortly after Martin Luther King's death, Motown Records sent its leading stars, including Miss Ross and the Supremes, Gladys Knight and the Pips, Stevie Wonder, and the Temptations, for a benefit concert which raised $25,000 for the Southern Christian Leadership Conference. (Courtesy of Bob Johnson.)

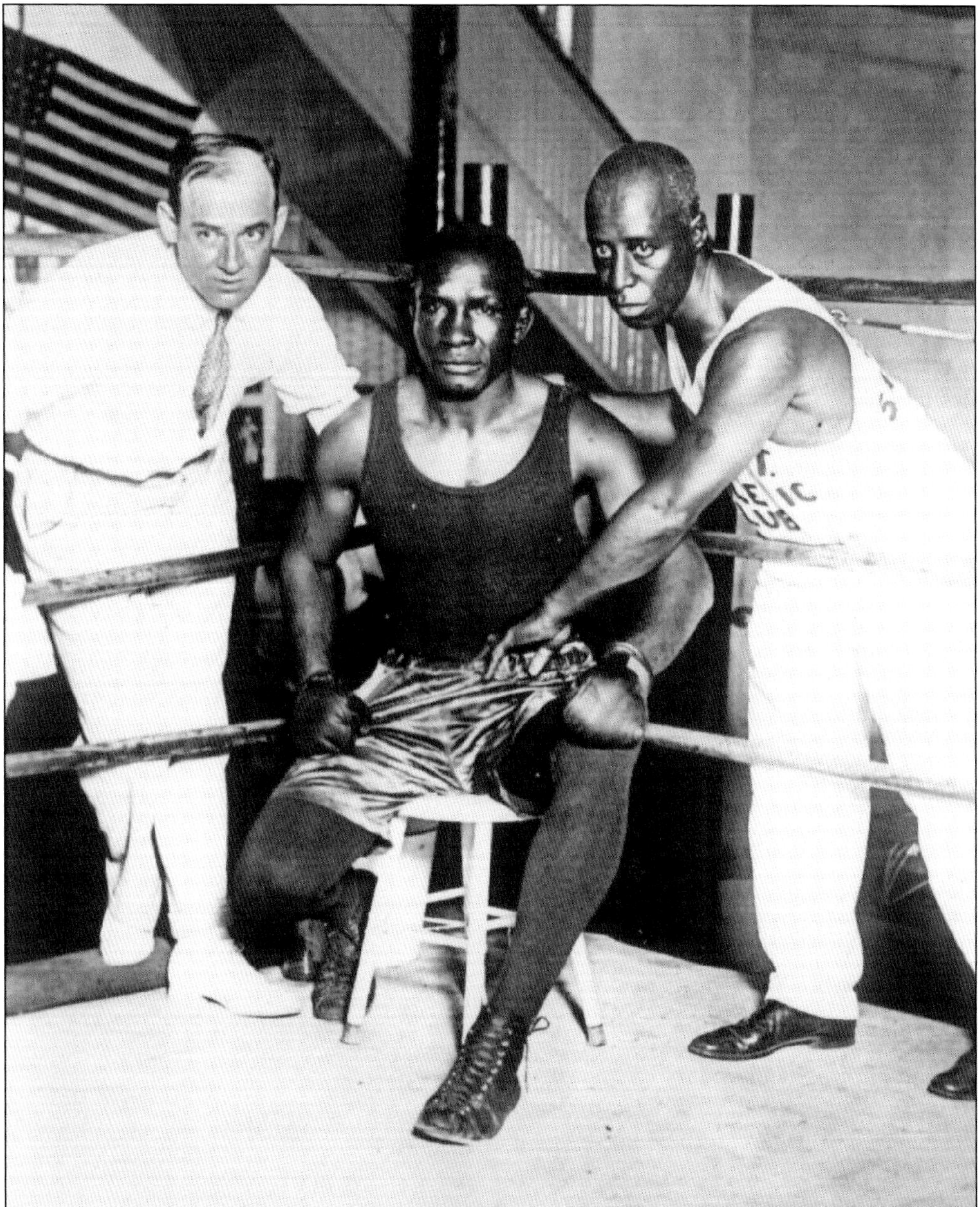

Theodore "Tiger" Flowers was born in February 1894 to sharecropping parents Aaron and Lula Flowers in the small southwest Georgia town of Camilla. At the age of six, his family moved to Brunswick, Georgia, where he attended Risley School and the Seldon Institute. His muscular, sculpted build had not come from weight training, but from his years as a call boy, stevedore, boilermaker, porter, steel riveter, laborer on a subway that was being constructed in Philadelphia, and in the shipyards constructing ships during World War I. (Courtesy Digging It Up Archives.)

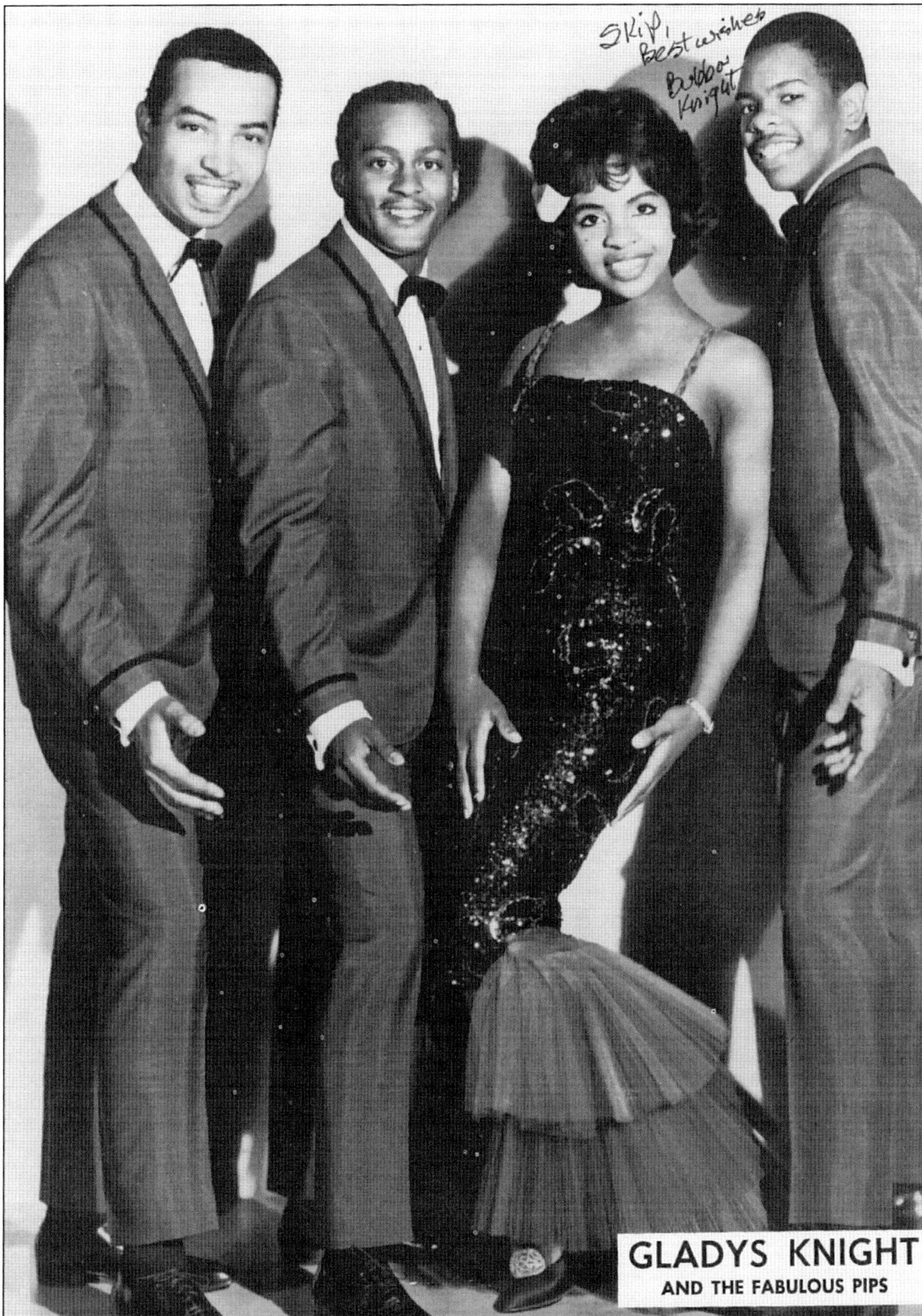

Here are the popular Atlanta vocalists Gladys Knight and the Pips in their heyday.

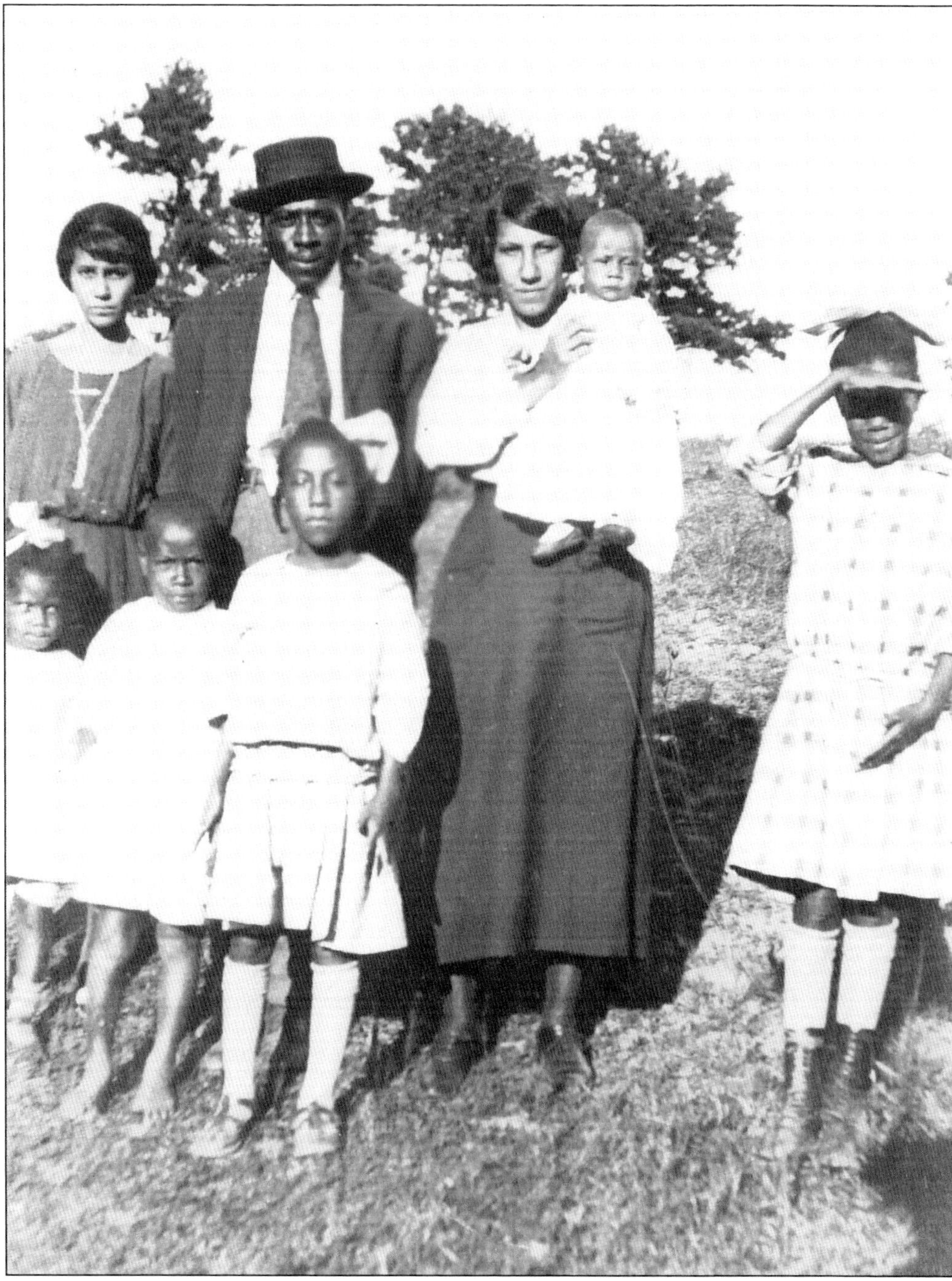

The family pictured here is representative of the many African-American families who, from the turn of the century to the 1930s, migrated to the small hamlet of Decatur from surrounding rural counties and settled in the town's black community known as Beacon Hill. While in many areas living conditions were substandard and below the poverty line, a sense of pride permeated the streets. (Courtesy of Skip Mason Archives.)

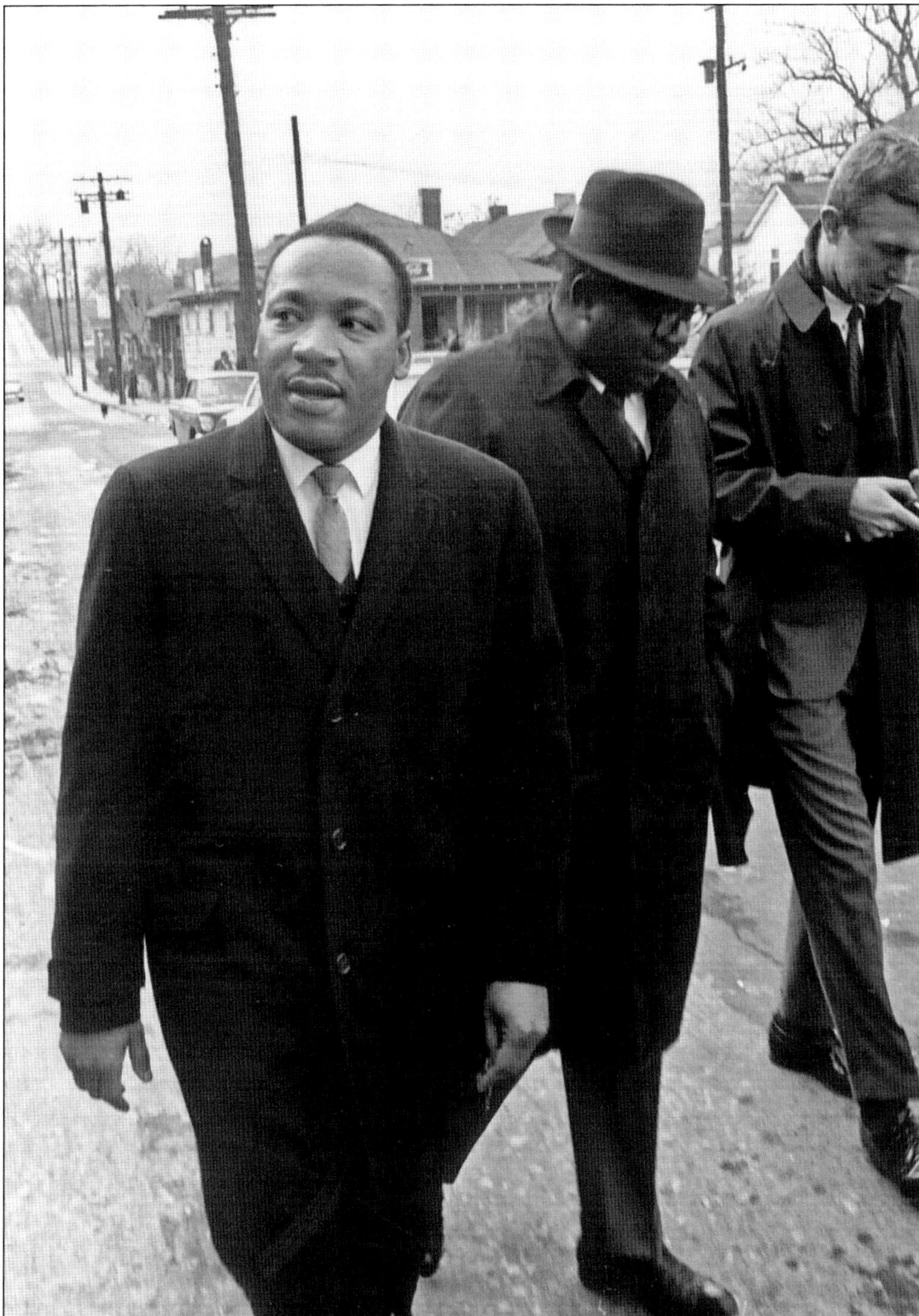

Martin Luther King Jr. is seen here during the Vine City housing protests, January 1966.

Arcadia would like to express its appreciation to the following organizations for their contributions to the Atlanta area titles:

Apex Museum
Atlanta Daily World
Atlanta History Center
Atlanta Independent
Atlanta Journal and Constitution
Auburn Avenue Research Library
Central Congregational United Church of Christ
DeKalb Historical Society
Digging It Up
Georgia Postcard Club
Herndon Foundation
Marietta Welcome Center and Visitors' Bureau
Morehouse College
Rockdale County Historical Society
St. James CME Church
Washington Memorial Cemetery
Westide CME Church